BuenosAires

BUENOS AIRES

A Cultural History

Jason Wilson

Interlink Books

An imprint of Interlink Publishing Group, Inc.
Northampton, Massachusetts

This edition first published 2023 by

INTERLINK BOOKS
An imprint of Interlink Publishing Group, Inc.
46 Crosby Street, Northampton, Massachusetts 01060
www.interlinkbooks.com

Library of Congress Cataloging-in-Publication Data

Wilson, Jason, 1944-
    Buenos Aires : a cultural and literary companion / by Jason Wilson.
       p.   cm. — (Cities of the imagination)
    Includes bibliographical references.
    ISBN 978-1-62371-739-1
    1. Buenos Aires (Argentina)—Description and travel.   2. Buenos
Aires (Argentina)—In literature.   3. Buenos Aires (Argentina)—
History—Miscellanea.   4. Buenos Aires (Argentina)—Social life and
customs. I. Title.   II. Series.
F3001.W68   1999
982'.11—dc21   99-36095
                                                                                              CIP

Design: Baseline Arts
Cover images: South American Pictures; Archivo General de la Nación,
Argentina; Nick Caistor

Printed and bound in the United States of America

10 9 8 7 6 5 4 3 2 1

Contents

PART FOUR
THE SOUTH

PART FIVE
THE WEST

Foreword

Like all great cities, Buenos Aires doesn't exist, except in the memory of those who live or lived there. It has no comprehensible form, no definable shape, it changes even as you walk through it, from corner to corner. Perhaps because there is too much of it, whatever it is: New York skyscrapers, Paris balconies, Madrid forged-iron windows, sidewalks from Damascus and Cairo, melancholy cafés and tree-lined suburban streets from places whose names are always on the tip of your tongue. Borges understood this when he declared "I've always been and always will be in Buenos Aires." It is a city that foreshadows all others. You never leave it entirely, you keep rebuilding it through the faded snapshots that your memory throws up.

Every city has its Virgil: Buenos Aires has Jorge Luis Borges. Once, walking with Borges through that area of Buenos Aires known as El Bajo, the old blind man described to me the seedy bars and gas-lit street corners which he had explored in his youth, when he could still see, and which for him had the solid presence of brick walls and shuttered windows. As we walked past what were now the high towers of the Sheraton Hotel or the expensive boutiques that sold leather-goods to tourists, Borges spoke of dim rooms where men in tight black jackets and white silk kerchiefs drank *ginebra*, while someone in the back strummed a *milonga* on a guitar, and of soft-spoken *guapos* who would mention, in passing and with a touch of nostalgia, that they had killed a man. Buenos Aires, apparently, had changed but the real, the unending Buenos Aires remained for Borges the same one of his earlier days.

My Buenos Aires, encountered after the fall of Perón in 1955 and until the first stirrings of the military dictatorship in 1968, is another. It consists of the neighborhood of Belgrano, where my family lived; a neighborhood of quiet streets shaded by jacarandas and small secret squares that opened suddenly at the end of them. Along the cobblestones outside my house, the horse-drawn cart of the man who sold soda-water would rattle in the early morning to deliver the wooden crates stacked with half-a-dozen green or blue syphons that the cook stashed away in the laundry-room. The rag-and-bone man would come, pushing his wheelbarrow, looking for old clothes to buy, and the knife-sharpener, dragging along his whetstone on a curious wheeled contraption, would blow on his harmonica to announce his passing. There was a chemist-shop at the corner that always smelt of eucalyptus, and down the other way, a stationery store that sold the most wonderful selection of notebooks and pens, and the adventure novels in the "Robin Hood" series where I discovered Jules Verne, Emilio Salgari and the saga of Bomba, the Jungle Boy, forever in search of his lost father.

Further south, towards the railway station, were the hillside gardens known as Barrancas de Belgrano, where we played on the swings under huge rubber trees and where the candy man sold long, rainbow-colored lollipops called *pirulines*. There was also a mysterious wafer vendor who carried his sugar wafers in a tall drum with a numbered disk at the top. After paying a coin, you were allowed to spin an arrow attached to the centre of the disk and, depending on the number the arrow selected, you were given one, two or (in very rare cases) three wafers. I found the man pleasantly frightening: there was a small building in the middle of the park, modelled after a round Greek temple, and I was told that this was where the wafer man lived and baked his wafers, and I imagined him throughout the dark night, under the crested dome, magically spinning his wheel in the silence of the deserted gardens.

Belgrano was home; the downtown core, known as El Centro, was the place of adventure. My high school stood a few blocks away from the political heart of the city, the Plaza de Mayo, where the first local government had been formed, a century and a half earlier, at the beginning of the wars of independence from Spain, and where, ever since, most of the uprisings that bled the country had started. It was also a short distance from the sexually charged and risky adult world: from the crammed shopping district of Calle Florida, from Calle San Martín with its banks and dirty cocktail bars and exchange bureaux, from Calle Lavalle lined with movie theatres for every taste, and from the old-worldly Avenida de Mayo where in the sidewalk cafés Spanish anarchists in exile would speak of literature and politics over a glass of sherry. Further north, past the wide Avenida del 9 de Julio and the Obelisk, lay the temptations of the bookstores of Calle Corrientes, dusty holes-in-the-wall guarded by sullen old men who made no distinction between the soft porn sold under the guise of a *Marriage Manual* and first editions of Julio Cortázar.

Afterwards, Buenos Aires became for me a city of absences: friends who had "disappeared," been kidnapped, tortured, killed or forced into exile.

Places where friends had met became places from which friends were taken; addresses were no longer the right addresses; certain corners, certain cafés became memorials.

Mere architectural change – streets widened, buildings torn down and rebuilt in ostentatious marble and glass, American shopping-centres created to replace the corner grocer and the specialty store – try to convince me that the new city is the one that now exists, the new city of which Borges's and countless others are but shadows. I don't believe it. As Jason Wilson's intelligent and comprehensive book shows, those shadows have a more durable, tangible reality than the transitory and capricious Buenos Aires built out of nothing but steel and stone.

Alberto Manguel
Calgary, October 1999

To Isabel Quesada & my Argentine family.

Preface

This cultural history and guide to a Buenos Aires filtered and reinvented through writing is a collective work, based not only on previous guides, historians and critics mentioned in the bibliography at the end, but on countless further contributors, although none is responsible for the final result. Special thanks to Isabel Quesada who posted numerous articles and books, Anthony Edkins always on the look-out for second-hand books, Andrea Parodi Wilson, our three daughters Tomasina, Lucinda and Camila, and our niece Cecilia Molinari, Kate Kavanagh, Nick Caistor, and Martín Cullen, with his vast store of *porteño* lore, and lastly to James Ferguson, astute and generous publisher.

This guide, aimed at foreigners to Argentine history and culture, strives to be informative, and arbitrary. Making sense of an ever-changing city is a creative act, and always precarious. Let this guide be a starting-point, a prompter. Most of the writers cited here have been challenged by their own city and question and mythify the link between self and place. Buenos Aires, no static background, perversely contradicts the solidity of the tense "is" with "was", for mutation is its key. That a foreigner should compile this literary guide stems from the inevitability of over-familiarity, and from a sense that writers best perceive place from outside their own cultures. Jorge Luis Borges confessed: "If I had never gone abroad I wonder if I could have seen the city with the power and splendor it now induces in me."

Reading is a kind of meditation. Hectic cities like Buenos Aires offer less and less time for reading as, Isidoro Blaistein recently complained: "First, nobody reads. Second, everybody writes. Nobody reads what others write and some don't even read what they themselves have written." Thus this book. Its dense information has been double-checked, but notoriously facts have a life of their own. My translations allow for an underlying Argentine Spanish to be sensed.

Jason Wilson
Buenos Aires & London

Buenos Aires Centre (by permission of Vacation Work Publications)

PART ONE

An Introduction to the City of Buenos Aires

"*City, as a foreigner I sing of you.*"
Rafael Alberti

An old man asks the gourmet detective Pepe Carvalho in Manuel Vázquez Montalbán's novel *Quinteto de Buenos Aires*, [Buenos Aires Quintet, 1997] what he knows about Buenos Aires. Carvalho answers: "Tango, the disappeared, Maradona." The Argentine novelist and psychoanalyst Marcos Aguinis asked himself the same question and came up with Che Guevara, Evita, and for the more bookish, Jorge Luis Borges. Perhaps, in Britain and the US we should add the Falklands/Malvinas war, Patagonia and *gauchos*, but not much else. Such icons and clichés change with time, but are always shorthand for partial and prejudiced understanding, even for Argentines. For example, in 1966 poet and biographer Horacio Salas (1938-) was driven by nostalgia to select emotionally charged national figures; "From time to time I read Borges again. / When I go to bed I patiently repeat the name of the Boca forward from the 1950s / Or I listen to Gardel to ward off silence." Football, Borges, Evita and tango lead us into the *porteño* soul, the inner being of the inhabitant of Buenos Aires.

The Spanish novelist Antonio Muñoz Molina (1956-) claimed in a journalistic piece that Buenos Aires "is one of the capitals in the great world map of literature." It is certainly the capital of Argentina. The expatriate and playful Argentine writer Julio Cortázar (1914-1984) began publishing under a pseudonym, Julio Denis, and taught at the University of Cuyo in Mendoza before exiling himself in Paris for good because of his opposition to Peronism in the 1950s. He wrote a letter to a friend in 1939, claiming that "Argentina is Buenos Aires, and then the countryside." Most writers, local and foreign, would agree. Ernesto Sabato (1911-), a Dostoevskian chronicler of secret Buenos Aires, often refers to his city as "Babylonic"; a common adjective, used also by novelist and essayist Eduardo Mallea (1903-1980). "Babylon" suggests the earthly, infernal, alienating city, in opposition to the heavenly, utopian city of God. Albert Londres (1884-1932), a French investigative journalist intent on exposing the white slave trade and prostitution in the 1920s, called the city a "Babel," as have many others. When the California-based English novelist Christopher Isherwood (1904-1986) arrived in Buenos Aires in 1948, during the heyday of Peronism, he found it to be the "most truly international city in the world." Mexican novelist Carlos Fuentes (1928-), who also lived in the city in the 1940s as a sixteen-year-old, modified this superlative status to encompass Latin America only: "Buenos Aires was then, as always, the most beautiful, sophisticated, and civilized city in Latin America."

Not all versions have been so complimentary. Contrary to Fuentes, Lucio Mansilla (1831-1913), author of the fascinating travel chronicle, *Una excursión a los indios ranqueles [A Visit to the Ranquel Indians, 1870]*, found this same Buenos Aires to be "a vertiginous agitation, in the middle of narrow, muddy, dirty, fetid streets that block out the horizon and the clean, pure sky... all crowded together by egoism, like a bunch of disgusting shell fish." Rafael Barrett, a Bilbao-born anarchist, concurred with Mansilla in 1904, labeling Buenos Aires "the city of egoism." In 1929, the French architect Le Corbusier complained in a petulant lecture: "Buenos Aires is the most inhuman city I've known. In fact, one's heart feels martyred there." In the same critical mode, Dr. Plarr, Graham Greene's (1904-1991) cynical exile in the novel *The Honorary Consul* (1973), saw Buenos Aires as "the great sprawling muddled capital with its *fantástica arquitectura* of skyscrapers in mean streets." Another European, the English expatriate writer Gordon Meyer (1919-1968), who adopted the River Plate as his home from the 1950s, wrote about Buenos Aires through his protagonist Jane, divorced from her philandering Argentine husband, in his first novel *Sweet Water and Bitter* (1962):

> What emerged instead suggested a vast second-hand shop without classi-
> fication. Every type of juxtaposition existed: curious, amusing, bizarre,
> tragic—a fashionable eighteenth-century church nudged by a grubby
> tailor's shop, an obscure, shabby army department protected by a moon-
> faced conscript with a machine-gun; a small palazzo—what other word
> to describe those fantastic, splendid homes of the wealthy, reproducing
> whole features of European palaces?—backed by corrugated-iron roofed
> shacks; an embassy backing on to an unofficial rubbish dump loud with
> decaying corpses of dogs.

I remember my first astonished view in 1970 from the windows of a Viscount flying across from Montevideo to the Aeroparque airport of an unexpectedly vast urban space cluttered with spiky buildings, spreading to the horizon under a pall of light smog. I know a 13th-floor view from María-Teresa Quesada's flat on Avenida Córdoba, where the city unfurls to the horizon without even a smudge of green tree or park.

There are many, many versions of Buenos Aires, one for each inhab-itant, one for each visitor, but for all it is a very *urban* city. This guide will pursue Buenos Aires as setting, protagonist and character, with writers and other observers offering their testimonies as witnesses, their "personal perspective" in the words of geographers Peter Preston and Paul Simpson-Housley, who define the process of absorbing a city "as an experience to be lived, suffered, undergone." The question I will be constantly address-ing is the problematic uniqueness of Buenos Aires, as opposed to its mimicry of just another modernizing metropolitan city. I shall also be pinpointing its "lieux de mémoires" in Paul Nora's phrase, its most signif-icant and sometimes enigmatic landmarks.

Modernity and Plagiarism

Roberto Arlt's (1900-1942) protagonist Balder, in his novel *El amor brujo* [Bewitching love, 1932], about seduction and sex, saw two versions of Buenos Aires superimposed: "the boxed-in one of skyscrapers, and the lower one, extending its fractured horizon of masonry." This cultural guide to the textual city relies on words, trying to characterize a city constantly mutating, that refuses to remain the same, except for the grid of streets—and even street names change. Argentina's great acerbic thinker Ezequiel Martínez Estrada (1895-1964) observed in 1940 that Buenos Aires "has advanced erasing its past," knocking down and rebuilding, rewriting its short history. Jorge Luis Borges (1899-1986) noted this constant process of urban regeneration: "The image we have of the city is always somewhat anachronistic. The café has degenerated into a bar; the hallway that let us glimpse patios and a vine is now a blurred corridor with a lift at the end. Thus I believed for years that at a certain point in Talcahuano street I would find the Librería [bookshop] Buenos Aires; one morning I discovered that it had been replaced by an antiques shop."

Mutation indicates modernity, how cities adapt to new architectural trends and desires; E. M. Forster saw London as in a "continual flux." Time dominates, and time passing creates new urban emotions. Alejo Carpentier (1904-1980), the Cuban novelist and musicologist, saw all Latin American cities in a "process of symbiosis." At an architectural level, few eighteenth- and nineteenth- century buildings still stand in Buenos Aires' rush to modernize. Certainly the adobe brick of colonial buildings has crumbled into dust. In 1947, Julio Rinaldini saw this building mania as a *porteño* characteristic: "But Buenos Aires has no interest in preserving anything. It goes on building and developing..." It is a mentality that is perhaps changing.

By the time Buenos Aires filled with immigrants and wealth, its style had become hybrid, eclectic; according to José María Peña, director of the Museum of the City of Buenos Aires, a diversity of styles, in his words, an "incongruous mix" characterizes the city. The Paris-based Argentine novelist Juan José Saer (1937-) employed the same word in 1991 to describe *porteño* architecture: "In Buenos Aires, incongruence is the norm. Heterogeneous constructions co-exist in every block... A twenty-floored building sticks up, improbably stable, next to a modest house, with a little garden in front. Even in the city centre, though less frequently, this architectural anarchy remains the norm." For Carpentier, Latin American cities are unique because "all imaginable styles are intermingled." In 1923, the visiting Colombian writer José María Vargas Vila (1860-1933) saw this eclecticism negatively: "the Absolute Lack of Originality is the distinction of Buenos Aires... all imported, all transported, all imitated... it's the Patria of Plagiarism." In *El paseo de Palermo* [The promenade of Palermo, 1874], the Argentine doctor-writer Eduardo Wilde (1844-1913) agreed: "the Argentines imitate everything, we're ridiculous, especially because we copy badly." To encapsulate this hybridity, the ironic Bruce Chatwin, who loathed being called a travel-writer, observed: "The history of Buenos Aires is written in its telephone directory," and randomly listed the names Romanov, Rommel de Rose, Radziwil and Rothschild as symptoms of a cultural jumble.

In this history, Buenos Aires is a palimpsest city, as all differing textual versions of it remain available, even visible, in words and illustrations in books. Crucial literary voices define this cacophonic city. During his long life, Borges wrote three poems entitled "Buenos Aires." In one he outlined how he sought to find his city in Palermo and in the Sur; but "now you are inside me." In another he asks: "What will Buenos Aires become?" and answers with a long list of places important to him from the Plaza de Mayo to calle Quintana, the docks, a house on calle Perú, the old National Library where he worked, a street corner in the Once where he chatted with his mentor, the experimental writer and thinker Macedonio Fernández (1874-1952), and also all the parts he never got to know, in a hidden, alien Buenos Aires.

In his earlier years Borges was a great walker (as recalled by his best biographer Estela Canto). Later, he was a familiar figure in the streets, lunching in the same restaurants, a man of rigid routines (perhaps because blind). He described himself as "a man of the city, of the *barrio*, of streets; / distant trams ease my sadness / with the long complaint they release in the evenings." His "patria" was Buenos Aires. In 1972, the wandering novelist V. S. Naipaul recklessly decided that "Borges has not hallowed Buenos Aires" because his city was a private city "of the imagination," which is clearly nonsense. Earlier, in 1967, Borges had lamented: "Buenos Aires is such a boundless city that nobody can know it."

A city like Buenos Aires seems to change more dramatically than other settled, historical cities like London or Paris because it demolishes its past in the rush to modernize. In 1904 the flamboyant Lucio Mansilla exploded: "Eh! They have changed my Buenos Aires so much that it is easier to remember names than the exact place where they can be found."

"a crucible of souls and races"
"I feel more porteño than Argentine." Borges

However, a city is also its inhabitants, here the *porteños* (those who live in the port)—who stimulated the great Nicaraguan poet Rubén Darío (real name Félix Rubén García Sarmiento, 1867-1916) to eulogize the "*porteño* fervor" of sheer bustle, chatter, and movement—hurry. For Darío, a provincial Central American, Buenos Aires was "Cosmopolis," a Paris without Parisians, "a crucible of souls and races." In his book about the future greatness of Latin America, *La raza cósmica* [The cosmic race, 1925], the Mexican philosopher and educator, José Vasconcelos (1882-1959), echoed Darío's (and countless others') comparison with Paris: "but day by day Buenos Aires is turning into the centre of Iberoamerican thought; Buenos Aires is our Paris, the capital of our América."

But this cultural mixture or immigrant cosmopolitanism was not always to everyone's taste. In 1886, the Argentine novelist Julián Martel (real name José Miró, 1867-1896) ranted against "the cosmopolitanism that is taking on such grand proportions with us, to the point that we do not know who we are, whether French or Spanish, Italian or English... because the foreigner who comes to our land, whether naturalized or not, does not give a damn if we are well or badly governed." The unjustly neglected Catholic-Peronist novelist Leopoldo Marechal (1900-1970) looked more kindly on this immigrant "melting-pot," and in his novel *Adán Buenosayres* (1948), evoked a street scene with "the Iberians, the Basques, the Andalusians, the industrial Ligurians, the Neapolitans, the Turks, the Jews, the Greeks, the Dalmatians, the Syrio-Lebanese and the Japanese." But he too had his misgivings about the future: "In fact there were people from the four corners of the world, here to fulfill the lofty destiny of the land named-after-a-pure-metal [i.e. Río de la Plata = Silver River]. And inspecting those unlikely faces, Adam asked himself what their destiny might be, and great were his doubts."

This notion of a Babel city was already formulated in 1848 by the traveler William MacCann in his *Two Thousand Mile Ride Through the Argentine Provinces* (1853):

> *The varieties of complexion and costume, including specimens of the human race from almost every country of the world, and the Babel of tongues from all nations, so confound the senses, that it is difficult to describe the effect. Surely no other city in the world could present such a motley assemblage; and the diversity of physiognomy is so great that one might doubt if mankind are all descended from a common stock.*

In 1882 Victor Gálvez (real name Vicente Quesada, 1830-1913, one-time director of the National Library, with a library of his own of some 82,000 volumes donated to the Instituto Iberoamericano in Berlin)

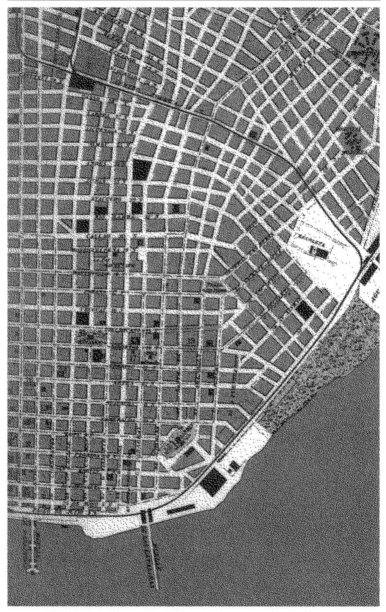

Buenos Aires, 1884 "one of the most regular cities in the world"

invented a North American female traveler called Lucy Dowland. In doing so, he fooled his contemporary Domingo Sarmiento, who, in a review, praised her perceptiveness. She described Argentines as an "active people, preoccupied above all by the wish to get rich" and less interested in solving their immigration confusion. Argentines, she concluded, "do not have their own identity, being an assimilation of people from everywhere, every kind of custom... you could call it a city in transit... the street crowds are just passing by... there are no national characteristics, no nation-people, they are fragments of many peoples."

That many people were drawn to Argentina to "make America" and become rich is a fact, as the Spanish republican writer Vicente Blasco Ibáñez, who visited the city to give lectures in 1909 and wrote an 800-page book *Argentina y sus grandezas* [Argentina and its greatnesses, 1910], wrote: "Buenos Aires. That name makes all the desperate people in the world dream. Repeating it mentally, one feels stronger..." According to historian José Moya, *porteño* culture had defined itself by the 1920s as "one of the most distinct and vibrant urban cultures in the world." He adds, "the Porteños' perpetual complaints (or boasts) about their lack of an autochthonous culture became itself an idiosyncratic mark of it." Here, Buenos Aires is perceived as a vital city of ethnic pluralism and conviviality, as Moya's analysis turns this synthesis of urban immigration into something unique, certainly in Latin America.

Grid City

Buenos Aires is a grid city, with avenues and canyon-like streets at right angles to each other. In 1833, Charles Darwin, a young naturalist on the *Beagle*, singled out this grid geometry and felt that Buenos Aires was "one of the most regular [cities] in the world. Every street is at right angles to the one it crosses, and the parallel ones being equidistant, the houses are collected into solid squares of equal dimensions, which are called quadras [*cuadras*]." Víctor Gálvez noted the same in the 1860s: "The city of Buenos Aires offers a singular aspect: its streets are narrow and its buildings usually one floor high... it looks just like a Spanish city," but he cursed "the crushing uniformity of its straight lines." In the 1920s, Albert Londres exaggerated this insight: "Buenos Ayres is a vast flat expanse on which houses have been planted acre by acre. These square blocks are cut off from each other by narrow trenches—roads, in fact. Walking about Buenos Ayres is like playing draughts with one's feet. You feel like a piece being pushed from square to square on a draught board."

This rigid patterning of blocks of 120 square yards and streets thirty feet wide led the Argentine architect Alberto Prebisch, associated with the local 1920s avant-garde, to complain that "Buenos Aires is one of the world's cities with the lowest proportion of green spaces." The poet and city-chronicler Baldomero Fernández Moreno (1886-1950) discovered this grid city inside his mind: "My brain is formed of grids / like your streets, o Buenos Aires!" His tellingly titled short poem "Compenetration" ends: "If I am asked why my verse / is so precise, so regular, / I would tell everybody that I learned to make it / on the geometry of your streets."

In conjunction with this grid uniformity, in 1948 the exiled Isherwood found the public buildings "ponderous," and they are certainly still ostentatious on the outside, constructed as imposing facades. Walking the streets today, your eyes feast on these solid, ornate facades bulging forward with pillars, caryatids, sculptures, domes, towers and balconies, what Chatwin called "pie-crust architecture". Víctor Gálvez complained about this showy aspect of the urban landscape, where a typical example, the Escuela Normal, has a "grandiose facade, but whose interior is diminished; everything has been spent on the external pomp." Literary traveler Philip Guedalla (1889-1944) in *Argentine Tango* (1932) found these ponderous and pompous facades unique to Buenos Aires: "But there can be few cities in the world which carry dignity in architecture to the impressive lengths of Buenos Aires. Almost any of the twenty monumental buildings might be the General Post Office; potential Law Courts abound on every hand; and the solemn frontage of the Opera might be the National Assembly, while by a natural compensation the Assembly looks very like a palace of the arts."

Far from this vision of a dignified, formal city, Martínez Estrada, always an acute historian of Argentine flaws, felt that it was an individualistic, whimsical place, with buildings at odds with each other, a city without secrets, without intestines or deep folds, with everything visible. The naturalist Gerald Durrell, brother to poet and novelist Lawrence Durrell (who also visited Argentina but loathed it), described the Aduana building as a "cross between the Parthenon and the Reichstag" in his *The Whispering Land* (1961). Like others, Durrell ascribed to Buenos Aires' buildings the tendency to emphasize the external facade, so that outer show conceals an inner poverty.

When Buenos Aires inhabits books it changes, becomes quirky, subjective, partial. Bruno, Ernesto Sabato's alter-ego writer in *Sobre héroes y tumbas* [*On Heroes and Tombs*, 1961], questions the task of shrinking a city into words: "How can that innumerable reality be represented in one hundred pages?" He lists the city's ingredients: "Six million Argentines, Spaniards, Italians, Basques, Germans, Hungarians, Russians, Poles, Yugoslavs, Czechs, Syrians, Lebanese, Lithuanians, Greek, Ukrainians... The largest Galician city in the world, the largest Italian city in the world... More pizzerias than in Naples and Rome together... a gigantic, murky conglomeration." Can any one person ever evoke a city? Gordon Meyer thought not: "But how the city really was who could say? One did not see it as it really was, but as one's self really was." The city reflects the observer, the many observers.

A Brief History of Buenos Aires

The city was first founded in 1536, somewhere near the now sluggish and polluted river called the Riachuelo, in today's touristic La Boca *barrio* (more or less on today's streets Humberto I and Defensa). The Querandí Indians were nomadic and aggressive, and by 1541 had driven off Pedro de Mendoza's (1499-1537) starving soldiers, whose abandoned horses and cattle thrived on the grasslands. The city was given its name Buenos Aires [Good Airs] not because its winds are good (strong winds rush in from the empty pampas called the *Pampero*, or from the south called the *Sudestada*, hence the saying, "wind from the South East / rain like the pest "), but in honor of the patron saint of sailors, the Virgin of the Buen Ayre. In 1947, despite this disclaimer, Julio Rinaldi defined Buenos Aires as "the playground of the winds. It knows the lassitude of the hot, heavy north wind, the relief of the south-west wind..."

The best witness to the first founding is the German chronicler Ulrich Schmidel in his *Derrotero y viaje a España y las Indias* [Log of a journey to Spain and the Indies, 1567] written after spending more than twenty-four years as a mercenary soldier between what today are Argentina and Paraguay (there is a statue of him in Parque Lezama). He mentions the seventy-two horses brought over with Pedro de Mendoza, the simple fort, with three-foot thick mud walls, remarking that "people were dying of hunger," eating their own horses, even each other ("it so happened that a Spaniard has eaten his own brother who was dead"). One of the constant concerns was food—an irony given the myth of abundance, the image of Argentina as a cornucopia, centuries later.

Cannibalism in early Buenos Aires (from Schmidel's account)

The city was refounded by the Basque Juan de Garay (1528-1583) in 1580 on his way down river from Asunción, Paraguay. His statue by the German sculptor Gustav Eberlein stands on the spot where he was meant to have established it, just north of the Casa Rosada. The first time that the word "Argentina" (falsely promising silver) was printed was in Martín Barco de Centenera's (1544-1602) long didactic poem *Argentina y la conquista del Río de la Plata* [Argentina and the Conquest of the River Plate, 1602]. In the 1840s, according to José Mármol (1817-1871), traces of Garay's early founding could still be seen in some of the ancient houses. In Mármol's *Amalia* (1851), Argentina's first novel but published in Montevideo during the exile of anti-Rosas intellectuals, the narrator describes the place where it all began: "A few paces away, he knocked at the door of a house whose look gave it a respectable air of antiquity, revealing it to be if not the daughter at least granddaughter of those who began to build on that Wednesday 11th of June in the year of grace of 1580, in which the governor don Juan de Garay founded the city of Trinidad and port of Buenos Aires, distributing the city into one hundred and forty-four blocks..." Argentina's greatest writer, Borges, wrote an ironic poem, which he continuously tinkered with, about this inauspicious start called "The Mythical Foundation of Buenos Aires." Here he rewrites history to claim that the city was founded in his *barrio* of Palermo, not in La Boca, for its "pavements," with street organs, *compadritos* [local tough guys], shops, Yrigoyen supporters and tangos, is more deeply Argentine than Genoese La Boca.

Garay founded a checker-board city, following the Laws of the Indies, divided into *manzanas* [blocks]. As it was a port, the Plaza Mayor [main square] was by the river rather than in the centre. At that time the river came up to the banks (the *barrancas* or the *bajo*). Round the main square were built the Cathedral, the Cabildo [town hall—but also the first prison], the fort and further churches. By the 1840s, the city was dominated by the Cabildo's church bells (confirming the slow passing of the hours in the novel *Amalia*). In 1870 Juan de Garay's house still stood, according to the eccentric Scottish writer Robert Cunninghame Graham (1852-1936), "a long low brick or mud adobe edifice, close to the corner of the square," but was demolished by his second visit. Through E. Vidal's watercolors in his *Picturesque Illustrations of Buenos Aires* (1820) you get a sense of the city house facades (Vidal never painted any interiors), made not of rare stone but of baked adobe bricks called *chorizos*—sausages. These early dwellings were not rendered and had high doors and protruding iron-grilled windows, with flat roofs (*azoteas*) ornamented with railings and stone pineapples or vases. The inside, according to Blas Matamoro, was based on the Roman Pompeian plan, with a first inner patio with a well or rain-collecting tank (*aljibe*) and where the owners slept, then a second patio where the children slept, and a third patio for the servants. None of this could be seen from the streets.

For most of the colonial period Buenos Aires was a small village, far from the Spanish Crown's monopoly ports like Cartagena in present-day Colombia, and locations of mining wealth in Peru and Bolivia. But Potosí's fabulous silver trade passed more quickly down river to Buenos Aires (two months) than over mountains to Lima (four months). Argentina's population in 1508 of 2,000 rose to 24,200 in 1779, while Buenos Aires's 580 people in 1580 jumped to 7,500 in 1700. The city survived on smuggling, tallow and cured hides. In 1618 Buenos Aires was made a seat of governorship. The Jesuit Antonio Sepp left an image of a small backwater in 1691: "the little village of Buenos Aires does not have more than two streets in the form of a cross." Things were not very different in 1727 when the German Jesuit Miguel Herre wrote: "Buenos Aires is called a city, but in Germany many villages are larger... In itself Buenos Aires is ugly; it only has three churches, with ours, the worst, found near the centre, by the fort. On one side is the Franciscan convent; on the other the attractive cathedral built in lime and bricks and covered in tiles; all the buildings are built with sticks and mud, like swallows nests." Herre then comments despairingly on the *porteños*:

> *In this part of the New World those who come from Spain are held as nobles, that is, all are white. You can distinguish them from the rest by how they talk and dress but not by how they live for they live like beggars. However, this does not prevent them from being arrogant; they scorn the arts and those who enjoy working, while those who know nothing and live idly are called nobles. In Germany men cut their hair and women wear it long; here everything is upside down for women shave their heads and man have long curls.*

The reality of illegal trade ensured that by 1776 Buenos Aires was nominated the capital of the Viceroyalty of the Rio de la Plata, with don Pedro de Cevallos its first viceroy, and was allowed to trade directly with Spain and its other colonies. But dissatisfaction with the Spanish colonial system was mounting.

Events that helped define the pre-independence *porteño* identity were "the English invasions." The first invasion took place on June 26, 1806, when General Beresford landed with 1,560 soldiers at Quilmes. He had liberated the Cape of Good Hope from the Dutch, and lured by possible booty and gold, thought he could repeat the same feat in the River Plate, but, apparently, without official British government support. On July 2, 1806 the unprepared city of Buenos Aires surrendered and Beresford became its governor. The Spanish Viceroy fled inland to Córdoba, while Beresford allowed the locals freedom to worship, own property and trade within the British Empire.

But swapping one empire for another was not to *porteño* tastes, and Juan Martín de Pueyrredón trained a resistance army of 12,000 who crept into Buenos Aires through the Tigre Delta. These 12,000 patriots, under the Frenchman Santiago de Liniers (1753-1810), forced the British to retreat first into the Retiro bull-ring where the Retiro station is today, then to the Cabildo, and finally to the fort (today's Casa Rosada). Eventually Beresford surrendered (later Liniers was sentenced to death by *harquebus*, and gave his name to today's main slaughterhouse). The invading British had been in power for forty-seven days. The cowardly Viceroy Sobremonte was voted out by the open-air assembly (*cabildo abierto*) and sent packing to Spain. This was the *reconquista* of the street name in Buenos Aires, a name echoing the other famous *Reconquista* of Spain from the Moors in 1492.

The British sought to recapture Buenos Aires with the help of Sir Home Popham's fleet. After taking Montevideo, General Whitlocke landed at Ensenada, near La Plata, on June 28, 1807 with 8,400 men and marched into the city. So as not to destroy the city, Whitlocke disastrously refrained from using artillery and sent his men in columns down the narrow streets. A Spanish merchant, Martín de Alzaga, organized the defence (La Defensa, another street name) from rooftops and windows, with the inhabitants pouring boiling water and dropping stones onto the heads of the hapless British. Whitlocke lost 2,900 men out of 7,000 and within nine days had surrendered. During the fighting British soldiers hid in the Santo Domingo church on Defensa and Avenida Belgrano, and it is here that the regimental colors hung after the surrender. Cannonball hits still scar the tower. Argentine patriots had formed an army, and by tasting their own power and asserting their will, had got rid of two empires and were the first to find independence in Latin America. Vicente López commemorated this deed in a pompous neo-classic poem of over one thousand hendecasyllables, *Heroic Poem in*

Memory of the Heroic Defence of Buenos Aires against an Army of One Thousand Men that Attacked it Between the 2nd and 6th of July. At that time the city held just 33,822 inhabitants.

After the expulsion of the British from the city, Charles IV appointed the French-born Liniers as interim viceroy, but events in Europe led to dramatic changes after France invaded Spain and placed Napoleon on the throne. In the ensuing confusion the Spanish colonies no longer had a king to obey. A meeting was organized on May 25, 1810 in the Plaza Mayor (today's Playa de Mayo) called the Cabildo Abierto, where those who could vote (some 476 men) appointed a *junta* to run the colony and so ushered in independence from Spain. The first *junta* (its president was Cornelio Saavedra) had to deal with dissension and executed Liniers in Cabeza de Tigre, Córdoba, as well as Alzaga, the hero of the British invasions, in the Plaza Mayor, which saw countless further executions. By 1813 the ex-colony refused to give its oath of allegiance to the restored Spanish monarch Ferdinand VII, and with Carlos Alvear as president, Argentina could be said to have become fully independent.

From these years right up to 1880, Argentina, or as it was called then, the United Provinces of Río de la Plata (under Rosas it was called the Argentine Confederation), fought a virtual civil war over tensions between the provinces and the capital city. There were also violent conflicts between those who remained loyal to the monarchical ideal and Jacobins such as Mariano Moreno (1777-1811), the translator of Rousseau's *Social Contract*. While some factions supported a federal ideal preserving Spanish customs, others envisaged a country with a dominant capital and a modern capitalist project. Constant invasions, rebellions, secessions, foreign interventions and blockades (especially British and French) paralyzed the utopian ideals of the thinker (and eventual president) Bernardino Rivadavia (1780-1857). In the first five years of freedom from Spain there were six governments. Finally, from the city of Tucumán came the declaration of independence on July 9, 1816, still an important day in the official calendar.

But independence did not bring stability. Social life was polarized in often violent tussles between *porteños* and *provincianos* as to how to run the country. Only when strongman Juan Manuel de Rosas (1793-1877) stepped in as the Restorer of Laws in 1829 with his federal government, was some order forced on to the mess. Rosas had no time for the modernizing, pro-European liberals of Buenos Aires (called *unitarios*), with their call for immigration and dependence on foreign capital. He imposed his federalist will by espousing the cause of the masses and land-owners, installing a personality cult and a secret police, and pushing the Indians back. He was a traditionalist, a patriot and a Hispanophile. He hung on to power until 1852 when, tired, he was finally defeated by General Justo José de Urquiza (1801-1870) at Caseros and quietly retreated onto a British warship and into exile.

Rosas in Napoleonic pose (Organization of American States)

The "capital problem" was seemingly resolved by President Bartolomé Mitre (1821-1906) in 1862 when he defeated General

Urquiza and when Buenos Aires, enriched by its customs taxes, dominated the rest of the country. Over the next twenty years under presidents Mitre, Sarmiento, Avellaneda and Roca this position was consolidated with the establishment of public schools, a national bank, an army and legal reform. As immigration changed the country and railways opened out the wide tracts of lands regained from the Indians by General Julio A. Roca's (1843-1914) campaign against them in 1879-1880, the role of the city as port and industrial centre became increasingly important. However, only in 1880 was Buenos Aires finally proclaimed federal capital of Argentina after a brief civil war and the temporary transfer of capital city status to nearby Belgrano.

From Village to City
The image of the city as a small provincial settlement was enshrined in Lucio Vicente López's (1848-1894) fictionalized memoirs of his childhood in Buenos Aires called *La gran aldea*, [The great village, 1884]. The book evokes the city just as it mutated into the richest city in Latin America in the 1850s. By 1885 Buenos Aires had 663,854 inhabitants. López's title became a set phrase, a nostalgic synonym for the city.

Between May 1895 and December 1912, the population of the country doubled (3,954,911 to 7,570,400), thanks to immigration. Some 56 million Europeans emigrated during this period, with the United States attracting over 32 million, and Argentina in second place with some 6,500,000. But Argentina had a higher proportion of foreigners over natives than the States (30 percent in 1914 according to Francis Korn, 42.7 percent in 1914, according to Horacio Vázquez Rial; ah, statistics…).

Immigration was welcomed and encouraged. Spanish colonial policy had excluded foreigners, but as the rich *pampas* were purged of the fierce nomadic Indians, and cattle and sheep farming led to economic booms through salting and freezing plants, so the land and the industrial city needed workers and immigration became an issue. An early advocate of such immigration was Argentina's first president Bernardino Rivadavia, who in 1826 dreamed of British immigration and offered free passages, free land and start-up money. Then, under Rosas, immigration was halted from 1829 until 1852, when the jurist Alberdi famously announced the solution to his country's development problems in his battle cry "to govern is to populate." Immigration became government policy, with five free days in the Hotel de Inmigrantes on arrival. By 1914, four-fifths of the Argentine population was immigrant-based, mainly Italian and then Spanish. Because vast tracts of land were owned by the select few and agricultural colonies tended to fail, most of these immigrants remained in the city.

Buenos Aires continued to grow. The historian James Scobie has shown how by 1910 Buenos Aires had progressed from being a plaza-orientated city to one with a downtown and suburbs as a result of Argentina's two economic booms, in 1884-1889, and again in 1905-1912, becoming "the showplace of Latin America." If the whole metropolitan area is taken into account, then the population growth between 1914 and 1970 was from 2,035,031 to 8,352,900. There are now larger cities in Latin America (Mexico City and São Paulo), but of all Latin American cities Buenos Aires still possesses the highest percentage of the total national population (11 million out of Argentina's 33 million in the mid-1990s).

A good description of central Buenos Aires in 1870 comes in Cunninghame Graham's sketch "Le Chef":

Just at the corner of the streets called Twenty-fifth of May and Calle de Cangallo stood Claraz's hotel. On those days, long before the city of La Plata rose and fell, before La Unión Cívica was known, and whilst the echoes of the Paraguayan War were still resounding in the River Plate, it was a busy spot. The life of Buenos Aires ran before the door. Only three squares away the two great Plazas, with their palaces and barracks, basked in the sun, or shivered in the wind, according as the Pampero whistled, or the hot north wind blew. The Stock Exchange was near; the mole within a stone's throw, and up the deep-cut Calle de Cangallo, which looked more like a dry canal than a great thoroughfare, stood several of the principal hotels. The house was built all round a courtyard, with a great archway over which were rooms upon an upper floor where Claraz kept his saddlery, his books. The rest of the establishment was but one story high, though being built upon a bank it looked right out across the River Plate, in Buenos Aires nearly thirty miles in breadth, so that the houses in La Colonia, on the other side, are only visible upon the clearest days.

In *La gran aldea* (the title suggests that the city is the protagonist), Vicente López anatomized the changes in Buenos Aires between the 1860s and the 1890s, concluding: "Buenos Aires was not then what it is today." He takes the shops as symbols of this mutation: "The European shops of today, hybrid and rickety, without local color, have banished the *porteño* shop." Just as today antiseptic Americanized shopping malls are replacing the small shops on every block. These European shops had windows that "sweeten the eyes without satisfying the need to touch," while the old shops were stalls where you could finger the produce. By the first edition of the prestigious German *Baedecker* guide (1900) on Argentina, the city had a "modern elegant aspect, like that of the most advanced towns. The private edifices, the luxurious premises of the shops, the pavements of asphalt, give to Buenos Aires the cachet of the great metropolis," making it larger, by area, than Paris and Berlin.

The Port

Fifteen different steamship companies reached the port in 1900. More than elsewhere, it was the port that reflected this leap in modernization. Originally, goods and passengers were carted off the boats from the shore. José Antonio Wilde evoked this shore-port in the 1830s as "a messy patch of land covered in rubbish, sand and whatever the tide left; great quantities of fish chucked away by the fishermen could be seen, often rotting, for it was also where people dumped their rubbish and dead horses." The city seen from the shore by arriving passengers was a "strip of poorly built, low houses, all looking the same." To improve this port, the Riachuelo was dredged and ships docked in La Boca. Subsequently, Puerto Madero, named after Eduardo Madero and his tendering group backed by British capital, was completed in 1898 and expanded in 1925–26 (the Puerto Nuevo), to give Buenos Aires its grand (and decaying) port look. In 1921 Baldomero Fernández Moreno wrote a Cubist poem about the port seen from his city rooftop: "Zinc grain elevators, / brick warehouses, / formidable black cranes, / the gray sticks of boats. / Chimneys, lightning rods, / trees dried by the cold, /

points, angles, triangles, / roughness, brushings, noises.../ And a white sail / on the gracious calm river." A character in Eduardo Mallea's nine-part novel about Buenos Aires, *La ciudad junto al río inmóvil* [The city next to the immobile river, 1936] looks down on the living port: "The port opened its monstrous mouth, night traveled, the beautiful nocturnal waters shone. The complaint of a powerful animal vibrated; piercing sirens of factories broke the throats of the estuary, moved the masts, skeletal castles." Marechal saw this port as the engine-house of the city in the extravagant opening of his novel *Adán Buenosayres*:

> Sonorous, black ships anchored in the port of Santa María de los Buenos Aires, throwing on to the docks the industrial harvest of both hemispheres, the color and sound of four races, and iodine and salt from the seven seas; and at the same time, jammed with the fauna, flora and minerals of our land, tall, solemn boats left for the eight directions over water amidst the harsh farewell of naval sirens. If from there you went up the Riachuelo to the frigorífico factories, you could admire chutes bursting with cattle and the skilled knives of the slaughterers ready to offer a catastrophe to satisfy the world's voracity. Orchestra trains entered the city or left for the greenery of the north... from the factories of Avellaneda to Belgrano the metropolis was ringed by smoking chimneys.

The port was visible from everywhere. Ernesto Sabato's protagonists sit on a bench in the Plaza San Martín, looking down on the "Torre de los Ingleses... the mass of the CADE, with its great, squat chimneys, and the Puerto Nuevo with its grain elevators and cranes; abstract, antediluvian animals with steel beaks and heads of gigantic birds bending down, pecking at the boats."

Manuel Gálvez's love-sick poet Carlos Riga in *El mal metafísico* [The metaphysical sickness, 1916] goes to the port to see his loved one taken off on her European tour for four years. (Borges' family, too, went away for seven years, as it was cheaper to live in Europe at the turn of the century than in Buenos Aires):

> At last the Cap Ortegal began to move. From under parasols flew farewells, trivial phrases. Some sent kisses, all waved handkerchiefs until the boat was in the middle of the dock. Lita had run to the poop... The poet was then inspired. He left the wharf and ran like a madman. He went towards the end of the long dock, a narrow canal along which the steamship would pass

as it brushed the walls. Riga ran and ran, arriving breathless. The transat-
lantic steamer approached sluggishly, dragged by a tug.

Juana Manuela Gorriti's (1818-1892) orphaned *folletinista* [pamphlet writer], in her short novel *Oasis en la vida* [Oasis in life, 1888] arrived back in Buenos Aires after fourteen happy years in Paris, a *desterrado* [an exile] in his native city. His ship docks, he sends his luggage by coach and walks, perceiving the city through the rose-tinted glasses of nostalgia, moved by the change from "village" to modern city since he had been abroad:

And Mauricio walked along the Avenida Montes de Oca and from there
went between villas [quintas], chalets, gardens and orchards.

The sad thoughts that had assaulted him on arrival, vanished before
the grand spectacle he was looking at.

Of the Buenos Aires he remembered, he only recognized the name
into which the glorious metropolis had turned. Its leveled streets, with
lights, furrowed by metal rails, with wide pavements, and richly paved;
its renovated houses, transformed into palaces; its squares become gardens
adorned with statues; avenues with palm-trees, that reminded him of the
fabulous riches of India; its schools which mimic sumptuous palaces; its
theatres visited by world famous celebrities, with a public of exquisite
tastes that judges severely and pays generously.

The port, then, has traditionally been the place of arrivals and departures, a space of intense emotions, offering first and last sight of the metamorphosing city. Silvina Bullrich's (1915-1990) anguished painter in her satirical novel *Calles de Buenos Aires* [Streets of Buenos Aires, 1939] drives around the port; fantasizing about escaping his city for Europe, he "sighed looking at the transatlantic liners that evoked new horizons."

One building in the port that held nostalgic associations for arriving passengers was the vast and palatial Aduana, or Customs. When we arrived in the port on a ship that took thirteen days from Genoa in 1974, this awesome Customs building was where we opened trunks of clothes, books and toys (we had decided to live in Buenos Aires for at least a year), nearly lost everything to a greedy official, and were only saved by dollar bills tickling palms. Gerald Durrell caught this Aduana ambiance: "At the precise moment we were heading towards the massive building... in whose massive interior lurked the most formidable enemy of sanity and liberty in Argentina: the Aduana, or Customs. On my arrival, some three weeks earlier, they had let all my highly dutiable articles of equipment into the country without a murmur... but, for some reason known only to the Almighty and the scintillating brains in the Aduana, they had confiscated all my pets." The Loire-château-ish Aduana building was opened in 1910 on Plaza Justo, overlooking the Avenida Belgrano bridge between Dique 2 and 3 of the port, after several earlier sites were used. Its grandiloquence is a reminder of the wealth and importance of smuggling during the colonial period when Buenos Aires was not allowed to trade except through the official ports thousands of miles away to the north (Cartagena in Colombia).

But today this port has lost its passenger facilities, thanks to cheap air travel and to container shipping, and since 1989, like London's docklands, has been reclaimed for the city dwellers, the urban regenerators respecting the original red-brick warehouses. Puerto Madero is almost a new *barrio*, the solidly built dockside warehouses that sit in a row several miles long have been stylishly converted into offices and expensive restaurants. There are plans for a Museo del Mar, a Museo de Ciencia, the Universidad Católica Argentina and a cultural complex. In 1999 this renovated dock area stood for Buenos Aires at its most New Yorkishly modern, where filmmaker Beda Docampo Feijóo set his over-acted parable about teenage awakening to life, *Buenos Aires me mata* [Buenos Aires is killing me] in a nightclub in a quay-side warehouse.

The Airport

Most arrivals and departures, with their emotional highs and lows, now take place at Ezeiza airport (officially known as Aeropuerto Internacional Ministro Pistarini), roughly twenty-five miles from the city centre. People still throng the roof and shout at family and friends staggering out of planes after long flights (Buenos Aires is not a place you happen to pass through; a direct flight from Madrid takes slightly less than twelve hours). The road to Ezeiza was the scene of a bitter and bloody confrontation between the left-wing urban guerrillas and the right-wing Peronists awaiting Perón's return from exile in Franco's

Madrid in 1973, narrated in detail in Tomás Eloy Martínez's *La novela de Perón* [*The Perón Novel*, 1985]. In 1983, after seven years in exile, the novelist and satirist Osvaldo Soriano (1943-1997) arrived back at Ezeiza. After passport control, customs and changing money, he took a *remis* into town (*remises* are the equivalent of London's mini-cabs and cannot be hailed from the streets) along the new concrete and tolled overhead highway: "Forty kilometers of motorway built by the military. The toll is so expensive that you hardly see cars. This monstrosity [*mastodonte*] is like a dumb monument to that vain and pretentious Argentina that the Proceso de Reorganización Nacional [military dictatorship jargon] tried to invent and that's now moribund." He drives over the demolished houses, reads the political slogans and graffiti. This empty overhead entry into Buenos Aires, the Autopista 25 de Mayo, the first sight for most arrivals, makes the city look very urban and cement-gray, like an overcrowded cemetery.

The other airport for entry to the city, usually for internal flights, is the Aeroparque Jorge Newbery, on the Costanera Norte. You can hear the jets revving, or air-braking, all over the heart of the city.

History of Buenos Aires (continued)

"*I do not doubt that politics is a real shit.*" Pacho O'Donnell, playwright and ex-Minister of Culture

The Intendente (or mayor) most responsible for modernizing the city was Torcuato de Alvear who, as the first mayor from 1880 to 1887, paved streets, planted trees in the plazas, made the Plaza de Mayo into a single square by demolishing the Recova and planting palm trees, and began work on the expansion of the Avenida de Mayo. It amounted to the "Parisification" of the city, echoing the opening up of Paris into grand avenues under Baron Haussmann, the Prefect of Paris, in the 1850s.

Far more important to the creation of modern Argentina was the building of the railway, linking Buenos Aires to the wealth of the ranching interior and making the port central to the Argentine economy. The first six miles of track were laid in 1857 to Flores; then in 1864 twenty miles north to Tigre; then in 1866 seventy miles to Chascomús. By 1884 there were tracks to the southern port of Bahía

Blanca, and by 1886 to Rosario and to the Atlantic resort of Mar del Plata. Most of the lines and trains were owned by four British-based companies, all of which were nationalized by Perón in 1945.

May 1910 was celebrated as the centenary of independence and as the coming of age of the modern, prosperous Buenos Aires, though Manuel Gálvez (1882-1962) set his novel *Nacha Regules* (1919) in 1910 to show the hellish side to this material prosperity, with its white slave trade, and infernal slums. Argentina was a country of more than seven million and optimistic about its future, as seen in Rubén Darío's paean to Argentine progress *Canto a la Argentina* [Song to Argentina, 1910]. The year 1910 saw a great march past on the Avenida de Mayo, with the guests including the *infanta* Isabel, aunt to Alfonso XIII of Spain. But behind the facade, the workers were angry, and confrontations between anarchists, socialists and those in power led to the thousand killed during *la semana trágica* [tragic week].

Arrest of an anarchist (Archivo General de la Nación)

Immigration had changed the face of the city and created a new urban proletariat, organized into unions, with socialist, communist and anarchist elements. Anarchists were responsible for a bomb placed outside the Casa Rosada and for the assassination the chief of police in 1909. Political ferment led to the creation of trade unions and the troubled rise of the Radical party under the populist Hipólito Yrigoyen

(1851-1933), who came to power in 1916, thanks to obligatory universal suffrage (for men) created by the electoral reforms of Sáenz Peña in 1912. A symbolic year highlighting this new immigrant unease was 1919, with the *semana trágica* and general strike in January, leading to street battles between the anarchist left and Catholic right. The omnipresence of strong trade unions in social and political life began here. But immigration also caused nationalist backlashes, and was at the heart of the debate as to who constituted the true Argentine, as it exacerbated the on-going tensions between the cosmopolitan city Buenos Aires and the provinces.

A dialogue in Gálvez's novel, overheard by the idealist forty-year-old Monsalvat (undergoing a mid-life crisis) between so-called friends at a smart dinner party, catches this mood:

> *An infinity of distinguished foreigners, from ambassadors to ladies, even European nobility, come to our country. And what did the rabble do? Take revenge on their idleness, damage our fatherland, ensure that the fiestas fail. A scandal, isn't it? What would these illustrious Europeans have thought about these immigrants? ...*
>
> *"All the foreign strikers and subversives," said the doctor, snorting with rage, "and the immoral Argentines who follow them, should be, were I in charge, shot in the Plaza de Mayo."*

The history of the city of Buenos Aires is inscribed and fragmented in different sections of what follows in this companion, and so a brief outline of how the city and its history intersect in the twentieth century is helpful. The next key date is the 1930 coup that toppled Yrigoyen in the wake of the world financial crisis and the subsequent *década infame* (1930-1943), with conservative power maintained through electoral fraud, military collusion and the exclusion of the Radical party. Behind this decade can be seen the intellectual hand of the poet Leopoldo Lugones (1874-1937) and his motto "La hora de la espada" [The time for the sword], a call for army intervention to return Argentina to its roots and break with North American meddling in local affairs. Lugones was associated with the rise of a sinister nationalism, close to proto-Nazism. The year 1930 was also the beginning of the long period in which the military took on the political role of intervening if it thought that civilian leaders were not patriotic enough. Fascist-Nazi sympathies ran deep in Argentina (as anti-Semitism still does), and the country did not side with the Allies in the Second World War until the war was almost over.

The city's turbulent political history took a new turn in 1943, with a military coup that ended the decade of conservative corruption, introducing Colonel Juan Domingo Perón (1899-1974) as Minister of War and of Labor, who rose to be vice-president under General Farrell in 1945. Perón was then overthrown and imprisoned for eight days on the island of Martín García. A vast popular demonstration in the Plaza de Mayo on October 17, 1945 led to his release and forms one of the magical dates in the Peronist calendar. Perón, a charismatic *caudillo*, in the manner of Rosas and Yrigoyen, had attained power with help from his wife, María Eva Duarte (1919-1952), whom he had married that same October and who had been instrumental in leading the movement to secure his release. In her autobiography *La razón de mi vida* [The reason for my life, 1952], "Evita" Perón recalled those days:

> *I flung myself into the streets looking for friends who could still do something for him. So I went from door to door. In that arduous and incessant walking I felt my heart glowing from the flame of the fire that consumed me absolutely... I walked through the neighborhoods of the great city. As a result, I know every type of heart that palpitates under the sky of my Fatherland...*

Perón was voted into power by the trade unions and masses in general in 1946 with fifty-four percent of the vote. He set about transforming Argentina through rapid industrialization, employing the internal migrants who flooded into the city from the country and nationalizing the British-owned railways, gas, and telephone companies. Perón's nine years in power from 1946 to 1952, and 1952 to 1955, saw the rise of a new mythic heroine, Evita, who gave women the vote in 1947, looked after the poor, and encouraged the *descamisados* (shirtless ones) and the *cabezas negras* (black heads) to take part in civic life and to benefit from social justice. Under Peronism pensions and wages were raised, and paid holidays made obligatory. The demonstrations in support of the Peróns in the Plaza de Mayo are legendary, and criticism of the voted-in "dictator" by the intelligentsia was bitter. As will be seen, Julio Cortázar left the country because Perón severely limited the importation of

European books and films, while Victoria Ocampo and Borges' mother were imprisoned for demonstrating against the government.

The end of Perón came with Evita's slow death from cancer (she died on July 26, 1952). The military had not allowed Evita to become vice-president in 1951, despite her adulatory following among the Buenos Aires masses. A year later, on April 15, 1953, bombs were set off while Perón spoke from the Casa Rosada, leading to "mobs" burning down the Jockey Club. Perón was finally ousted in September 1955, after the bombing by the airforce of the Casa Rosada in June, an atrocity that killed over 300 people in the Plaza de Mayo. In response, countless churches were burned down by anti-clerical Peronists, including Santo Domingo, San Ignacio, La Merced and San Francisco. The military again took over and banned Peronism, so that when they did allow elections it was candidates from the Radical party who became presidents. Arturo Frondizi (1958-1962), then briefly José María Guido and finally Arturo Ilía (1963-1966) held tenuous power amidst many military *golpes* (misleadingly called revolutions). Perón, meanwhile, awaited his return from exile in Franco's Spain.

The example of the Argentine Che Guevara and the Cuban Revolution led to the rise of urban guerrillas in the form of the People's Revolutionary Army (ERP) and the Montoneros, who took their name from an earlier generation of rural guerrillas. Both groups were active in Buenos Aires from the late 1960s on. They were characterized by their impatience with liberal democracy and army interventions, showing a Robin Hood flair and attracting thousands of radicalized students and ex-Peronists.

After long years of military repression and civil strife, General Alejandro Lanusse finally opted for a return to civilian rule and allowed Peronists to stand in elections in 1973, a move which led to the victory of Héctor Cámpora, whose presidency was merely intended as a prelude to the return of the "great leader." This eagerly-awaited event ended in violence and tragedy when rival left-wing and right-wing groups engaged in a shoot-out at Ezeiza airport, where an estimated two million Argentines had turned out to welcome Perón. In the following months chaos reigned, as Perón was elected for the third time with almost 62 percent of the votes. Veering to the right and embracing repression, the champion of the masses seemed strangely out of touch and became more and more involved, through his third wife Isabel, with right-wing death squads. After his death in July 1974, his wife took over the presidency and the crisis deepened. Everyday life in the city was tense; the death squads fought with the guerrillas, who included many poets and writers from Juan Gelman to Miguel Angel Bustos and Paco Urondo—the latter two were killed fighting. A daily spate of bombs, power cuts and brutalities took place until a deadly military crackdown in 1976. The ensuing military regime exacted a ghastly toll of nearly 9,000 *desaparecidos* or "disappeared" (some calculate as many as 30,000), but led to further resistance, embodied by the brave *madres de la Plaza de Mayo* [Mothers of the Plaza de Mayo], who later became the *abuelas* or grandmothers. It was during this dictatorship that Argentina won the soccer World Cup in 1978 in a brief, nasty resurgence of manipulated patriotism.

The stupid gamble the military took by invading the Malvinas/Falklands islands (rather than negotiating for the bleak outpost that Britain no longer wanted) led to war, pointless deaths—now commemorated in the Plaza San Martín—and a confused patriotism that again saw the Plaza de Mayo crowded with mindless, chanting jingoists. The only positive outcome of this war was to speed the restoration of democracy in 1983 with Radical Raúl Alfonsín elected. He was beset by staggering economic problems (5,000 to 28,000 percent inflation during his presidency and massive speculation), but tried to set up trials and establish exactly who had "disappeared." After Alfonsín, Peronism returned in 1989 under the colorful but astute Carlos Menem. His love of women and fast cars, his *caudillo* sideburns and worship of Rosas, as well as his public soap-opera disputes with his wife and the sad death of his son, became daily gossip. Yet he tamed inflation, stabilized the economy and changed the constitution (scrapping the no re-election clause) to remain in power for a decade. His intended aim was to push Argentina back into being a "first-world country" (as it was in the 1940s), with his *dolarización* (dollar parity) of the *peso*.

All this and far more has permeated city life, entered the collective urban psyche. New and sometime bitter landmarks range from former torture houses to the military-built overhead highway, from the symbolism of the Plaza de Mayo to the marble memorial in the Plaza San Martín. Other modern transformations testify more to wider trends and fashions: the ecological park off the docks, the banning of burning garbage in tower blocks, the tidying and privatization of the plazas, and the gentrification of the port area. Massive European immigration has changed the city forever from its Latin American roots, although later immigration under Peronism from the provinces and neighboring countries like Bolivia and Paraguay has re-Latinamericanized the city. This continuum of events has been filtered and recreated through writers, whose different takes on the city's history have been brought together in this book.

The Escudo (Coat of Arms) of the city depicts two sailing ships, sails furled and at anchor, with a dove symbolizing the Holy Spirit (enlarged in the original colonial coat of arms) flying above them over a calm sea (or river). Leopoldo Marechal wanted to change this dove into a hen in *Adán Buenosayres*: "The hen, perfect symbol of Buenos Aires!" He has his Jewish, bohemian philosopher Samuel Tesler explain: "you will find a clucking people who scratch the earth with their industrious legs and peck about night and day without remembering sad Psyche, without raising their eyes to heaven, without listening to the music of the spheres." Marechal's novel debates the destiny of its artist characters in this "hen's city," all the time conscious that *gallina* [hen] was slang for a whore.

Ezequiel Martínez Estrada claimed two miracles happened in Buenos Aires: the first was that it snowed in 1919 (the *Guía Pirelli* corrects this date to 1918; it snowed once more on June 6, 1955); the second was the unexplained arrival of thousands of swallows in 1932. The hottest day on record was January 30, 1957 at 43.3°C (110°F) and the coldest on July 9, 1918 at -5.4°C (22°F), according to the same *Guía Pirelli*. At the end of the news comes the weather. A riverine city with high humidity makes both the winter cold seem colder and the summer heat hotter. When I first arrived in Buenos Aires in August, I was shocked at the number of people in fur coats complaining of the cold. The Spanish avant-gardist Ramón Gómez de la Serna (1888-1963) joked about this riverine humidity: "Humidity ensures that the virginal envelopes that we keep in the drawers of our desk seal themselves and become mysterious, as if they had a letter inside, which eases the tedious labor of writing because all you have to do is address them." Not that Argentines are great letter-writers. The summer is unbearable (Gómez de la Serna called summer "the empire of sweat"), with fans and air-conditioners overworking and dripping water on to the pavements. He explained to fellow Spaniards: "This is a fantastic and capricious climate, in which you never know which season it is, because there are summer days in winter, and many spring days in autumn." Clearly, this unpredictability and extremity link the climate with the nature of the people. The consensus, though, is that spring is the best time to be there—from mid-September on. As Manuel Gálvez wrote in 1919: "September. Spring. Buenos Aires with its tree-lined streets, its parks, its squares, the long walks that make an enchanting path along the river, suddenly flower, stained with green, all shades of green... Oh Spring in Buenos Aires!"

Porteños

"*I think that there is something essentially porteño in me... In my dreams I am always in Buenos Aires.*" Borges

There have been many attempts to characterize the typical *porteño* through time, though the "port" today is no longer the economic hub of the city. Perhaps history best captures local uniqueness. In the 1840s the exiled patriot Mármol described the *porteños* thus in his novel *Amalia*: "These porteño people who pass with facility from tears to laughter, from being serious to being puerile, from great things to trivialities: a people of Spanish blood and French mind, although that wasn't Dorrego's opinion when from the tribune he shouted at the crowd who heckled him: 'Silence, you Italians...'" Already by the 1840s, then, Buenos Aires was something of a cultural melting-pot. A little later in the 1870s the Scottish adventurer and scribbler Robert Cunninghame Graham remembered the upper classes in his sketch "Le Chef" as thinking of themselves as "the first of humankind," and noted that they scorned the English "gringos," the Italian "carcamanos," the Spanish "gallegos," and the Brazilian "macacos" (monkeys). Women were "dressed in a loose black skirt with petticoats much starched and laced" with "mantas" over their heads as disguise, and only walked the streets to mass. He found that society followed semi-Moorish rules, with the "men at parties congregating into knots, smoking and talking scandal, and the girls seated upon chairs, whispering in undertones whilst managing their fans." It was without doubt a view of the élite who despised the immigrants.

The Spanish philosopher José Ortega y Gasset (1883-1955), a one-time resident in Buenos Aires, located *porteño* typicality in the male *guarango* [literally, a lout] who had an enormous appetite to become someone admirable, superlative, unique, but failing to attain this desired future, turned aggressive; hence the *guarango's* "imaginary superiority over the rest." Later in the 1940s and 1950s Evita Perón was called a *guaranga* by her class enemies. Borges in 1931 sought this dubious national essence in the more or less untranslatable figures of the *compadrito* and the *guapo*, knife fighters and singers who lived in the outskirts, descendants of the *gaucho* and immigrants from the countryside. The historian of Buenos Aires, James Scobie, described this *compadrito* (neighborhood tough) with "high-heeled boots, a silk handkerchief knotted at the neck and a slouch hat"; it was an exaggeratedly *macho* look, though the individual was usually harmless. From the 1930s on, isolated, alienated individuals in a vast urban metropolis became the constant objects of diagnosis for writers from Roberto Arlt to Raúl Scalabrini Ortiz. The latter's study of the "*porteño* man" titled *El hombre que está solo y espera* [The man who is alone and waits, 1931] examines the *macho* stare, the rampant individualism, the constant improvisations, the judging of the person not ideas, the primacy of intuition over intellect. He wrote: "The *porteño* does not read, does not make any preparations in life, is a man of sudden intuitions." This typical man he famously called "the man of the street corners of Corrientes y Esmeralda," this city corner having turned into the magnetic pole or pivot of Buenos Aires. The key to his soul is that "he recognizes himself in the words of tangos."

The historian Luis Arocena changed this pessimistic diagnosis to one of a people with a "satisfied knowledge of their urban rootlessness." One possible definition of the *porteño* is hence his or her love for the city, despite everything. Silvina Bullrich's neurotic painter in *Calles de Buenos*

Aires epitomizes this trait: "He wanted to distract himself but only managed to return to another obsession: his city." So many books, films and tangos reflect this *idée fixe* in their titles (I hear in my head Gardel singing "Mi Buenos Aires querido..."). The obsession has led to countless local histories (I know of four books on the Avenida de Mayo, and several on each *barrio*), a mass of documentation which boasts of a pride in the city that differentiates the *porteño* from, say, a Londoner or New Yorker.

The prolific novelist, biographer, and, at the end of his life Catholic nationalist, Manuel Gálvez saw many kinds of *porteños*, but singled out for satire the type of the "good porteño" who naively "admires success." Certainly, to triumph abroad earns fame at home (Borges won the Formentor prize in 1961 with Samuel Beckett, only then to become famous in Buenos Aires; Hollywood Oscars nominations pull people to national films they otherwise avoid). Receptivity to foreign approval remains strong. Foreigners are generously welcomed, as Lucio V. López observed in *La gran aldea*: "because in Buenos Aires we are so friendly that it's easier for a foreigner who has just arrived to have the doors opened to high society, no matter who he is, than for a son of this country who has never traveled abroad." I myself can attest to this openness after countless trips to this generous city.

The Marxist Juan José Sebreli came up with many *porteño* types, from the "medio pelo" or middle-class upstart, who could be a rich industrialist or general, decried by the supposedly aristocratic, to the "petiterismo" or snobs associated with the Avenida Santa Fe's Petit Café in the 1950s, who mimicked upper-class tastes and fashions. Sebreli linked the *cabecita negra* [little black head], another national stereotype to Argentina's industrialization and the rise of a genuinely national proletariat, under Perón. Gradations and nuances of color, race and class have always been part of the city's typology. A *negro*, for instance, could be blond if he came from the working class. The *atorrante* was an immigrant who hadn't made it, who lived homeless in the gutter; a poet could be an *atorrante*. As a city of immigrants, foreigners become stereotyped: there was the *gringo* [derived from *griego* meaning Greek], at first a term applied to Italians, the largest immigrant group who were also known as *tanos* (Napolitanos); the *gallego* (meaning a "dumb" Galician), the second largest group, mostly from Galicia and still the butt of Argentine jokes;

the *turco*, anyone from anywhere in the Middle East; and the *ruso*, usually a Jew (there are today over 300,000 Jews in Buenos Aires) but in fact an ample, imprecise adjective applied to Poles, and Central Europeans. Often these categories can be used as nicknames.

In my experience, though, the terms *vivo* [clever, vivacious] and *viveza criolla* [native wit] stand for what is most peculiar to the city. To be *vivo* is to be street-wise, agile, cunning—all desirable, if arguably anti-social, attributes. Florencio Escardó (1904-1992), a medical doctor and popular writer, saw the *vivo*'s "mental agility" and "rapid communication" as typical of the *porteño*. In traffic jams they hoot not out of impatience or frustration, but to say "wake up sleepy" to the car in front, find a way out of this mess. In 1955 Miguel Delibes, the Spanish novelist, noted the unique *porteño* method of parking cars by bumping them together and leaving no gaps, a technique that requires everybody to leave their hand brakes off. This is still a widely practiced response to a shortage of parking space as well as another expression of *viveza*. In 1965 Gordon Meyer thought that "none of the dozen or so dictionary renderings convey the essence of viveza criolla", choosing himself "that of being smart at the expense of another, a quality of smart-Aleckness." All that matters in a discussion, he remarked, is the "lightening riposte." In 1998 Miranda France translated *viveza criolla* as "creole cunning", artful lying and cheating, with footballer Diego Maradona its supreme embodiment. This *viveza* is to be found in certain forms of behavior, but especially in verbal wit or cheek. Delibes found the whole city constantly *talking*: "In Argentina everything talks from taxis to trams, to shop-windows, even the stones on the Andes mountains... Everything talks, shouts, in Argentina: about Perón, about Evita, the shirtless ones [*los descamisados*] and five-year plans. It doesn't matter: the point is to talk." The *vivo* is the improviser, the quick fixer, the street-wise survivor. The opposite of the *vivo* is the *boludo*, a term meaning "heavy-balls", constantly overheard in street talk, with its synonym *pelotudo*. Just before he escaped to die in Geneva, Borges said that he found *porteños* boasters, and accused them of being "superficial, frivolous, snobs"—another, less benign, interpretation of *vivo* behavior.

In defining the uniqueness of the *porteño*, Escardó argued that "the porteño self can only be understood in active combination with his city" and that to understand the one you must study the other, for city and inhabitant mutually create each other. Escardó saw the city taxi-driver in his yellow and black car, often festooned with religious paraphernalia with radio blaring tangos or rock, as the *vox populi*, not as a provider of a service but as a travel companion. The taxi driver is the thermometer of people's reactions to politics, the hoarder of street gossip. He represents his city (I know many people who report gossip with a taxi driver as real sources of information, as authoritative fact rather than the Chinese whispers that enliven city life).

Foreigners who seek to categorize *porteños* often stress attributes of collective melancholy and seriousness, best typified by the solitary male in tango lyrics, philosopher Ortega y Gasset's "sombre machos." Marechal's fictional Jewish philosopher Samuel Tesler has a go at these foreigners in the novel *Adán Buenosayres*: "It is time that porteños abandon their stupid reserve. The thirty-two foreign philosophers who have dishonored us with their visits, after taking the pulse of Buenos Aires by plunging a thermometer in its anal orifice, diagnosed that our city is sad... These gringos forget that Buenos Aires is an archipelago of island-men unable to communicate with each other." Earlier, in the 1890s, the Nicaraguan poet Rubén Darío at first found the Argentine "cold" and "indifferent." Other Latin Americans might add further unflattering adjectives such as pompous and pretentious, as seen mockingly in Peruvian novelist Mario Vargas Llosa's witty novel *La tía Julia y el escribidor* [*Aunt Julia and the Scriptwriter*, 1985]. There are countless anti-Argentine jokes in other Latin American countries, which normally poke fun at the allegedly widespread national belief that Argentina is really a part of Europe and has nothing to do with its poorer, dark-skinned, indigenous-influenced neighbors. North American essayist Waldo Frank, who suggested to Victoria Ocampo that she should found a journal that became, in 1931, *Sur*, had noted Argentina's unpopularity in 1944: "Argentina is a peculiar nation. Nobody likes it. Not the United States. Not Brazil. Not a single Spanish-speaking sister-nation!" The art critic Damián Bayón accounted for this distaste by separating the city from its hinterlands: "Buenos Aires is a world apart in Latin America, with its own cultural laws and fashions." This is the case, even within Argentina. Albert Londres wrote:

"I have never seen anyone laugh or smile, stroll or meditate, or wait for something, or nothing, in the streets of Buenos Aires." Borges, in his seminal essay about being Argentine, "The Argentine Writer and Tradition" compared the poet Enrique Banchs' symbolist poems with Ricardo Güiraldes' folkloric *gaucho* novel *Don Segundo Sombra* and asked which of the two was most Argentine, strangely picking Banchs for his mood of "constraint." Borges himself admitted to an "Argentine reserve, distrust and reticence," the "difficulty we have in making confessions, in revealing our intimate nature."

If this was the typical Argentine of the 1940s, almost a clone of Borges himself and surely an Anglophile, does it still convey today's *porteño*? You can still see the stiff suited, dark-blue-blazered, *engominados* [brilliantined] men, but they are dwindling, surviving mainly in the City, the financial quarter, or as diplomats representing Argentina abroad. Street poet Raúl González Tuñón (1905-1974) accepted this dour and negative trait: "And although my hat and my tie and my swine's mind / may be perfect European products / I am sad and cordial like a legitimate Argentine." The outrageously satirical comedian Enrique Pinti plays on this national self-perception in his show *Salsa criolla*, categorizing Argentines as "grey," repressed, not daring to break out: "We are the land of half measures and tepid water." Among the young there is still a conformist streak in dressing, with the ubiquitous clean jeans, the pony-tails, the wind-jackets. That old Spanish *qué dirán* [what will the neighbors say?] still haunts the city.

Language, Food and Smells

A *porteño* is also defined by his *porteño* talk which can almost seem like a dialect (which in the case of *lunfardo*, a dockside, underworld slang, it is indeed). Many words in daily use, like *guita* for money, *laburo* for work, *cana* for police, *fiaca* for laziness, *morfar* for to eat, *mina* for woman, *bancar* for to put up with, *trucho,* for fake or false, come from Italian and *lunfardo*. *Lunfardo* was at first the in-language of the underworld. Writer Fray Mocho, a policeman, has a section cataloguing the different kinds of criminals in Buenos Aires in his *Memorias de un vigilante* [Memoirs of a policeman, 1897], called "*lunfardo* world." This criminal's dialect was made popular through tangos. There is an

Academia Porteña del Lunfardo on calle Estado Unidos 1379, with José Gobello, author of a *lunfardo* dictionary, as its secretary, with the objective of promoting *lunfardo* writers and songs. Linguistically speaking, the *voseo* differentiates the city from the provinces (though it applies only to the present tense: *vos sos, vos querés* etc). The slushing sound of the consonants "y" and "ll" make Argentines recognizable to all Spanish speakers, and there is also an Italian lilt. The use of the word *che*, roughly meaning "hey", is also a hallmark, so much that "los che" stands for "los argentinos." Key Argentine words explain the quality of city life. Miranda France picked on *bronca,* meaning anger, and *chanta,* meaning fraud or cheat, as capturing the bad temper, the queues, the telephone hassles of the 1990s. I find it amusing that the English word "sorry" (*sori*) erupts constantly in *porteño* speech. A writer like Julio Cortázar so mimicked *porteño* speech in his short stories that when García Márquez visited Buenos Aires, he thought everybody spoke like characters from Cortázar's fiction.

A *porteño* is characterized, too, by how much he or she talks in a deafeningly noisy city (contrasted with the granite-solid silence of the *pampas*), as already noted by Delibes. According to the newspaper *Clarín* (August 13, 1998), the noisiest street corner in Buenos Aires was Santa Fe and J. B. Justo, recording 104.5 decibels. People talk at each other, vie to get their words in, usually in a confessional mode (backed up by years of Freudian, then Lacanian psychoanalysis), and gossip rules. There are the official stories, and there is gossip where everyone has a say about what is really happening. This gossip tells us about the inner city networks and how small the *porteño* world can seem. Already in 1932, the English literary critic and biographer Philip Guedalla realized that "until you have spent a month in Buenos Aires, you do not know what gossip is." Silvina Bullrich dissected this gossip (*chismes*) in the *barrio norte*, where everybody spied on everybody in order to spread scandal (its roots are in the Spanish panic of *qué dirán*). The district, she wrote, revolved around "scathing criticism, morbid pleasure in being the first to know a scandal and spread it." She blamed the men for spreading *chismes*: "they are the true masters of this art," worse than *solteronas* [spinsters]. Gossip still rules, but the world has spread beyond Bullrich's idle upper class, and is now fuelled by TV chat shows (my favorite being

Mirtha Legrand's lunch with celebrities) and gossip mags, from *Hola* downward.

A *porteño* is further a product of what he or she eats. Meat-eating is a sign of belonging —at one time the average meat eaten per capita was 78 kilos (172 pounds) a year—as is the male belly or *panza* (Perón once called Argentines *panzistas*, perhaps derived from Sancho Panza). The cake and pastry shops—*confiterías*—with the *media luna* and *sandwich de miga* (thin wafers of white bread sliced from giant loaves with numerous fillings) or the *empanadas* (pasties best filled with meat or cheese and onions and which the poet P. J. Kavanagh called "the most delicious snacks in the world") are an intrinsic part of city life. So too are the pizzas and especially the *dulce de leche* (once translated as milk-jam). But to me Buenos Aires is the capital of pasta; there are fresh pasta factories in nearly every block. There is even a *porteño* tradition of eating a plateful of *ñoquis* on the 29th of every month. But if pasta is the Italian inheritance, the Spanish colonial one thrives with maize-based dishes like *humita*, *locro*, and the baked *carbonada*. Germinal Nogués claims that *revuelto gramajo* (scrambled eggs, ham and potato sticks, my daughters' preferred *porteño* dish) is unique to the city.

Barrio café, La Boca (Harriet Cullen)

A symbol of creole Argentine identity, more associated with country customs and *gauchos*, is the use of the gourd with a straw called the *mate* and *bombilla*, often encased in elaborate silver and filled with bitter *yerba mate* (*Ilex paraguariensis*). This beverage also called "Jesuits' tea" because the plant was grown by the Jesuit order in Misiones in Northern Argentina and in Paraguay. Boiling water is added and it is passed round for all to sip. The drink can be sweetened and is a caffeine-rich stimulant.

But meat still rules; to set up an outdoor *parilla* [barbecue] on any roadside and grill strips of meat is an Argentine act of national solidarity. There was once a smell of Buenos Aires, especially at midday – the reek of barbecued beef [*asados*] from the countless building sites, although today's workers have mostly adopted sandwiches. Cortázar described a summer city-smell as "a mixture of petrol smells, heated asphalt, eau de cologne and wet sawdust." In the steamy summer months, there is also an overcrowded city drain smell, but nothing like the one described by naturalist W. H. Hudson in the 1860s:

> the principal and sublime stench in a city of evil smells, a populous city built on a plain without drainage and without water-supply beyond that which was sold by watermen in buckets, each bucketful containing about half a pound of red clay in solution. It is true that most houses had aljibes, or cisterns, under the courtyard, where the rain water from the flat roofs was deposited. I remember that well: you always had one or two to half a dozen scarlet wrigglers, the larvae of mosquitoes, in a tumblerful.

Hudson paid for this situation with typhoid fever. The drainage and water supply were put right by British engineers in the 1870s, for by 1918 there were some 3,000 miles of sewers in the city, and, like elsewhere, today's safe drinking water reeks of chlorine.

The way in which the city gets rid of its smelly rubbish has been observed by Gerald Durrell:

> a covey of dustmen indulging in their early morning ballet... The great dustcart rumbled down the centre of the road at a steady five miles an hour, and standing in the back, up to his knees in rubbish, stood the emptier. Four other men loped alongside the cart like wolves, darting off suddenly into dark doorways to reappear with dustbins full of trash balanced on their shoulders. They would run alongside the cart and throw the dustbin effortlessly into the air, and the man on the cart would catch it and empty it and throw it back, all in one fluid movement. The

timing of this was superb... Sometimes there would be four dustbins in the air at once. The whole action was performed in silence and with incredible speed.

Because people live in high-rise flats, rubbish piles up and has to be collected every night. I too have watched the skill with which these dustmen, invariably Indians, dispose of the trash; the technology might have changed since the early 1960s, but not the artistry. *Porteños* cannot believe that rubbish is collected only once a week in London.

People make the city, and racially mixed *porteños* are very attractive to look at in the streets and cafés, especially the young, as the exiled Polish writer Witold Gombrowicz, of minor nobility, recorded: "There is no Notre Dame cathedral or a Louvre, however, you often see stunning teeth, magnificent eyes, agile and harmonious bodies in the street." In the end, observers can only offer generalizations and prejudices. After a long effort novelist Marcos Aguinis simply gave up: "To understand the Argentines is a hopeless task."

Walking
"My poetry tries to represent present-day Buenos Aires, the amazement and wonder of the places my long rambles lead me to..." Borges

Buenos Aires is a city for walking around, as the Chilean poet Pablo Neruda (1904-1973) discovered (he met his second wife, Delia del Carril, an Argentine some twenty-four years older than he, in Madrid in 1934). In his 1933 poem with its title in English, "Walking Around," Neruda rails against the excessive and oppressive urban quality of the city, with its "tailor-shops," "barbers' shops," markets, lifts, dentures in coffee pots, clothes on lines in patios, and lost spectacles. The poet felt so estranged that he wanted to scare a "notary with a cut lily" or a nun "by hitting her with an ear." This book will be organized as a form of walking-around, in something like the *flâneur* tradition, along crucial currents or flow charts, both visible in the city maps as streets (the *Guía Peuser* being the best) and in the verbal imagination of writers and singers. It will be a sort of literary arm-chair stroll.

President Domingo Sarmiento, in Paris in the 1850s, adopted the pose of the *flâneur*, defining it as "the right to poke your nose into anything." We will follow this approach. After months in trains sliding down South America, the novelist Paul Theroux wrote with relief about Buenos Aires: "It was a wonderful city for walking, and walking I decided it would be a pleasant city to live in." To Theroux's surprise, he "found the city safe to walk in at all hours, and at three o'clock in the morning there were crowds in the streets." The American poet and translator Willis Barnstone agreed about Buenos Aires: "this is a city of walkers, whether at four in the afternoon or four in predawn dimness, there is hardly a deserted street in this capital, and cafés and kiosks are open to serve the pedestrians." Today, however, "security" has become a constant topic in the newspapers as assaults and muggings are on the rise. Carlos Riga, the starving poet in Manuel Gálvez's novel *El mal metafísico*, lives in the streets that he walks all day long. Here is his day: "In the morning, following my doctor's advice, I usually go to Palermo, to the Recoleta, to the Zoo, sometimes with a friend. After lunch I go to the cafe *La Brasileña*, where I stay a long hour, and then I browse in bookshops, chat in the street with chance acquaintances. At night, straight after dinner, I go back to the café; and then frequent newspaper offices."

But despite its grid streets, its sheer size and often the height of its buildings deter walkers from making sense of the city, as Gómez de la Serna lamented: "The hardest city to see is the capital of Argentina. After many years strolling all over the place, night and day, getting to know all its barrios, nooks and crannies, I still haven't found its synthesis." This despite being married to the Argentine writer Luisa Sofovich, living in the city from 1936 to his death in 1963, and being a friend of many local writers, including Oliverio Girondo and Norah Lange.

To be able to walk at all is the first difference between Buenos Aires and many other American cities, from the car-dominated Los Angeles and Caracas to the dangerous, extensive Lima, Mexico City, São Paulo and Rio de Janeiro (for a start), where you walk at your peril. To walk in Buenos Aires is to inhale foul exhaust from internal-combustion engines, to tolerate decibels beyond belief, and to navigate holes in the narrow pavements, but even so, it is still a walk-about city. Alberto Salas, in his succinct study of what's unique to Buenos Aires, *Relación parcial de Buenos Aires* [Partial account of Buenos Aires, 1955], claimed that there is no verb in Spanish to describe this city-strolling; he rejects *callejear, pasear*, to prefer *vagar* [to wander]. For Salas, such wandering is "that pure exercise of freedom, that strolling without compulsions and urges, a true enriching experience that allows you to pass the time walking the streets for the pure pleasure of it." This sort of walking is close to reading, to day-dreaming or to meditation. Yet in Buenos Aires you cannot walk fast. You have to follow the slow drift as the pavements are narrow and crowded, and *porteños* talk-walk (note, nobody in Buenos Aires ever walks up or down escalators. You have to be patient).

An early great street-walker (in an innocent sense) was the poet Baldomero Fernández Moreno who, after returning from seven years in Spain in 1899, saw his city with fresh eyes and wrote a book called *Ciudad* [City, 1917] which Borges described as the "complete possession of the city, total presence of Buenos Aires in poetry" and a "perfect" book. The tone of these poems comes from a line like "I have wandered like a vagabond all afternoon" or "and my worn-out heels sound loud on the pavement", for the poems are subtle links between city observations and the poet's state of mind. The street is therapy: "Wandering the streets you forget your troubles, / I tell you, I have wandered so far."

The novelist Alicia Jurado stressed in her memoirs *El mundo de la palabra* [The world of the word, 1990] how Borges enjoyed walking his city: "we always spent hours walking round the Plaza San Martín and sitting now and then on benches to talk, of course, of literature. He would take me to his favorite places: Constitución bridge, to the Parque Lezama, to Adrogué..." Borges viewed the urban thoroughfares as lifeblood in his poem "The Streets": "The streets of Buenos Aires / are already the core of my soul." In his love for his native city he internalized these avenues, roads and alleys, especially the *barrio* back streets. Streets are "a promise of adventure" and Borges resists the "imprisonment of houses." These same streets that haunted the aging Borges depressed the poet Alfonsina Storni (1892-1938) who struggled all her life to retain her dignity as a woman in the *macho* literary world (before committing suicide). Her poem "Lines to the Sadness of Buenos Aires" begins:

"Streets that are sad, grey, straight and equal / where sometimes you can catch a patch of sky, / its dark facades and tarred ground / stifled my tepid spring dreams." Like Borges, she too has internalized these streets as a mood: "My soul now suffers from its monotony." But it is the altogether more cheerful Baldomero Fernández Moreno who captures the thrill of street life for, he wrote, even if he had a castle with a great leather chair, when night falls "I would rush out to the street / to the street and the café."

Only by walking the streets can a city become familiar. Fernández Moreno again: "Look how faithful I am to you, o my city! / Again in the streets like before... in the bustle of its people / I'm still searching for something." A city promises some revelation, some life meaning in its labyrinth of streets, and you have to walk to find out. Baldomero's poet son César Fernández Moreno opens his poem "To the City of Buenos Aires": "Before I saw you as a great, dark mass, / with streets like intricate labyrinths", but then he learned "the simple miracle of your structure" and by learning its street geometry he felt the city completely his. This labyrinth of streets suggests something unique about the city. Manuel Gálvez's idealist protagonist, desperately seeking the whore Nacha in the crowded city streets, is described thus: "and so his shadow crawled the streets, deaf to the thousands noises, to the hooting cars, and tram bells, to the enormous street lights, to the lighted advertisements, to the luxury of the shop-windows, of the jewels, of the flowers, of the books, of the theatre enacted in the cosmopolitan, complicated and dynamic streets of Buenos Aires."

The novel that most persistently takes Buenos Aires's streets as metaphors of the city's soul is Silvina Bullrich's tellingly titled *Calles de Buenos Aires*, her first, self-published novel (later she became one of the few professional writers in the city). The novel explores critically, through chance meetings and love affairs, the lifestyles of a group of upper-caste dilettantes in the late 1930s. The prologue sets the scene: "The streets of Buenos Aires are a faithful portrait of the city's soul. Hurry, nervousness, indifference, pushing to pass first and, if possible, to be the only one to pass. That's how, day after day, this is the city that never sleeps. To say city is to say insomnia." The only character with the inner resources to escape her class destiny is Gloria, a budding writer who loves walking, hands in pockets: "She loved the noisy streets, the smell of petrol, the haggard faces of those who need clean air... She was a porteña to her soul. She moved freely in the crowds, knew every corner of her city." To know the streets was to confirm her roots. Gloria liked wandering without a purpose, a *vagabundeo* [drifting] that led her to the heart of the labyrinth. To be a vagabond is to be free, to be guided by desire and instinct (the Parisian surrealists loved their city streets for the same adventurous reasons).

Street names have, annoyingly, changed. In 1998 the novelist Mempo Giardinelli (1947-) underlined "porteño governments' proverbial mania for changing street names." The street that was Comercio in Mármol's *Amalia* is today Humberto I, Cuyo is Sarmiento, and calle de las Artes is Carlos Pellegrini. Sometimes the new official street name is ignored by some; calle Perón is still called Cangallo, and Raúl Scalabrini Ortiz is still known as Canning. Borges defined Buenos Aires as "that vain tangle of wool / of streets that repeat bygone names." Not knowing to whom the street name refers to is a common experience. Street names reveal the "newness" of history, as new names are added to the nomenclature in a kind of musical chairs, the older names being relegated to oblivion. The corners formed by two streets are given as places to meet in *porteño* lingo. People say they live on Santa Fe and Ecuador, meaning Santa Fe at the level of Ecuador. Street names are also a kind of *aide-mémoire*; they remind passersby of Argentine history, of writers, of musicians, of painters, of scientists (in Belgrano you walk across Darwin, Humboldt, Bonpland and Fitzroy). Gómez de la Serna decided that this "street nomenclature broadens our horizons." There are also categories, from the grand "avenue," the "street," the "passage," to the humble *cortada* [short-cut].

Walking the streets, you can enviously glimpse down the hallways that lead to imposing art deco and nouveau apartments. Here stand the *porteros porteños*, often of Galician descent (i.e. *gallegos*) who polish and sweep and guard the opulent front doors to the blocks of flats. But they do not let you in. To enter you must use the *portero eléctrico*, where you push the flat number for someone to open from inside. Earlier, the streets communicated with the inner patios and the privacy of home through *zaguanes* [hallways], eulogized by Borges as relics of a vanishing, colonial city. Enrique Amorim, in his sketches *Buenos Aires y sus aspectos* [Buenos Aires and its aspects, 1967], has a section tellingly called "Eulogy of the Zaguán," recalling "that it was through the *zaguán* that we looked out on to life. The place of farewells. The place of anxious waiting." Baldomero Fernández Moreno's poem "Zaguanes" ends by extolling his "love for the half-open door... sprains, glances, profiles."

Subways, Buses, Trams and Taxis

Buenos Aires is an urban island, bounded by the fifteen miles of the Avenida General Paz opened in 1941, the canalized and sluggish river Riachuelo, and the vast, muddy estuary of the river Paraná. In the often imaginary journeys and sites visited in this book, walking and reading are not the only modes of transport. If you prefer not to walk, the quickest way of travelling the city is on the subway. The *subte* or *tranvía subterráneo* [underground tram], South America's first underground system, was opened in 1914 and completed in 1944, with 2,500 miles of lines. Buenos Aires was the twelfth city in the world to open an underground service. The routes spread out like the branches of a tree from the city's heart, the Plaza de Mayo, from where this guide will begin (though Miguel Delibes found this outgrowing of lines "very restrictive"). In Sabato's novel about the decadence of the ruling class in Argentina, *Sobre héroes y tumbas*, Fernando explains how his paranoia about blind people began on the underground: "I studied the behavior of a blind man who worked on the underground to Palermo: a short, solid, dark man who was very active and badly brought up; a man who wandered the carriages with a restrained violence selling shirt stiffeners in the compact crowd of squashed people." He then trails the blind man from the Plaza de Mayo underground station where chapter one begins. The *subte* today is the most efficient, and cheapest (at 50 *centavos*) way to travel the traffic-choked city. Stations are being restored (many with attractive tiled murals) and lines have extended to Belgrano, even though travelling can be suffocatingly hot and slow . Soon there will be poems in the carriages, in the wake of London's poems in the underground, as a competition has been set up. People hawk goods in the carriages, even poems, as Ramón from Almagro did, handing out a sample to passengers and hoping they would buy his self-printed book of ballads.

Alternatively, you could take a bus. And buses criss-cross the city in bewildering and illogical ways. These Mercedes-Benz buses are called *colectivos,* a typical *porteño* creation. So much so that César Fernández Moreno claimed that "the colectivo is one of the ideal structures of the porteño: in it he can express his skill in improvising his irony. The colectivo, like the porteño, rides roughshod over you." *Colectivos* first began in 1928 when taxis became too expensive. The early taxis that took fixed routes became small buses, and today there are 182 lines that frantically roam the city. There is sometimes sitting room, but usually over-crowding means standing room only, a situation that makes it hard to peer out of the windows to see where you are. These Mercedes Benz "dragons" once characterized the city's motoring bravado, where the skilled drivers used to hand out tickets and change and race off at the same time, competing with each other for passengers. Today there is a ticket machine and you must have loose change. The design of the buses has become duller, more like buses anywhere, unless you go to the outskirts, like Bánfield, and spot the old, glaring-faced *colectivos*. Baldomero Fernández Moreno dedicated a poem to *colectivo* number 26: "Through the barrio flies the extravagant, / blue, emerald, black, / number twenty-six: / one hundred wheels and not one brake." His son, César, picked on traffic noise made by these buses, for as already pointed out, Buenos Aires is an ear-deafening city: "The colectivo, the omnibus, the taxi and the tram / hootings of a savage symphony." My own favorite *colectivo* routes are those of the 152, and especially the 60 to Tigre.

Julio Cortázar's weird short story "Omnibus" is set in Villa del Parque, with a journey to the centre on the *colectivo* 168. Francisco Sanctis, in Humberto Costantini's novel *La larga noche de Francisco Sanctis* [*The Long Night of Francisco Sanctis*, 1984], refuses to board a smart number 60 *colectivo* and instead leaps onto a 28: "(Estación Saavedra to Puente Uriburu), a peeling, wheezy old rattletrap, still miraculously in service, [that] splutters laboriously out of the darkness of a side street. First gear slips, the bus lurches forward a few yards in a series of coughs, fits, and starts. Back in elusive first gear, it sticks its hesitant muzzle out into Maipú Avenue." The further you go from central Buenos Aires the more battered are the *colectivos*. For those who can pay more, there is a sitting-down-only bus, called the *diferencial*. Knowing your buses and avoiding being pick-pocketed are skills that differentiate the *porteño* from outsiders.

Before the *colectivos* there were trams, "a veritable porteño institution," according to Alberto Salas. You can still see the iron tracks in some streets. The first electric trams, introduced on April 22, 1897 and running from today's Plaza Lavalle to the Portones of Palermo, were seen as modern and beautiful. By reaching fifteen miles an hour they speeded up travel (and increased accidents). By 1905, the Catalan economist Federico Rahola could ride "the tram through 65 kilometers of perfectly paved and urbanized streets." The trams that linked up the *barrios* tended to follow rail and road; they had begun in the 1870s as horse drawn. By 1922, the tram epitomized modernity as evident in Oliverio Girondo's irreverent *Veinte poemas para ser leidos en el tranvía* [Twenty Poems to be Read in a Tram]. Leopoldo Lugones had previously published a poem ("Citizen Moon") about a man fancying a young woman during a tram journey "whilst the tram crosses a poor area / in the suburbs..." Unfortunately, she alights before he can react so that the sarcastic poem ends with his defeat: "Some meetings are truly without happy endings!" Baldomero Fernández Moreno dedicated his first book of poems *Las iniciales del misal* [The initials on the missal, 1915]: "To the tram company called / the Anglo-Argentina / and Lacroze / in whose grimy and pharaonic carriages passed / obscurely the best / hours of my happy youth." The same poet wrote in 1915: "At night it's beautiful, / to watch in the streets below the trams, / with dust of stars on their wheels / and a little star on the tip of the trolley." The poet Elvira de Alvear coined a clever image for the tram: "Trams, illuminated flutes, / circulate through the forgotten plazas."

In the suburbs the tram was not so modern. Marechal's bohemian artists in *Adán Buenosayres* took "a broken-down Lacroze tram, that moaned down to the smallest of its screws." Even so, a guide book called Buenos Aires "the City of the Trams," while the London *Times* acclaimed it as "one of the most remarkable tramway systems in the world... three times the mileage of London's!" In urban development terms the tram created the city and linked up its *barrios*, just as the car created Los Angeles.

Clara, the nonchalant whore in Luisa Valenzuela's (1938-) first novel *Hay que sonreír* [*Clara*, 1966], loved travelling in trams:

Nothing more pleasurable than a tram journey. When it's hot, fresh air pours through its windows as one sits in the middle of the street. When it's cold it's a glass cage that crackles, snores, purrs as it crosses the city and carries you protected amidst bells and death-rattles. The only inconvenience are the many old people who travel, the pregnant women, and all those you have to stand up for if not it's a disgrace... And what's great about tram journeys is passing near to the houses, along narrow streets, bumping over cobbled roads, and one can watch indoor life, the geraniums that hang from windows, and sometimes people between half-closed shutters. Bleep, bleep, the tram passes along Tucumán Street. This is truly life.

Unfortunately, the tram as a kind of café on tracks, a casual meeting place, a way of exploring a city or seducing a passenger, is no longer available to *porteños* as trams were disbanded in 1962 as too old-fashioned for a modernizing city. However, an Asociación Amigos del Tranvía was founded in 1976, opened a library on calle Paraná 755, piso 11, and publishes a magazine and books devoted to trams. All over the city, rails wait under the asphalt for the return of trams.

Finally, there are the swarms of yellow and black taxis, symbols of city life on four wheels, with those talkative, inquisitive drivers with ready-made opinions on everything, especially politics, football and tango (though many are not officially registered, and some drive like maniacs). The economic state of the city is mirrored in the condition of these taxis. Philip Guedella spent a month in Buenos Aires in 1931, just after the coup that ousted Yrigoyen. He remarked that "few cities express their more exuberant modes in taxicabs" more than Buenos Aires, and compared the comfort of local limousines to a "Chicago gunman's hearse." He described the hair-raising rush of "Juggernauts at speed (for Argentine automobilism is nothing if not spirited) down narrow alleys planned by Spanish forefathers to be traps for shade in the noonday heat, their silence quite unbroken except by the click of an occasional mule. This superposition of a modern city upon an old Colonial ground-plan has strange results." Guedella observed that the way to allow more traffic flow had been to narrow pavements to single-file pedestrian ways, while taxis hurtled past, as they still do, if not so luxuriously.

Sitting and Cafés

If you do walk around the streets of Buenos Aires it's a relief to drop into a café and sit down. Cafés are ubiquitous. The first café to open in Buenos Aires was the Café de Catalanes in 1799 during the Viceroyalty on the corner of San Martín and Cangallo (it lasted until 1873). It set a precedent and created a fashion that characterizes Buenos Aires social and literary life. Novelist Ernesto Sabato intoned proudly: "There are so many cafés in Buenos Aires." Alberto Salas called the café the city's "meridian." Miranda France wrote in 1998 that "the quality of cafés was extraordinary," and, when she left the city, concluded: "I knew nowhere in the world where the bookshops and cafés were more inviting." The Nicaraguan poet Rubén Darío wrote in his memoirs that he met his young literary friends at night in the 1890s in cafés and beer cellars and named three, Monti, Luzio (on Sarmiento and Maipú) and Auer's (on Corrientes and Esmeralda). Sabato's protagonist Martín in *Sobre héroes y tumbas* enters the Moscova and celebrates how cafés and bars are refuges from foul, egoistic city-life in Buenos Aires, for inside "coarse external reality was abolished." Bars, then, are places to meditate in. Humberto Costantini's middle-aged ditherer in his novel *The Long Night of Francisco Sanctis*, set in the Buenos Aires of 1977 with its kidnappings and ironic, final "disappearance," justifies bars:

> *A bar, as everyone knows, is usually the best remedy for temporary sensations of unreality or other lunacies. Tables, windows, chairs, the predictable Spanishness of the waiter, the bottles of Chissotti and Anís Ocho Hermanos behind the counter, are elements that, because they are familiar, because they have been witnesses to and accomplices in hundreds of past lunacies, tie one to reality with solid bonds... This, on the whole, is what Sanctis must be thinking as he reaches Cabildo, setting out for a small place he knows at the corner of Ciudad de la Paz and Lacroze.*

Alberto Salas defined the café as "the negation of time, where one is available for anything," the ideal place for "lazybones" and "idlers."

In his novel about the rise and fall of a right-wing thug and hired killer in the Buenos Aires of the 1960s and 1970s, *Historia del Triste* [*Triste's History*, 1987], Horacio Vázquez Rial (1947-) explains café life in the city to his Spanish readers (Vázquez Rial lives in Barcelona):

> *the impenetrable atmosphere of the café, centre of dealings and disagreements in the life of Buenos Aires, the marginal and the other city, urban advance party in the less domesticated zones around the city: the exterminators of Indians who successfully completed their campaigns on Rosas' orders first, then later followed Roca's, sowed in the infinite shock of the pampas the first signs of this transcendental social institution known as the pulpería [a bar and store], baptized and attended by Galician immigrants who last saw a pulpo [octopus] when they left for America in search of their fortune... in 1957, porteño cafés were all this and some more: places to while away time, to listen to the radio, bet at illegal billiards or darts or card games with Spanish naipes, to hire go-betweens or thugs of all kinds, to acquire debts or pay them back, or scribble poems on paper napkins, or novels based on overheard conversations: porteño cafés were also where the infamous went...*

Vázquez Rial outlines a social history of the café in a novel, where ironically Triste's sinister assignments are given in the famous café Tortoni on Avenida de Mayo.

Most people live in flats, and often remain in families until married. Cafés, bars, beer cellars, even *confiterías*, offer escape from cramped, promiscuous living, from family prying, but were mainly for men until the 1960s. Cafés are discreet places for illicit meetings, or public arenas for literary or political gossip. Buenos Aires also inherited the Parisian café trend, as well as the Spanish, usually male, tradition of the *tertulia* where men talk, play cards and hold literary gatherings, as in the Café Pombo, made famous by Ramón Gómez de la Serna in Madrid. Estela Canto noted that "Buenos Aires was a literary city and Borges, despite his solitary passion for the Nordic and Anglo-Saxon world, was a man of cafés, as all Spaniards and South Americans usually are." Manuel Vázquez Montalbán's greedy detective Carvalho praised Buenos Aires cafés with their "marvelous atmosphere... far above the foul organicism of most Spanish cafés."

Cafés do not last, are demolished, lose clientele through fashions, though some of the more famous literary ones have survived. But what has changed is the nature of leisure. The café as the "small fort of friendship" (in Scalabrini Ortiz's phrase), as the *cafetín* [little café] that the tango songwriter Enrique Santos Discépolo blessed ("you gave me in gold a handful of friends") is being replaced as the café in which to have a quick chat and move on.

In his novels Ernesto Sabato, more than any other writer, has made the casual or chance "meeting" in public places, especially cafés, a characteristic of Buenos Aires street life, like the following with the tango innovator Astor Piazzolla (1921-1992). Sabato, a character with his author's name, was "in Suipacha street. He stood for a moment pretending to look into a shop window, calmed down, and looked for a café to drink something. He was just next to TÍO CARLOS. Kuhn was not at the cashier's, so he looked for any table just as he spotted Astor Piazzolla who was smiling at him. 'Hey, did my beard scare you?' he asked."

Tomás Eloy Martínez (1934-) evoked the Café Tabac on Libertador and Coronel Díaz in his novel *Santa Evita* (1995) as catering for special and typical café habits:

> One of the advantages of the Tabac is that, by the windows, inexplicable, soundless oases appear. The maddening din by the bar and in the corridors dies down and by the edges of these privileged tables you can talk without being heard by the next table. Maybe that's why they're always empty. In Buenos Aires, many people only wake up at midnight from their long siestas and go out to stalk life. Some of this fauna were waking up and stretching in the Tabac.

This is the café as a place to be alone in, or as a place to eavesdrop or meet friends, a nerve centre in the city.

A café, La Antigua Perla del Once (in the Once *barrio*), is visited by Martín in Sabato's *Sobre héroes y tumbas* and offers another image of the centrality of cafe life in the city's network. Martín's first need is to urinate: "Whilst I got ready in the foul, smelly room, I confirmed my old theory that the toilets are the last remaining place for philosophy in its purest state and began to decipher the scrawled inscriptions." There are many who have read there the real history ("the other side of the coin") of Buenos Aires. This is the same café where Borges would meet his mentor, the speculative philosopher, Macedonio Fernández, who,

Borges wrote, tried to convince him that "death was a fallacy". The café is also the place to write in. Luisa Valenzuela explains the genesis of her satirical novel *Strange Things Happen Here* (1979): "Buenos Aires belonged then to violence and state terrorism, and I could only sit in cafés and brood. Till I decided a book of stories could be written in a month, at those same café tables, overhearing scraps of scared conversations, seeping in the general paranoia." She once told me she wrote a novel on a café's paper napkins.

Another kind of establishment is the tango café where the lads—*los muchachos*—would meet, a *barra* of friends and contacts. The most famous was Gardel's regular (but no longer there) called the Café de Los Angelitos [Little Angels], mentioned in Catulo Castillo's tango of the same name: "café of the Angelitos / Gabino y Cazón's bar, / that I cheered up with my shouts / during Carlitos" [Gardel] days on Rivadavia and Rincón street corner."

Ultimately, the café stands for a respite from the city bustle, a moment to contact real life. Juan Dahlmann, Borges' protagonist in the story "The South," feels himself "deeply Argentine" on his way to Constitución station to escape from the city and recuperate from a stupid wound to the head. He drops in for a coffee in a bar on calle Brasil near Yrigoyen's house (which has a plaque on it) and tastes the sweet coffee as he strokes a fat cat that lives in another time dimension. While in Buenos Aires it is easy to sit and read in cafés, feeling like Borges' cat, in another sort of reality. Tango poet Enrique Santos Discépolo praised the "Cafetín de Buenos Aires" as a "school for everything."

The River Plate

The eastern frontier of the city is water, the "fresh-water sea" [*mar dulce*] as Solís called it, the city's washing and bathing place before the arrival of piped water. It remains the source of drinking water despite the fact that today it is dangerously polluted. In this name River Plate (Río de la Plata) lies the root of many illusions. Silvina Bullrich wrote of "a dirty, dark river, strange paradox for a limpid, metallic noun," for there was never any silver in Argentina, despite the country's name. Riches came through cattle and wheat, late in the nineteenth century, and immigrants from Europe, especially Italy and Spain, came to "make

The River Plate (Nick Caistor)

America" because the country was seen to be fertile and under-populated, fulfilling Alberdi's dictum "to govern is to populate."

The river mouth of the Paraná and Uruguay river-systems characterizes Buenos Aires. From the humid air, which at the height of summer makes you feel you are swimming underwater, to the horizon of muddy waters that isolates the city between flat fresh-water sea and flat *pampa*, it is omnipresent. The river banks have shifted out as land has been reclaimed in the course of the twentieth century (the waters used to lap today's *barrancas*, or the *bajo*). The *bajo* (the low part), which used to be water, is now the Retiro station and all of the port. Socialist poet González Tuñón complained of this removal of the river from its original riverbanks: "They robbed the city of its river. / An iron and cement wall separates them. / But you sense its presence, in everything / in every stone / in every bandoneón [the tango accordion]." The riverbanks were once the site of beaches and swimming places, especially on the *costanera norte* [northern river promenade]. With its famous Club del Pescador, a fishing jetty, tree-lined river walks and popular outdoor restaurants and marinas, it used to be an area where people could stroll in fresher air, but today they have to swim in pools.

The name *Paraná* comes from the original Indian sounds, meaning "river related to the sea," although there were several other indigenous names from *aos* ("seals") to *Paraguay* ("meeting of the rivers"). At its mouth this river is some 140 miles wide; Argentines claim it as the widest river in the world (though it is only fourth in terms of water volume).

The novelist Juan José Saer catalogued some of the different color adjectives that Argentine poets have applied to this river, from Lugones' "dark-skinned" and "great lion colored river" to Baldomero Fernández Moreno's "milky coffee river." Borges called it a "chestnut current" but also *azulejo* [blue-grey, applied to horses], linking the water's blueishness to the Argentine flag. A literary critic, Delfín Leocadio Garasa, compiled a similar list to Saer's in his *La otra Buenos Aires: paseos literarios por barrios y calles de la ciudad* [The other Buenos Aires: Literary walks through *barrios* and streets of the city, 1987], adding Roberto Arlt's "reddish plain," Capdevila's "chocolate" and Mallea's "green and metallic blue." Certainly, the river's color depends on the moment of day and the light. In her autobiography Victoria Ocampo described the river thus: "A coveted strip of warm mud... It was water that from the banks seemed pink, lilac, blue, and when you touched it with your hand, the color of dulce de leche, a watery one." Perhaps this *dulce de leche* color is the most appropriate, given the honored place this milk-jam has in the *porteño* palate. Ezequiel Martínez Estrada opens a poem dedicated to this river with "this sea of linseed and caramel." The socialist poet Alvaro Yunque noticed not the color but the size of the river: "Other beautiful rivers / have many colors, / you, Río de la Plata, / have the horizon." Its color, he finally decided, was "wide copper-colored pampa." Andalusian poet in exile Rafael Alberti decided on a "dun river," while the traveler Philip Guedalla called this same river "yellow" in 1932. Alberto Salas generously noted: "this river contains all the colors, all the nuances lent by the sun, by clouds, by the wind." Leopoldo Marechal's metaphysical poet Adán tries to lend human attributes to the river: "The River Plate! It has raised its venerable body along the waters: its forehead is covered with *camalote* plants, and intones a mud song, its mouth filled with mud, its beard dripping mud." He adds: "He who has never heard the River Plate's voice will never understand the sadness of Buenos Aires. It's the sadness of mud pleading for a soul." The pretentious Adán is then mocked by his friend, the philosopher Tesler: "Bah! A dead river: a cocktail of water and mud."

"Playground of the winds", 1834

PART TWO

The Centre

"To understand a city it is not enough to stroll its streets. You must live in it, deal daily with its professionals, its shop-keepers, its millionaires."
Alejo Carpentier

Plaza de Mayo
The historical heart of the city is the Plaza de Mayo, so named after the May 1810 public demonstration that led to Argentine independence. It is from this official square that my excursions begin. This was the original plaza, traced by Juan de Garay in 1580, with the fort (now the Casa Rosada), Cabildo [town hall] and cathedral around it. Once known as the Plaza de la Victoria (named after the victory over England), it was not in the middle of the town, as was the norm in Spanish colonial urbanization, but near the shore as Buenos Aires was conceived of as a port. In 1802 the arched Recova (or Recoba) was built on the south side between the fort and the Cabildo to house forty-eight stalls to sell market produce. William MacCann described the Plaza de la Victoria in 1848 as composed of "beautiful piazzas, for the most part flagged with lozenge-shaped pieces of black and white marble; and under the well-formed arches [are] shops tastefully ornamented." He also mentioned the unfinished cathedral, the Cabildo and police department. This same plaza was described by Lucio V. López's narrator as he witnessed the public celebrations of Mitre's victory over Urquiza at the battle of Pavón in 1862, a victory that confirmed the ascendancy

of Buenos Aires over the provinces: "The city was completely covered in flags...We entered Plaza Victoria, opposite the main Police Station [and] saw an arch adorned with our national flag and great branches of weeping willows." He goes with the crowd to watch the boats bringing the victorious soldiers home: "We went down to the river shore by Rivadavia street. A huge crowd filled the sidewalk and street and crushed against the iron balustrades along the seashore." It was suffocatingly hot, and church bells and fireworks made a din.

The arched Recova in the plaza became associated with beggars and was demolished in 1884, when Buenos Aires' Intendente (Mayor) Torcuato de Alvear unified the two plazas into one, and asked Prilidiano Pueyrredón, the painter, to plant the palm trees (*Phoenix canariensis*). In this plaza is an equestrian statue of Manuel Belgrano (who designed the blue and white Argentine flag) erected in 1873, with Belgrano sculpted by Albert Belleuse (1824-1887) and the horse by an Argentine sculptor, Manuel de Santa Coloma (1829-1886), the son of the first Argentine consul in Europe.

The Plaza de Mayo has always been the symbolic centre of the city, as the novelist Julián Martel noted: "The Plaza de Mayo was... a curious, anti-aesthetic showcase of all the splendors and miseries that make up great Buenos Aires' social life." The critic Blas Matamoro agreed with Martel's aesthetic judgment in 1971 when he lamented that the Cabildo, the Casa Rosada and the cathedral were not demolished to give a view of the river. He called the Plaza de Mayo "that out-of-proportion wasteland."

The Cabildo is described by Martel in his novel about the disasters of speculation, *La bolsa* [The stock market, 1886], as "sad through the loss of its beautiful ornament, the tower, that rose next to the wide breach in the avenue, similar to the enormous skeleton of an antediluvian mameluke." As the *Guía Pirelli* points out, the present Cabildo has undergone several facelifts since it was first built on the same spot between 1725 and 1765 with the city's first public clock. In 1894 it even lost its tower in the widening of the Avenida de Mayo. The tower was restored in the current version, based on the original plans and finished in 1940. Today it is a museum, a fiction of itself. It was also designated the first prison in the city by Garay in 1608, and those executed in the plaza emerged from a jail underneath the Cabildo, covered with iron bars where prisoners could talk to passersby. José Antonio Wilde called the Cabildo prison "a focus of dirt and immorality" and saw it as "an affront to a civilized country." Not until 1877 did the Penitenciaría Nacional replace it, opening on Avenida Las Heras.

The cathedral, spiritual core of the city, is an "immobile *porteño* bulk on the Plaza de Mayo," in Baldomero Fernández Moreno's line. Leopoldo Marechal in his novel *Adán Buenosayres* reinvented it, with its "two needles of Nuestra Señora de Buenos Aires" that "teach the suburb the way to the paths above" (it has a dome, not spires). His protagonist the poet Adán imagines "the inside of the basilica, its altar shaped like a shrine, and that image of a woman on a high-up throne, with the infant Christ in an arm and a boat in the other. How good it would be to stand now in that deserted public place, under the light filtering through the stained glass!" The current neo-classical fronted cathedral is the sixth to be built on the spot picked by Juan de Garay. In 1848 the sober traveler William MacCann described this cathedral for his English readers as a "large cruciform brick building, originally of Moorish style, and still unfinished; the front, facing the Plaza Victoria, consists of a modern-built Corinthian portico of twelve columns, supporting a well-proportioned pediment; and the edifice is crowned with a large dome, which looks poor and naked in consequence of the smallness of the mouldings." He continued: "The beauty of the interior is enhanced by its contrast with the outside" and referred to the black and white marble paving stones, the massive square pillars with gilded capitals, the richly carved pulpits, the thirteen side-chapels, the altar that reached the roof as "beautifully carved, gorgeously painted and gilded" and concluded that the "whole is brilliantly illuminated" and "magical."

According to the *Guía Pirelli*, the first bishop arrived in 1618 and the first cathedral was inaugurated in 1622. The sixth version had many architects and took over a hundred years to complete, thanks to what Horacio Vázquez Rial called "a combination of misunderstandings, deficiencies and inefficiencies." Blas Matamoro called this cathedral "a malformed mix of Italian-colonial- Magdalenian style." The baroque altar was designed by Isidro Lorea and the polychromed Christ by Manuel de Coyto, who was punished by the Inquisition and exiled for four years in Patagonia. The reliefs on the front were sculpted by Joseph Dubourdieu, and represent Jacob meeting Joseph, or allegorically Buenos Aires meeting the Confederation. Argentina's great liberator, "the sworded-saint" [*el santo de la espada*], General José de San Martín (1778-1850), lies embalmed in a mausoleum at the side, as he was a freemason; this side chapel was being restored in 1998. It is continuously guarded by Grenadiers named after San Martín, who also guard the Casa Rosada as the official presidential guard (their barracks are a grand house on the Belgrano *barrancas* on calle Luis María Campos).

The boy narrator in Julio Cortázar's bizarre story "After Lunch," is forced to go for a walk with a backward brother, perhaps a dog, perhaps his own guilt, for we never find out, and dreams of taking a tram to the Plaza de Mayo: "I like it because of the pigeons, because of Government House and because it reminds me of so much history, the bombs that fell during the revolution, and the horses they said were tied to the Pyramid." The narrative thus ingenuously mixes the fall of Perón with *gaucho* leaders like Rosas.

This Pirámide, erected in 1811 to commemorate the May 25th revolution against Spain, was first built forty feet high in bricks, designed by Francisco Cañete and crowned with a *bola* [a stone ball used with a leather thong by *gauchos* and Indians to trip and immobilize horses and cattle]. The painter and architect Prilidiano Pueyrredón enlarged and covered it to 55 feet and added a statue of liberty sculpted by Dubourdieu in 1860. It was moved in 1912 to its present place after the Recova was demolished and the two plazas united.

The Plaza de Mayo is famous today for two kinds of events. The first was when the plaza "really began to be the pole of political and social attractions," in Mempo Giardinelli's words, recalling October 17, 1945, when thousands of workers crowded the square demanding Perón's release from prison on the island of Martín García. Following this popular revolt, Perón (elected president in 1946) and his wife Evita continued to encourage the orchestrated congregation of workers, the *cabecitas negras* (little black heads, a racist term) or *descamisados* (the shirtless ones, Evita's term), hectoring them from the balcony of the Casa Rosada. These stirring scenes were recreated with Madonna in

Alan Parker's film version of the musical *Evita*.

Eva Duarte Perón has always been close to the hearts of the poor, gave extravagantly through her Fundación Eva Perón, got the vote for women in Argentina in 1947 and was for many a lay saint who promised redemption (*Santa Evita* in Tomás Eloy Martínez's title for a novel). She also wrote an autobiography-cum-manifesto *La razón de mi vida* [The reason for my life, 1951]. She returned after her death as a symbol of social justice for the left-wing guerrillas in the 1960s, but was boosted to the status of world icon by Andrew Lloyd Webber's catchy song "Don't Cry For Me Argentina" and the musical, *Evita*, in which she figured, absurdly, with Che Guevara. Such was the scandal of this British musical in nationalist circles in Buenos Aires that an Argentine counter-version, *Eva*, was staged, written in 1986 by two well-known leftish writers Alberto Favero and Pedro Orgambide, with the actress Nacha Guevara playing Evita and rising to heaven in her death-bed at the end.

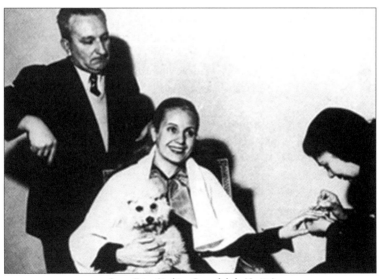

Santa Evita (Archivo General de la Nación)

The Peronist meetings in the Plaza de Mayo followed the tradition begun in May 1810 when people crowded the square to support Argentine independence. The English poet and critic G. S. Fraser saw Evita in 1947 from this plaza: "It was pretty full, but not jam-packed. A loudspeaker kept announcing that the president and his wife would soon appear, a brass band occasionally struck up martial airs. Groups of young men and women moved through the crowd in single file, bearing aloft placards on which there were gigantic smiling portraits of Perón and Evita." Finally Evita "a slim figure, with neat fair hair, in a light beige costume" appeared on the balcony of the Casa Rosada and read from a typescript in a high "strident" voice; "she was fierce and emphatic" and attacked the newspaper *La Prensa*. After the meeting, mobs smashed windows in the *La Prensa* building nearby in the Avenida de Mayo. Later, on April 15, 1953, as Perón was talking from the balcony, two bombs went off and killed six people. Perón incited the angry crowd to attack the oligarchy, and supporters duly burned down the Jockey Club.

In his novelistic recreation of Evita Perón's embalmed corpse and its bizarre afterlife (*Santa Evita*, 1995), Eloy Martínez described how Evita's mother set off by tram after the 1955 "revolution" (a misnomer for the ousting of Perón, who fled to Paraguay in September 1955) to recover her daughter's corpse from the embalmer Dr. Ara. Arriving in the plaza, she noted "the bullet-holed marble of the Hacienda palace, the palm trees shredded by machine gun fire, the portraits of Evita fluttering in the hostile weather, the statues without noses, without hats, in ruins." The Hacienda palace, today the Ministerio de Economía on Yrigoyen and Paseo Colón was built in 1940 and is still pockmarked by bullets from the 1955 bombardments. Doña Juana approaches the building where her daughter Evita worked: "Bland and vulgar on the outside, the CGT [Confederación General de Trabajo] building was on the inside a string of corridors that ended in labyrinthine staircases." Miranda France, looking for traces of Evita in the city in 1997, passed the Ministerio de Acción Social on Defensa and Yrigoyen where Evita had her office and asked a policewoman if she could visit. "To my amazement she led me to the elegant wood-paneled room and left me there alone. Minimally furnished, the office was dominated by Evita's desk, the very heart of the Peronist revolution, where she had sat, for hours on end, receiving her *descamisados*..." But she found no special Evita atmosphere. The grim building that used to be the Banco Hipotecario was started in 1947 and finished in 1956. Inside can be found the old Congreso de la Nación that was used from 1864 to 1905, now open to the public for two hours a week. Like a horseshoe-shaped theatre, the former Congress, with its tight leather seats, was where Mitre and Sarmiento spoke and voted in their laws. The original gates, railings and blueish glass-domed ceiling are also preserved within the newer building. Upstairs is the Academia Nacional de la Historia (also on Balcarce 139), which houses a good library.

The second reason for the plaza's fame concerns the Mothers of the Plaza de Mayo (and then the *abuelas* [grandmothers], and their organization HIJOS). Led by Hebe Bonafini, beginning in 1977 these women paraded courageously every Thursday at 3:30 around the Pirámide, protesting the "disappearances" of their children in the military's *guerra sucia* [dirty war] against left-wing "subversion." Today, they continue to protest against the forced adoption of 172 babies by the military authorities and the impunity enjoyed by those responsible for wide-scale human rights abuses; they have recently opened a Café Literario de las Madres on Hipólito Yrigoyen 1440. The military and paramilitary suppression of left-wing movements was documented by the Comisión Sobre la Desaparición de Personas (CONADEP) under writer Ernesto Sabato's editorship in the compilation *Nunca Más* (1984), where nearly 9,000 cases are studied in gruesome detail, though the total figure could be around 30,000. Poet Juan Gelman lost his grandson after his son and daughter-in-law were disappeared. He exiled himself a second time after the military and the torturers were given amnesty, first by President Alfonsín and then by President Menem in 1990, and wrote a harrowing poem dedicated to the Mothers. Lawrence Thornton makes of these women the silent heroines of his novel *Imagining Argentina* (1987), a book that dramatizes the disappearances:

> *The Plaza de Mayo was less than a mile... the Casa Rosada, the seat of the government lay just across the street from the Plaza. All Carlos' attention was on the obelisk rising from the Plaza, which was topped with the statue of a woman in flowing robes who carried a spear. They were still too far to see the circular promenade, and for a moment his eyes drifted from the obelisk to the spire and cupolas of the buildings beyond, the thrust of palms and jacarandas and palo borrachos trees, the bell tower of the odd church. But when they crossed through the traffic of the round-*

> *about his gaze fell level with the Plaza where upward of fifty women*
> *were walking in a slow, ritualistic procession. Each wore a white scarf*
> *which bound them together in some as yet unknown sorority... They all*
> *carried signs so that at a distance they appeared like a gathering of reli-*
> *gious zealots... the signs were epitaphs and the women were bound by*
> *motherhood. Photographs of the disappeared were centered in each sign.*

The radical Uruguayan essayist Eduardo Galeano has a succinct entry on the Mothers in his alternative history/compilation of Latin America, *Century of the Wind*: "The Mothers of the Plaza de Mayo, women born of their children, are the Greek Chorus of this tragedy. Brandishing photos of their disappeared ones, they circle round and round the Obelisk, before the Pink House of the government." For many foreigners, Argentina came into focus on the political world map thanks to the media coverage of these brave women.

The bombing of Perón on June 16, 1955, the first strike by the anti-Peronist alliance, followed his excommunication the day before after a long struggle with the Catholic Church over state control of education. What was supposed to be a fly-past by the naval airforce became a bombing and caused many deaths (historian David Rock claims several hundred). It led to a counter-attack by Peronist mobs, who burned several churches and destroyed precious religious artifacts. This sequence of events is included in Ernesto Sabato's novel *Sobre héroes y tumbas*, which recreates the history of the city through a love affair between Alejandra, an upper-class incest victim, and the hero Martín. The bombing is a chaotic moment: "people shouted *Plaza Mayo*, among lorries filled with workers driving madly there, and confused shouts and dizzy image of the planes skimming the skyscrapers. And then the din of the bombs, the rattle of the machine guns and anti-aircraft guns. And always people scampering about." Expatriate English writer Gordon Meyer's protagonist Jane, divorced and living in Britain, remembers her Argentine days when she too witnessed the bombing from a skyscraper roof, in the novel *Sweet Water and Bitter* (1962):

> *It was the first time I had seen this view: the vast estuary encircling two-*
> *thirds of the city, apparently empty of shipping. In the west and south rose*
> *the city itself, a uniform gray under the gray sky, solid, stacked up, square-*

toothed, in ugly cubist masses—a tremendous unsorted jumble of child's bricks and squares, here and there punctuated by towers, spires, masts, stretching in the west as far as the eye could see, stuffed with four million humans... To the south, near the river, reared the bulk of the gray-roofed War Ministry, its chimneys smoking like a coal-burning ship's funnels. It was from that direction, where stood the government house, that the noise of gunfire came... An airplane turned towards us, heading silently for the government house area. We watched it begin its dive...met by violent anti-aircraft fire, it disappeared below the line of buildings; a moment later the sound of a dull explosion was hurled into the air.

Horacio Vázquez Rial's street-wise thug also witnesses the bombing in the novel *Historia del Triste*:

Triste was in the plaza at two-forty-five, when the deafening sound of airplane engines made him instinctively throw himself under the galleries along most of the buildings there, the colonial Town Hall, being the nearest: seconds later, three planes from the naval aviation began bombing Government House and the Army Ministry... from his position, crouching and squashed against the old wood, he saw everything: how the planes dropped their bombs on the Government headquarters where the General was supposed to be, on the plaza, where nobody was supposed to be and on the solid, modern structure of the Army Ministry, behind the Casa Rosada, on Azopardo street... Triste saw a bomb smash on to the presidential palace: saw how a second bomb fell on a bus full of passengers... saw how a bomb hit a cornice on the Ministry of Hacienda [i.e. the Treasury], *knocking off plaster work.*

The Plaza de Mayo symbolizes the place where a populist, national unity can be re-enacted. In the novel *The Story of the Night* (1996), Irish novelist Colm Toibín has his gay Anglo-Argentine narrator, a witness to US involvement in the dirty war of the late 1970s, participate in a rally on the Plaza de Mayo. Outside the Casa Rosada, a crowd gathers to support General Galtieri after the military *junta* invades the Malvinas to claim them as Argentine at last. Toibín describes a sense of belonging as the crowd shout "Las Malvinas son Argentinas" [The Falklands are Argentine]. After the years of dirty war the narrator "felt the pure wonder of us being there together, people who had been unable to speak to their neighbors, who were afraid on the street, and the venal generals who had been our enemies, all of us now were together for these days, proud of our country." It dawned on him that "we had come after all these years to possess this square once more." The plaza is still used for demonstrations. This August we crossed the cordoned-off square packed with hard-faced men in blue overalls, lolling about. Only next day did we read that these were *colectiveros*—bus drivers—protesting to President Menem.

On the plaza, then, is the asymmetrical, even lopsided Casa Rosada (Government House but meaning "pink" house as opposed to Washington's "white" house), so-called because of its red sandstone. The original color was achieved, according to Miranda France, by mixing pig's blood with whitewash, while poet Baldomero Fernández Moreno attributes its color to a "gentle blushing." It stands on the foundations of the original fort and dry moat built by Garay, parts of it now exposed to view. This fort, seen from the sea in many sketches by travelers, was finally demolished and reconstructed as different buildings by two Swedish architects, and then joined together under President Roca in 1879 into what can be seen today. In the opinion of Manuel Vázquez Montalbán's gourmet detective, the Casa Rosada is "one of the most famous Government houses in the world."

Despite its name, the tyrant Rosas did not live there. According to José Mármol, the inhabitants of Buenos Aires were dismayed by the dictator's neglect of the building, "residence of past governors, before and after the revolution, now abandoned and turned into barracks and stables during don Juan Manuel de Rosas' destructive reign." Presidents only began to inhabit the palace from 1862. The literary traveler Philip Guedalla paid a visit in 1931 to General José Felix Uriburu who had recently sacked Argentina's elected President Yrigoyen, and described the body-guards, with condescending wit:

> It was always mildly thrilling to penetrate the guarded precincts of Government House; and as one penetrated further, they grew still more guarded. One felt with a delicious frisson, as we walked down the final corridor under a close scrutiny, that it would be highly injudicious to insert an artless hand into a trouser pocket; and two figures in the last ante-room of all compelled a deeper awe. For those broad-shouldered gentlemen in unimpressive ready-mades were the embodiment of force

itself; their ill-fitting suits clothed the basis of all government. They were not tall, but their surprising breadth made up anything they lacked in height. The hair upon their heads was smooth and dull and black, and their impassive Indian faces had been cast in some material more durable than flesh...

After that, no Dictator could hope to be impressive, unless he happened to breathe fire or strangled anacondas in the intervals of dealing with his correspondence. Our host, indeed, was quite the reverse— a darkish military man with kindly manners and a charming smile.

G. S. Fraser interviewed Perón in 1947 in his Casa Rosada office and noted on his personal desk a "beautiful" photograph of Evita, pictures of workers, and a stuffed condor. Perón appeared to be in his late thirties (in fact was in his fifties), was broad and strong, with a "very likeable, slightly shy smile." Surprisingly unaffected and simple, he talked for an hour and a half about his policies. Earlier, the Argentine poet Carlos Mastronardi witnessed the renunciation of President Yrigoyen in 1920 and walked with the famously taciturn president (he was nicknamed "the armadillo" because he never left his hole) from the Casa Rosada on foot back to his house in calle Brasil, that is, a journey "from palace to cave." Later, Yrigoyen's house was sacked.

Yrigoyen was an extraordinary man, a legend in his time. Son of an illiterate Basque, he fathered children but never married, followed the philosophy of the German thinker Karl Krause (1781-1832), and helped found with his uncle Leandro Alem the Unión Cívica Argentina (the Radical party) along genuine democratic and pacifist lines. He refused to use the telephone, never saw a film, and hated flying. He was elected in 1916 after Argentina's first free elections (still for male voters only). Yrigoyen was adored by his followers after insisting on an eight-hour day, minimum wages, and improved housing. He also tried, unsuccessfully, to abolish prostitution. But after his second election in 1928 he was overthrown by General Uriburu's right-wing coup in 1930, ushering in the "infamous decade." The Casa Rosada also has a museum in its arched-brick basement, dealing with past Argentine presidents (entrance on Yrigoyen 219).

Below the Casa Rosada stands the monument to Colón (Columbus), though he never dreamed of reaching the River Plate. Sculpted by

Arnaldo Zocchi (1862-1940) in Carrara marble, it was a gift from the Italian collectivity for the 1910 centenary celebration of independence. In a poem, Ezequiel Martínez Estrada joked that this Italian Columbus is really "a tenor gripping a large musical score / preparing to sing a full-chested do." French journalist Albert Londres, in his *j'accuse* of the 1920s Argentine white slave trade, came up with an idea for an accompanying statue based on the *gallina* (whore) in 1928:

> *In a word, there is no lack of statues. More ingratitude; the Gallina has none! It should be in marble, white and stainless. Erected at the mouth of the harbor so that those arriving should salute it first.*
>
> *There is a square opposite the entrance to the new Post Office. I reserve the site. Thus our sister would stand between Christopher Columbus who discovered the continent, and San Martin who discovered Liberty. She, dear child, has discovered the Argentine.*
>
> *There she should stand with her long slim legs, and eyes full of languor, but so courageous.*
>
> *A pimp on the bas-relief below, of course.*
>
> *TO THE FRANCHUTA. THE GRATEFUL ARGENTINE PEOPLE*

The only other statue near the Plaza de Mayo, however, is one to the Basque Juan de Garay, the second founder of the city, on Leandro Alem and Rivadavia, built by Gustav Heinrich Eberlein (1847-1926). Near this statue is an oak donated by the villagers of Guernica to the resident Basque community in 1919 (before the Nazi bombing of Guernica in the Spanish Civil War on April 26, 1937).

One last building, just off the Plaza de Mayo, deserves mention, and is being renovated. Here in the *Concejo Deliberante*, sixty newly elected Buenos Aires city councilors and Mayor will sit. In 1952 Evita's corpse lay there in state for thirteen days because it was the building she worked in the most. The building dates from 1926 and was designed by Héctor Ayerza in the neo-classic style that bedevils Buenos Aires and gives it that atemporal, anachronistic feel. Four floors high, with a five-bell 300-foot octagonal tower, it will house a *confitería*, a library, and an art gallery with paintings by Quinquela Martín, Pueyrredón and Berni among others. Twenty-six statues stand outside.

Avenida de Mayo

Heading west from the Plaza de Mayo, the walker enters the wide Baron Haussmann-inspired Avenida de Mayo, created in 1885, with plane trees and pavement cafés. The narrow, checker-boarded city had needed wider streets. Víctor Gálvez moaned in 1882 that "Buenos Aires does not have one single boulevard." The Avenida has always been associated with Spaniards, and the Club Español (just off the Avenue on calle Bernardo de Yrigoyen 172), built by the Dutch architect Enrique Folkers in 1907, with its lavish facade and balconies, tiled dome, Moorish drawing room and collection of Spanish art testifies to this link with the *madre patria* [motherland]. Up a grand staircase the excellent restaurant is open to the public. Ramón Gómez de la Serna noted this link: "To try to define the Avenida de Mayo is like trying to define the intrinsic relationship Buenos Aires has with Spain. It has something of the Catalan Rambla, of Alcalá street and the entrance to the Gran Vía, confusing the feelings that Catalans have in Madrid and *Madrileños* have in Barcelona." Cádiz-born poet and painter Rafael Alberti, exiled after the Spanish Civil War in Buenos Aires from 1940 to 1964, wrote "The Avenida de Mayo shines in your crown / like the most precious rambla in Barcelona / night-loving Spain that reigns in the café / mixing shouts of *vos, chau* and *che.*" He regularly met fellow Civil War exiles in the Café Casa de Troya on this Avenida. When the *Granadino* poet Federico García Lorca came to Buenos Aires with Lola Membrive's theatre company on October 13, 1933 he stayed in room 704 of the Avenida de Mayo's Hotel Castelar (built in 1928) for five months, meeting fellow poet Pablo Neruda in 1934. They wrote a book together called *Paloma por dentro* [Dove on the Inside], with Lorca illustrating Neruda's poems, of which only one copy was made. Lorca put on his play *Bodas de sangre* [Blood Wedding] in the Maipo theatre, and gave five lively lectures that were broadcast on the radio. He had been invited to Buenos Aires by the *peña* Signo [a *peña* is a literary gathering], which brought together writers like poet Oliverio Girondo and his novelist wife Norah Lange (of Norwegian descent), and this was where Lorca heard the great feminist poet Alfonsina Storni sing a tango. A bronze plaque commemorates this stay. The hotel is famous for its Turkish baths, one for women, one for men (when I peered in I saw two large, naked men being pedicured).

Another hotel that evokes grand cultural days is the Majestic, built in 1906, where Nijinsky lived in a suite in 1913, and the French visionary architect and painter Le Corbusier made a temporary home in 1929. In 1930 it became a bank, and today it houses the offices of the Dirección General Impositiva. Its interiors remain a fine example of art deco and art nouveau. The run-down Hotel Majestic appears in Ricardo Piglia's (1941-) bizarre novel *La ciudad ausente* [The absent city, 1992]: "The Hotel Majestic, with its marble entrance and peeling walls, was there on Piedras and Avenida de Mayo. At the end of the staircase, on a landing, there was a desk, and behind it an old man stroking a white and brown cat... Junior saw a corridor with a carpet, several closed doors... and lit a cigarette." He takes a lift up: "The lift was a cage and its ceiling was covered in inscriptions and graffiti." He gets out into a corridor with yellow walls and thick carpets that muffle the street noise and rings at a door, which is opened by an aging cabaret dancer. The place gives him the sensation of "somewhere else," out of the city.

The newspaper *La Prensa* moved to the grand Gallic building in the Avenida on 567-575. One of its rooms is a copy of a room in Versailles; in another room doctors gave free medical advice free; there was also a free library, and rooms for visiting VIPs. The building is topped by a female holding a torch, symbolizing the freedom of the press. The newspaper was founded by the Gainza Paz family in 1869. Under Perón the newspaper was closed as too hostile to the regime and moved to Montevideo. The Radical French Prime Minister Georges Clemenceau found this building the most "sumptuous" in the city in 1910. In 1914 the traveler W. H. Koebel wrote: "Decidedly nowhere in the world can a newspaper office boast a facade such as this… one of the marvels of modern Buenos Aires." After the Gainza Paz family sold the newspaper, the Buenos Aires municipality bought the splendid building that today houses the Casa de la Cultura de la Ciudad de Buenos Aires.

Another fine building with literary echoes is on Avenida de Mayo 1330, where in 1926 Natalio Botana installed his radical and legendary evening newspaper *Crítica*, founded in 1913. The building was specially designed by the Hungarian architects Gyorgy and Andras Kalnay for a newspaper (including a gym and barbers), in a daring art deco style with

Aztec motifs and four statues on the facade. Among its famous contributors were a young Borges (whose work on *Crítica* has been collected), Enrique González Tuñón, and Roberto Arlt. At one time *Crítica* was selling over 600,000 copies, until it was closed in the 1930 coup, though the paper continued until 1963. In the Spanish politics of the avenue *Crítica* supported Republican Spain (against cafés that supported Franco). It is now the offices of the Police administration.

Two nubile caryatids on the Avenida de Mayo (Luis Martín)

The most extraordinary *porteño* building, also on the Avenida de Mayo, is the Palacio Barolo designed by Mario Palanti (1885-1968) for the Italian millionaire Luis Barolo. Construction started in 1919 and it was opened in 1921 on the six hundredth anniversary of Dante's death.

At the time, and for thirteen years, the Barolo was the highest building in Buenos Aires, with eleven wonderfully ornate lifts to its eighteen floors, and a dome that lit up at night. Everything was specially made, from door handles to the lifts. There is a vast arcade crossing through at street level to calle Hipólito Yrigoyen; from its middle you can stare up into the dome. The whole building is solid and sumptuous with a facade of myriad protruding balconies. The dome is to be opened as an art gallery. In a poem to the great gossip and chronicler of Madrid life, Ramón Gómez de la Serna, who lived and died in Buenos Aires, the exiled Peruvian poet Alberto Hidalgo wrote "The Barolo building halts the traffic on the Avenida de Mayo / hoisting the sole finger it was given, / so that you can pass by." Earlier, Leopoldo Lugones saw the Palacio Barolo (in mocking, untranslatable rhymes) with its "consabida torre de morondanga" [its usual, crummy tower] that "alza el budín de luces de la boda guaranga" [raises its pudding of lights in a vulgar wedding]. In fact, the tower was 300 feet high, and Barolo had an identical copy of it built in Montevideo on Avenida 18 de Julio. Baldomero Fernández Moreno lived on calle México 1320, 8–A, from 1924 onwards. From his roof terrace, he said, "the Barolo is the first thing that hits the eye."

The Mexican post-revolutionary Education Minister and writer José Vasconcelos visited Buenos Aires briefly in the early 1920s with fellow Mexican poets Julio Torri and Carlos Pellicer (1899-1977). They found the Avenida de Mayo cosmopolitan and thought highly of the pavement cafés: "Sometimes this sole fact suffices to mark out friendly cities, cities for walkers. Tables to drink coffee, to eat outside on the pavement, confirm that the street is not a site for passers-by, but to socialize and have fun. This would be inconceivable in New York or in London..."

The most prestigious literary café still standing in Buenos Aires, a pocket of static time, is the Tortoni on the Avenida de Mayo and Piedras, now on the tourist route. The establishment was once frequented by Rubén Darío, the Nicaraguan alcoholic and bohemian poet who lived in Buenos Aires from 1893 to 1898, and by the poet and daring single-mother Alfonsina Storni, who committed suicide in 1938 and is honored by a plaque and a room named after her. In 1926 the Italian playwright Luigi Pirandello gave a talk there, followed by a tango sung by Carlos Gardel, at an event organized in the basement by the

Peña Asociación de Gente de Arte y Letras, run by poets Raúl González Tuñón and Francisco Luis Bernárdez (1900-1978). González Tuñón remembers reading his poems there when unknown, and how a man came up and congratulated him. It was President Alvear "in the days when presidents could walk alone." By the entrance you can read the following couplet: "From a bar, rainbow I greet you / stuffed with coffee and melancholy." It was founded in 1858 by a Frenchman and named after the still existing Café Tortoni in Paris, and when it moved to its current site it held exhibitions downstairs (painter Quinquela Martín's first show) and still hosts literary events, tango shows and a radio station. I always stop by to have a hot chocolate and stare at the paintings, the moody brown columns, the art nouveau glass, the skilled waiters, the billiard players and the crowds of *porteños* who still drop in. Baldomero Fernández Moreno, who once lived on the Avenida de Mayo, described a session at the Tortoni: "In spite of the rain, I left home / to drink a coffee. I am sitting down / under the soaked and stretched awning / of this old, known Tortoni." A bronze plaque recalls this city-celebrating poet. Another poet, Carlos Mastronardi, remembered Saturday evenings in the Tortoni's overcrowded "catacombs"; once Rubinstein played the piano, and another time the philosopher Ortega y Gasset spoke there. Horacio Vázquez Rial in his novel *Frontera sur* [Frontier south, 1994] retells the history of this café for his readers with short memories;

> In 1858, the recently founded Café Tortoni had its entrance on calle Riva-davia. Thirty years later, the demolition of the south side of the block, to widen the avenue, affected its foundations. When the work was finished, the Tortoni had two entrances: the original one on Rivadavia, and the other, now the main one, on the avenue of luxury and progress. Nothing has changed since then. The owners placed tables and chairs on the pavement...

In 1991, Borges took the Mexican poet Octavio Paz (1914-1998) there, who described it to his Mexican readers as "famous for its mirrors, its gilded fittings, its enormous cups of chocolate, and its literary ghosts." A modern tango written by Héctor Negro summarizes the appeal of the Tortoni: "Tango of the old Tortoni / faithful refuge / of friendships by the little coffee cup / In today's basement, the magic is still the same."

The mood of the place is "brown," with mahogany, yellowish-brown sky lights; the Tortoni still attracts celebrities (there are photos of Gabriela Sabatini, Hillary Clinton and King Juan Carlos of Spain).

A block behind the Tortoni's Rivadavia entrance is the Plaza Roberto Arlt, complete with fountain, *palos borrachos* and statues by Libero Badii—an oasis of sunlight off pestilential streets. All Arlt's fiction recreated proletarian, immigrant Buenos Aires. His first novel, *El juguete rabioso* [The rabid toy, 1926] traces the picaresque adventures of Silvio Astier in a *lunfardo*-dominated world of tango situations (failure, betrayal by women, being a *gil* or loser) where survival is what counts. This novel was followed by *Los siete locos* [*The Seven Fools*, 1929] and *Los llanzallamas* [The flame-throwers, 1931], based on Erdosain, a lowly salesman who murders his teenage mistress and finally kills himself, surrounded by a motley pack of riff-raff. Arlt's Astrologer, who dreams of founding a new religion, foreshadows the sinister López Rega of the 1970s. José López Rega, known as *el brujo* (the wizard), was the personal adviser to Perón and his third wife Isabel in the 1970s. A dabbler in the occult, he reputedly communicated with the dead Evita and organized the right-wing death squads, the Triple A. Arlt also wrote plays, and collected his pieces about city life as *Aguafuertes porteñas* [Porteño etchings, 1933]. He gives the best underdog's vision of the labyrinthine city in its economic heyday, dramatizing the story of the poor immigrant whose dream of "making America" fails.

Further down the Avenida de Mayo, Vázquez Rial mentioned the Café London in his guide to the city, a modernized parody of what it was when Julio Cortázar frequented it. Cortázar grouped the lottery prize winners in his novel *Los premios* [*The Winners*, 1960] in this café on Perú and Avenida de Mayo, before they set off for the cruise ship and its mysterious break-down at sea. The overcrowded, overheated café, with bad-tempered waiters and uncomfortable seats, was, he wrote, "a café for pitucos" [snobs], as noisy inside as outside in the street where "the Avenida de Mayo insists on its usual chaos." The novel questions personal relationships and literature itself, as its characters end up in the same café in a vicious circle of frustrations. All in all, this avenue deserves Nogués' description as "a unique and marvelous architectural reserve in Buenos Aires," while Blas Matamoro claimed that you can read in the avenue's "facades the history of architecture of Buenos Aires."

The Avenida de Mayo ends at the grand Palacio del Congreso [Palace of Congress], with a 250-foot dome made with 30,000 tons of copper. Designed by the architect Víctor Meano, its facade is Greco-Roman and the dome green. Meano was murdered by his verse-writing butler in 1904 just before the Palacio was inaugurated, after the man had been accused of seducing Meano's young wife. Eloy Martínez described Perón's lying-in-state in the Congreso in his documentary novel *La novela de Perón* [*The Perón Novel*, 1985]:

> *The Great Man's coffin was already in the Blue Drawing Room of the Congreso. A Deputy proposed that it be left forever on the platform of the chamber so that his immortality could inspire the laws and decrees of the future. They dressed the corpse in his military uniform. His interlocked fingers held a mother-of-pearl rosary. The presidential sash crossed his breast. The crowd that waited to see him increased beyond 400,000 people. Only 2,000 per hour could reach the catafalque. It was an old man's wake in which people hardly cried and talked in philosophical tones. A railing draped with a blue rug separated the coffin from the people. It was soggy with tears, mud, the dregs from the street, but the pilgrims went on kissing it.*

The radical North American writer Waldo Frank, who had fought in the Spanish Civil War and been beaten up by fascist thugs in Buenos Aires, visited the Congreso in 1944:

> *Acting President Ramón Castillo goes to the Capitol this afternoon to open the national Congress with a message... The box in which we have seats, close to the rostrum where Castillo will read, gives me a good view. I see the body of Ambassadors, including the nut-like little Jap and the Nazi chargé d'affaires; I study the cabinet, including the vapid-faced Foreign Minister Guiñazú... The huge domed Palace has the embalmed dead air usual in legislative halls. Men get up and mumble incomprehensible reports to which no one listens. The ladies in the box across from ours, the wives of cabinet officers and high functionaries, discreetly gossip. Boredom is ubiquitous.*

In front is the grandiose Plaza del Congreso (1910) with a pond and a monumentally elaborate sculpture representing the Río de la Plata as a young man holding an oar in his left hand, and above two figures spraying fountain water, though in 1998 water no longer sprayed out. There are several further allegorical sculptures, with the main one representing the Dos Congresos (of 1813 and 1816), a vast Boadicea-like statue which people climb, sometimes placing a branch in the woman's raised hand. The steps leading up to this formidable white marble women were sculpted by the Belgian Jules Lagae. In the middle of the plaza stands an authorized copy (one of three) of Rodin's 1904 greening bronze "The Thinker," giving the city its "lesson in tranquil meditation," according to Guatemalan poet Gómez Carillo.

The North American novelist Lawrence Thornton in his *Imagining Argentina* (1987) clusters his view of the military "disappearances" around Carlos Rueda, a theatre director who hallucinates the truth about his disappeared wife and daughter. Thornton describes the plaza as a symbol of the military evil:

> *That dream is embedded as a bronze marker in the paving stones of the Plaza del Congreso. All distances in our country are measured from Kilómetro Cero which shines, bronze in sunlight, in the cold eyes of the generals and in the medals cascading over their tunics. In 1976 the generals drew a line around Kilómetro Cero. 'Step over it and we will kill you,' they said... They even invented a name for what they were doing, the proceso, the process, but those of us watching and suffering had another name, la guerra sucia.*

The Kilómetro Cero [Kilometre Zero] is the point from which all road distances from Buenos Aires are measured (the longest route is 3,390 km to Bahía Lapataia on the Chilean border). César Fernández Moreno joked that one must call Buenos Aires "by its real name: *kilómetro cero*," and explained how architect Alberto Prebisch placed a stone nearby with a rhyming poem (in the Spanish) by Guido Spano carved into it: "I was born in Buenos Aires / what do I care about being snubbed / by misfortune! / Argentine until I drop dead / I was born in Buenos Aires."

The Biblioteca del Congreso on Alsina 1835, founded in 1859 with its newly built Hemeroteca [newspaper library], has a vast collection of books and opens to the public twenty-four` hours a day. Edgar Bayley, poet and essayist, worked there for many years until his death in 1990. It is not to be confused with the library in the Palacio del Congreso, open solely for senators and staff.

Carlos Mastronardi's *Memorias de un provinciano* [Memories of a provincial man, 1967] recreated the atmosphere in Samet's bookshop on the Avenida de Mayo in the 1920s, where the latest avant-garde writing from Europe could be discussed. This is where Mastronardi met Güiraldes and Borges, with whom he later became close friends. A bookshop then was more than a place to browse and buy, but an institution in which to hold discussions and meet fellow writers.

The Confitería del Molino (so called because of its Quijote-associated windmill on the facade) on Callao and Rivadavia faces the Congreso and was thus peopled by politicians. It was founded in 1905 but even though threatened with demolition and today boarded up, it survives as a wonderful art-nouveau relic (Gómez de la Serna called it a "sumptuous place"). In a mocking poem in 1922 Oliverio Girondo compared the "sweet" eyes of girls from Flores with "the sugared almonds of the Confitería del Molino." In this *belle époque* café President Yrigoyen's fall was plotted, the Duke of Wales drank a coffee and the popular poet and diplomat Amado Nervo (1870-1919) would sit and meditate.

Nearby lived Gómez de la Serna on calle Victoria 1974, today renamed Hipólito Yrigoyen, and a plaque commemorates his stay of twenty-seven years in the city, calling him a "genius of contemporary Spanish literature." The plaque also quotes him: "When I die I would like all the caryatids in Buenos Aires to cry for me," a typical *boutade*, for some wonderfully exuberant female caryatids support the nearby Palacio del Congreso. In his flat he had an X-ray of his head which he called his self-portrait and which lit up. Gómez de la Serna was famous for his haiku aphorisms and witticisms called *greguerías*, and wrote quick, surreal novels and biographies, producing over 100 books in his lifetime. In Madrid he was celebrated for his *tertulias* in the defunct Café Pombo.

Costanera Sur

The filling in of the river to build the docks of Dársena Sur diverted the original promenade, called the Alameda. This walking-space, with fresh air from the river, became the Costanera Sur in 1924, designed as a "river balcony" with pleasing balustrades. Silvina Bullrich alluded to it in 1939 as the Costanera Vieja: "It was backed by gardens where on suffocating nights during the Argentine summer, the inhabitants of the airless city came to find fresh air, drink beer and pursue cheap emotions in the violent games played there." The Jewish *gaucho* writer Alberto Gerchunoff boasted: "Buenos Aires' lung is this artery that gives us an oceanic illusion." Alas, no more. This *costanera* has in turn lost its riverine aspect with landfills and silting for a highway that was never built, so that this second walk now looks on to land and a lake, the recently created, and wonderfully wild, Parque Natural Costanera Sur, opened in 1986. The old jetty (the grandly built *espigón*) thus incongruously sticks out into land (with a monument Al Plus Ultra, called after the first airplane that crossed the Atlantic from Palos de Moguer in Spain to Buenos Aires in sixty-one hours). We visited here in 1998 to find squatters living under the pier, so abandoned is this area.

Nearby is the Escuela de Bellas Artes Ernesto de la Cárcova, named after a socially-conscious realist painter who lived from 1867 to 1927 and is represented by a sculpted head. Inside the school itself is the Museo de Calcos y Escultura Comparada, containing 200 papier-mâché copies of the world's more famous sculptures. Germinal Nogués calls this museum "one of the places with the most *duende* and magic in the city [*duende* may be translated as spirit or inspiration]. It is strange to walk round these plaster copies, ghosts of the originals. Today the school is surrounded by parked tractor trailers, with engines on, though the surprising garden and tiled, spouting, Andalusian fountain mitigate the changed atmosphere. The once secluded Cervecería Munich, designed in 1927 by the architect András Kalnay, is now the Museo de Telecomunicaciones. Juana Bignozzi lamented this loss in her poem "Munich of the Costanera": "Many beers remained to be served / Concrete Bavarian of my childhood." She ends with the line that "someone will come back asking for a beer."

It was on the Costanera Sur that Dolores ("Lola") Mora (1866-1936), Argentina's first woman sculptor, has her set piece "Fuente de las Nereidas" [Water Nymphs' Fountain]. Made in Italy from Carrara marble, it has a naked Venus on a shell held by two mermaids. Built to stand in the Plaza de Mayo in 1903 but seen as too scandalous on account of its naked women, it was first moved to the corner of Leandro Alem and Cangallo (later Perón), and then to the Costanera Sur in 1916. Haroldo Conti, the Argentine novelist who was "disappeared" by the military in 1976, set his novel *Alrederor de la jaula* [Around the cage, 1967] on the Costanera in 1956, where his boy Milo works on a merry-go-round. At one time the boy passes Lola Mora's statue with his dying boss: "They spent some time by the fountain and Silvestre commented that it was covered in slime... By all those figures full of life it looked like bird-dropping." This area south of the Plaza de Mayo is described by Conti as Milo spends time with his girl friend Tita:

> They walked right round it, meaning from the river-front along the rambla [promenade] and then behind, through the trees, the abandoned games, the empty snack bars until reaching the Monument to the Spaniards, lying dark and solitary at the end of the route. They returned to the river-front and sat looking out to river on stairs worn away by the water. There were a few still boats beyond the canal and one that moved between the buoys towards the south. Some tugs sailed beyond the break-water.

Sergio Renán made this novel into a film in 1974 called *Crecer de golpe* [Growing up overnight] Today there are still the trees, the parapet, the sense of a promenade and the above-mentioned *Monument to Spain* by Arturo Dresco on a base of red granite, depicting the Discovery and Conquest. There are over twenty-four figures represented in this complex sculpture, including the poet Martín del Barco Centera, author of the poem that gave Argentina its name, Las Casas, the defender of the Amerindians, and Félix de Azara, the Aragonese naturalist who recorded life in northern Argentina and Paraguay.

When the city ended on what was then the Alameda, the most conspicuous sight was that of the washerwomen, the *lavanderas*, nearly all black, washing on the rocks and sand. A young W. H. Hudson recalled this scene in his memoirs *Far Away and Long Ago* (1918):

> Here on the broad beach under the cliff one saw a whiteness like a white cloud, covering the ground for a space of about a third of a mile; and the cloud, as one drew near, resolved itself into innumerable garments, sheets and quilts, and other linen pieces, fluttering from long lines, and covering the low rocks washed clean by the tide and the stretches of green turf

between. It was the spot where the washerwomen were allowed to wash all the dirty linen of Buenos Ayres in public. All over the ground the women, mostly negresses, were seen on their knees, beside the pools among the rocks, furiously scrubbing and pounding away at their work, and like all negresses they were exceedingly vociferous, and their loud gabble, mingled with yells and shrieks of laughter, reminded me of the hubbub made by a great concourse of gulls...

Hudson also remembered their foul language. These same washer-women became the dictator Rosas' best informants. There is a scene in José Mármol's anti-*Rosista* novel *Amalia* in which Rosas' sister-in-law promises to ask these washerwomen whether anyone has left traces of blood on linen and thus catch the bleeding fugitive *unitario*.

Newspaper vendor (Harriet Cullen)

PART THREE

The North

"The north is the imperfect symbol of our nostalgia for Europe."
Borges

Barrio Norte

This is where the elegant people, the *paquetes*, fled after the yellow fever epidemic of 1871 (which killed 13,614 *porteños*), and it now refers to a mentality as much as to a geographically defined place. Its exact boundaries are hard to place, although Florencio Escardó claims that Avenida Santa Fe is its "psychological wall." The Marxist-Sartrian Juan José Sebreli defined this *barrio* in his inquiry into the political geography of Buenos Aires as "enclosing, separating and protecting the rich against the poor"; and because the rich need to differentiate themselves from *parvenus*, it was, he thought, the least "neighborly" of the city's *barrios*. He underlined how different this area was from other monotonous *porteño* neighborhoods with its "European streets," little plazas (Carlos Pellegrini), fountains (Guido and Anchorena, Arroyo and Esmeralda), curved streets (Arroyo), streets ending in staircases (Seaver) and its labyrinths (Palermo Chico). Silvina Bullrich memorably captured the *barrio norte* caste mentality in her novel *Calles de Buenos Aires* [Streets of Buenos Aires, 1939] by identifying "petulance" and "exhibitionism" as its key defects: "In this barrio of rich and new rich everybody knows everybody, some better than others, and everyone spies on everyone, seeking in the mistakes of the rest an excuse, in the tragedies of others, gossip." In her time the *barrio norte* was a constantly bickering cocktail party of idle people, and outside its confines "human beings didn"t exist." *Barrio norte*, she wrote, was a sort of snobbish malady: "sybariticism, egoism, the eternal cunning and poisonous smirk of the upper class, that's the disease engendered by Buenos Aires."

After his childhood years in Palermo and adolescence in Europe, Jorge Luis Borges returned to Argentina to live in the *barrio norte* with his mother. Their address was calle Maipú 994, 6th floor, flat "B," near the Plaza San Martín (Borges had earlier lived on Quintana 222, then Anchorena 1662 from 1938 to 1943, and again Quintana 275). Today on calle Maipú 971 there is a map, the "Jorge Luis Borges paths," indicating those parts of the city incorporated into his work. Victoria Ocampo was surprised by Borges' love for his city: "Borges in the middle of the splendours of New York or Paris, remembered with an ache calle Maipú... Calle Maipú is not so beautiful that it leaves you breathless." Strangely, the Fundación Internacional Jorge Luis Borges is on Anchorena 1660, next door to where he once lived at 1662 (and wrote "The Circular Ruins" in a dreamy week). The pleasant, spacious house has a lecture room and offices, Borges' library is in the process of being catalogued, and a top floor is being converted into a *Hemeroteca* to be named after poet Alberto Girri, all under the guidance of Borges' widow María Kodama. The main collector of Borgiana and a good biographer is Alejandro Vaccaro, who has founded an Asociación Borgesiana de Buenos Aires, with a cllection of over 4,000 items (vaccaroal@ infovia.com.ar).

Borges's poem "Barrio Norte" laments the passing away of the original patios, *milongas* and guitars into the grand zone of the 1930s, and the later blocks of flats. Only the *gomero* trees reveal that "obscure loyalty that my words declare: / the barrio." Later in 1969 in "Elegy for the Dark," Borges accepts the *barrio norte* as his own: "Buenos Aires / which before broke up into suburbs / as it reached the ceaseless plains, / has become again the Recoleta, the Retiro, / the blurred streets of the Once." Estela Canto remembered Borges' Maipú flat in her biography: "It was a small flat: a tiny *living room*; a minuscule bedroom with a narrow bed, a table and a chest of drawers for Georgie [Borges' nickname]; the bedroom on the street corner, his mother's, with a large baldaquin bed filling out the room; the kitchen and maid's room. Norah [Borges' painter sister], who had married the Spanish writer Guillermo de Torre, no longer lived at home." The highlight of Paul Theroux's short stay in Buenos Aires in 1979 was visiting Borges in his dark Maipú flat on the sixth floor. Theroux noted little furniture, a cat, no carpets, and a gleaming parquet floor free of dust. He saw prints by Piranesi, and books, a collection of Everyman classics and shelves of poetry in no particular order, all battered and sprouting paper page markers, with "the look of having been read." Willis Barnstone was told by Borges about a meeting with the North American poet Robert Lowell in his Maipú drawing room, when, "suddenly, this cousin of Amy Lowell lay down on the floor, took off his trousers and, wearing nothing but his undershorts, began to scream. I don't know what he said. I thought he was a madman. I assure you, he didn't act like a gentleman." Borges never did read any of Lowell's poems.

But Borges was not the only writer to live in the *barrio norte*, as we'll see in later sections, for most writers have lived there at one time or another. A good example is the doomed poet Alejandra Pizarnik who lived on Montevideo 980 (let's hope a plaque will soon commemorate this). When I visited her there in 1970, her studio had poems pinned to the walls like paintings, and stank of stuffy air.

Strangely, Ernesto Guevara, baptized "Che" for being Argentine, lived on the fringes of the *barrio norte*, when he moved there with his family to study at the Medical Faculty in 1948. His flat was on Aráoz 2180, with a balcony looking onto the street and another, his bedroom's, onto an inner staircase. While reluctantly in Buenos Aires (he was no *porteño*), the asthmatic Che played chess in the student Olympics for his university and graduated as a doctor in 1953, before setting off again on his travels, ending up in Guatemala, never to return.

Roberto Arlt's character Erdosain in *Los siete locos* [*The Seven Madmen*, 1929] wanders the *barrio norte* streets of Arenales and Talcahuano, past the corners of Charcas and Rodríguez Peña and the junctions of Montevideo and Avenida Quintana "appreciating the spectacle of the magnificent architecture of these streets, forbidden to the down and out. It was another world within the rotten city that he knew, another world to him." In Arlt's first novel *El juguete rabioso* [The rabid toy, 1926], Silvio is told to bring books to a flat on Charcas 1600, and he is amazed at the luxury he encounters: "Strange and special are these luxury blocks of flats. Outside, their harmonious lines, with metopes that highlight the sumptuousness of the complicated and arrogant cornices, with their wide windows protected by wavy glass, make the poor devils dream of refinements of luxury and power." Silvio is stopped by a porter in uniform, sent to a lift and ushered into the flat by a maid in black with a white apron who had opened the door "like a monumental steel door in a safe."

In Arlt's strange novel about love and sex *El amor brujo*, [Bewitching love, 1932], the married Balder takes a tram ride with his sixteen-year-old pick-up through the *barrio norte*, turning into Arenales and along Talcahuano. They see "free spaces in the streets filled by private cars. Delivery bicycles leaning against each other outside luxury foodstores. Inside the garages groups of chauffeurs dressed like lackeys." A typical *barrio norte* flat, with its inhabitants, emerges from Julio Cortázar's story "House Taken Over," charting the alien forces that push a cultured brother and sister into the street (perhaps the forces of Peronism?). The flat on calle Rodríguez Peña is described in estate-agent details: "How could I forget what the flat was like. The dining room, with Gobelins, a library and three large bedrooms at the back. A corridor with a massive oak door isolated that part from the front with its bathroom, the kitchen, our bedrooms and the main drawing room. You entered the house along a hallway with tiles." The grand flat in question has probably been demolished to allow for a taller and more economically spaced apartment block; the good life is over for a dwindling middle class.

Barrio norte also suggests a certain kind of culture, often tainted by snobbery, with libraries and bookshops galore, including second-hand ones—a feature of the city. Casa Pardo, founded in 1892 on calle Sarmiento, off Florida, moved south in 1969 to the Barrio de San Telmo at Defensa 1170. The Librería Fernández Blanco, specialists in Latin American history and literature, is another excellent rare bookshop on Tucumán 712, as is Capítulo I, specializing in Argentine literature, history and the city, on Ayacucho 1206. The Plaza Lavalle has an open stall second-hand book fair on Sundays. The Biblioteca Lincoln (a library of US books) is on Maipú 686. In his biography of the suburban poet Evaristo Carriego Borges mentions his habit of sifting through second-hand books "in the murky purgatories of the secondhand bookshops on calle Lavalle." Silvio, Arlt's boy protagonist growing up on the mean streets of Buenos Aires, finds a job with Don Gaetano on Lavalle 800: "a huge room, packed with books. The space was long and shady like a cave. Wherever you looked there were books on tables made of planks on trestles, books on counters, in corners, under the table, in the basement." In short, a typical *porteño* bookshop.

Willis Barnstone recorded how his idol Borges would walk to the glassed-in Librería de la Ciudad in the *Galería* off calle Florida, very close to his Maipú home, and dictate his latest poem there. Borges hated phones and didn't mind being recognized. Barnstone explained: "Borges liked to work in company, since he was, as he frequently declared, a lonely, isolated man... The bookstore was Borges' habitat." In 1999 the passageway connecting Florida and Maipú was being modernized. This penchant for working in bookshops and cafés was not wholly due to Borges' loneliness, for it is common to most *porteño* writers. The exaggeratedly ironic poet Leopoldo Lugones, for instance, worked all his life in the Biblioteca del Consejo Nacional de Educación on calle Paraguay, where friends dropped in and where he had a portrait of W. H. Hudson on his desk. Lugones swung from being a socialist in his youth to being a fascist. He was a formidable "dictionary" poet, in Borges' words, stretching the language beyond feeling and sincerity.

The *barrio norte* has several old cafés and once had more. Violet Bell, who breaks out of her puritan anti-sensual prison in Isobel Strachey's novel *A Summer in Buenos Aires* visits the Confitería Paris in 1925, on the corner of Charcas and Libertad. Founded in 1917 but no longer existent, this was where Teatro Colón concert-goers would retire for tea, with its

> *magnificent interior of mirrored walls and marble floor and a heavy sweet fragrance of little buns and cakes piled on a baroque counter which wound along the glittering walls. These led into another larger hall containing little marble-toped tables with gilt chairs, long windows shaded with embroidered linen curtains and statues in the style of Ingres*

or Chardin in rounded alcoves in the painted walls. The tables hummed with fashionably dressed Argentines drinking coffee and chocolate while a string quartet played mazurkas in a recess.

Poet, erstwhile socialist and fascist, Leopoldo Lugones (Editorial Universitaria de Buenos Aires)

Victoria Ocampo was thrown out of the Paris for lighting up a cigarette. Gordon Meyer would go there after opera at the Colón: "Afterwards there was the 'Paris', the fashionable confitería in early twentieth-century style, with its imported marble, bronze capitals, crystal chandeliers, huge Sèvres vases, silk-curtained windows and devoted waiters. Here we would discuss the opera or anything else until 1 or 2 in the morning." Equally fashionable and elegant was the Confitería El Águila, founded in 1852 on calle Florida 102 and later moved to the corner of Callao and Santa Fe. This august establishment was even used for official government receptions, as for the President of Brazil, Dr. Campos Salles.

The *barrio norte* is also identifiable by its leafy plazas like Plaza Vicente López, Plaza Mitre or Plaza Rodríguez Peña. Buenos Aires is not blessed with green spaces, and can appear a very unforgivingly urban city with regular, narrow streets, although the English traveler Thomas Hutchinson noted in 1865 that Buenos Aires had "many agreeable squares," which he called the "lungs" of the city. The forgotten poet Pedro Herreros opens his "Buenos Aires Twilight" thus: "In the middle of the city / the plaza is an oasis." Gordon Meyer's short story "Exiles" describes a generic plaza and conveys a certain kind of architectural monotony evident throughout Argentina's towns, inevitably built around central plazas, usually with statues of General San Martín in the middle. Meyer's meticulous, slightly pedantic and ironic description of the plaza could only come from a foreigner:

For the periphery of that plaza in which you then lived was a cordon of jacarandá trees, all leaning over slightly, like a corps-de-ballet, inclined from the waist, hands entwined over heads. Other trees grew there—eucalypti, casuarinas, magnolias, and immensely tall palms exploding like giant roosters' tails. All failed somehow to beautify the square. They were city soiled.

In the centre of the plaza, on an unlovely grey block, stood the monument. You came to think that there was a fear of natural spaces; they had to be dominated. And by a French sculptor, if possible—that was important. Such was the copy of Bourdelle's "Hércules Saetando."

As for the subject of the monument in your own plaza, the inscription between his Roman gladius and the nineteenth-century trousered leg said

> *something or other "pro patria mori," which was orthodox enough; and*
> *closer examination showed that he had led an expedition into the desert*
> *(accompanied, as you knew from elsewhere, by a contingent of monks.*
> *"In order to finish with the savages once and for all"). After that—as a*
> *result?—he was made Minister for War... But now he stood: in the centre*
> *of the plaza, large than life, monochromatic, one hand outstretched,*
> *fingers extending upwards, like the opening lotus flower; and a pigeon on*
> *his head.*

My guess as to the model for Meyer's square is Plaza Rodríguez Peña.

Calle Florida

From the Plaza de Mayo you can stroll north along calle Florida, named
after a valley of the river Piray where a certain Colonel Arenales defeated
the Spaniards in Alto Perú (today Bolivia) in 1814. Florida is a
palimpsest street written about by most writers, an anthology street that
makes selecting particular versions of it an arbitrary process. So we'll
start with novelist Eduardo Mallea who called this fashionable street a
"canal" that cuts across Buenos Aires; it has remained the street that
offers *flâneurs* and saunterers the smart face of the city, always bubbling
with energy. From the city's earliest years, Florida was exceptional as the
first paved street when the other streets turned muddy with rain. Trams
never sliced along it, and it is now a pedestrian thoroughfare. It was also
the first street in Buenos Aires to have electric lights, in 1882. Lucio V.
López signaled a dramatic change in calle Florida between the 1860s
and 1890s: "the village of 1862 had many aspects of a city; many people
went to Europe; women cultivated letters." Even so, Florida was a street
where women and fashion set the tone: "not even philosophers could
stroll from four to five in the afternoon in winter along Florida street
without being moved by the fashionable women's bodies." With
changing fashions it wasn't "chic" to speak Spanish; "it was necessary to
splatter your chatter with some English words, and many French ones,
trying to pronounce them carefully." In fact, López waxes elegaic about
the transition from "that Buenos Aires of 1862 that was patriotic,
simple, part peopled by shopkeepers, by priests and still village-like" to
"a people with great European pretensions, who wasted time *flaneando*
[a neologism from the French flâneur] in the streets." In its fashionable

history calle Florida has had galleries, Bond Street lookalike shops, grand department stores like Gath y Chaves (founded in 1883 and demolished in 1974), and even a facsimile of Harrods with lavish window displays and a porter in green livery. Today, Harrods is no longer related in anything other than its name to its London original and is undergoing modernization.

The street also housed the original and exclusive Jockey Club (burnt down by Peronists in April 1953) and the modishly avant-garde Di Tella Institute at Florida 936, run by Jorge Romero Brest (founded in 1958 and closed in 1970) and famed for its happenings, "pop" art shows, experimental theatre and rock music. Like the street itself, this was always a place for those in the know. At the top end, near Harrods, is the Galería del Este, a closed passage that joins Florida with Maipú, one of the "hearts" of the city according to Manuel Mujica Lainez. Here is the glassed-in La Ciudad bookshop, where Borges would often sit and many others would sign copies of their latest books. Nearby on Florida 943 is the Spanish government cultural centre, ICI (Instituto de Cooperación Iberomamericano), designed by painter and architect Clorindo Testa (of the Biblioteca Nacional fame) which launches books, puts on talks and poetry readings, and has a library.

Calle Florida is definitely a place to be seen in and has been since the 1880s. The feminist poet Alfonsina Storni, an unmarried mother and finally a suicide in 1938, wrote a sonnet titled "Meeting," which describes how on a corner of the crowded calle Florida she bumps into an ex-lover and comments on his yellow teeth as she "plays with her gloves"; he rushes off, horrified, into the street's "dense crowd." You could and still can count on seeing wanted and unwanted faces in the crowds there. The city, as defined by the sociologist Richard Sennett, privileges the gaze rather than touch or discourse; there's something special about Argentine staring, a critical summary that looks you up and down quickly to note your social status, your poor or fine dress sense.

How have others seen this street? Manuel Gálvez's 1916 novel *El mal metafísico* [The metaphysical sickness] is set at the turn of the century and explores impecunious bohemian life. Carlos Riga, the poet, watches women who are so "beautiful and luxurious, so inaccessible that he stared at them every afternoon, avidly, on the corso that was calle Florida." During the early 1920s Florida was already the in-place; the Mexican educator José Vasconcelos remarked that "in calle Florida there's a drawing room intimacy; you don't know anybody, but we pass so close to each other that we become a family." In 1932 Philip Guedella contrasted fashionable Florida with its traffic-choked, parallel streets and called it "a *souk* left by the Moors in some old Spanish town for all the world to pace at ease between the little shops in the cool evening." Seven years later, Silvina Bullrich's alter-ego, the questing, walking writer Gloria, wanders into calle Florida: "She loved the bustle of that street, its shop windows, its lethargic traffic, its bottle-necks, that sensation of life of a great city. She strolled along happy and light... Men standing on corners stared at the well-dressed women who passed brazenly." The ritual of the lustful stare, the *piropo* [verbal flattery or sexual innuendo], are a male preserve, a symptom of "that male Argentine avidity that measures all possibilities."

Above all, calle Florida is the mental escape of gazing into "illuminated shop-windows." French novelist and biographer André Maurois (1885-1967) paid a fleeting visit to Buenos Aires in 1952 and compared Florida with the austerity of post-Second World War Paris: "The abundance in the shop-windows," he lamented, "is enough to wring the heart of a Frenchman." In 1980 Andrew Graham-Yooll bravely returned to Buenos Aires to testify against the urban terrorist Mario Firmenich, leader of the Montoneros who had kidnapped Graham-Yooll while he was a journalist with the English language *porteño* newspaper *The Buenos Aires Herald,* an act that necessitated Graham-Yooll's exile to London for seventeen years. Graham-Yooll had this to say about the fame—and escapism—of calle Florida: "*Calle* Florida, the most famous pedestrian shopping street in South America, looks like an elegant market place; foreign goods fill shop windows; import duties have been lifted. With the national airline office at one end of the street, and Harrods at the other end, Florida gives the impression of being a lane leading to a dream country of rich possessions, all behind glass and all within reach."

Marcos Sastre opened the first bookshop in Buenos Aires in 1837 on calle Victoria 59, today Florida (moving there from his earlier bookshop on Defensa in the Sur), patriotically calling it The Argentine Bookshop. This meeting place, El Salón Literario, attracted many writers including Esteban Echeverría, Juan María Gutiérrez and Juan Bautista Alberdi; the thousand volumes could be borrowed, but it only lasted a year until closed by Rosas. To put Sastre's bookshop in perspective, the first printing press in Buenos Aires had only opened in 1780, and the first newspaper, *El telégrafo mercantil* was not sold until 1801. In 1893 Rubén Darío, during his first year in the city, wrote an uncollected poem "Porteña" that opens "Yesterday the sonorous pavement of Florida / felt the trotting of horses from England / who dragged carriages where love calls / the dark face of the prettiest women on earth." Calle Florida still has good bookshops like El Ateneo on Florida 340. Mexican novelist Carlos Fuentes recalls the smell of "varnished wood and cattle leather" when he entered this bookshop to buy a book by Borges, as many Argentines liked binding their books in "leather." The Flashchoen bookshop in Gálvez's *El mal metafísico* benefited from being on calle Florida, the gossip-centre of the city: "Flaschoen's bookshop, situated on Florida, was usually full, every afternoon, with three or four poetasters and reporters, and was the most active centre of vicious gossip in Buenos Aires. Flaschoen, the bookshop owner, a lively restless Dutchman, amused himself chatting with his customers—who hardly ever bought or paid for anything—seeing how they stripped others naked." Of the Florida bookshops André Maurois noted enviously in 1952: "The bookshops are like palaces. At Peuser's, Kraft's and Viau's there are not only books in every language but exhibition galleries and lecture halls." There is literally a "Palacio del Libro" [Palace of the Book] on calle Rivadavia.

The Jockey Club, founded by Carlos Pellegrini and built in 1897 on Florida 102, exemplified the grandeur of this street. In 1910, W. A. Hirst asserted that this club was "probably unsurpassed by any club building in the world." Future French prime minister Georges Clemenceau visited Buenos Aires in 1910 for the centenary celebrations and found the Jockey Club very "American," with a luxury that did not bother to conceal itself and lacking British simplicity; he singled out the "great rotunda, empire style." Beatriz Guido (1924-1988), married to film director Leopoldo Torre Nilsson, fictionalized the burning down of this sumptuous building in *El incendio y las vísperas* [The fire and the days before, 1964]. Her novel charts the rich, cultured, sexually-liberal Pradere family from October 1952 to April 15, 1953, when the Jockey was burnt down by Peronist "hordes." Alejandro Pradere kills himself in the Turkish baths of the Castelar Hotel after witnessing the fire; his daughter and son help anti-Peronist terrorists, the family collaborates with the regime so as not to lose its grand *estancia*. The library of 50,000 books, a Goya, a Corot, a Fromentin, a Sorolla were lost. In Guido's novel, the reader follows Pradere into the club, up the soft carpet, past the Falquière statue of Diana (partially destroyed by fire, but now in the new Jockey Club house in the Plaza Carlos Pellegrini), to the solarium and into the second floor hallway. There stands "the Louis XIII Gobelin and that beautiful sixteenth century screen... He feels part of the tapestry," until he catches sight of the thugs. Victoria Ocampo adored this statue of Diana at the top of the club's grand staircase, and envied the statue's marble thighs that would never stain with menstrual blood, asking rather oddly: "Who would have made this statue of Diana with thighs stained by blood?"

Calle Florida was the scene in 1955 of a symbolic class protest against Peronism by Borges' mother Leonor Acevedo, as narrated by the writer's spurned lover and then biographer Estela Canto:

> *Calle Florida was always packed with people during the day and so the political tension was high. Suddenly doña Leonor, followed by friends, burst into insults against Perón and Evita... Then they sang the national anthem. The ladies were surrounded by a crowd, and the police, scared of trouble, arrested them and took them to the station. Norah Borges* [Jorge Luis's sister] *and a friend were taken to the Buen Pastor prison* [where Victoria Ocampo had also been imprisoned], *a prison for whores, where Norah spent a month sketching whores and thieves, who all looked like her husband Guillermo de Torre. Given her age, doña Leonor was put under house arrest.*

Eduardo Mallea's vain, philandering Carlos in *La ciudad junto al río inmóvil* [The city next to the immobile river, 1936] walks into calle Florida and sees that "the street of cheap and turbulent luxuries was in front of him. Salesman shout outside their shops, a smell of freshly ground coffee, a shining of glass, shop windows and violent advertisements on the streets fronts... and the march past of the buying hordes, that irregular, constant, avid, provincial army."

Apart from strolling and gawping along today's central pedestrian way (the Bond Street of the city, for comparisons with other great cities are ingrained in the *porteño* mind), the visitor can find in calle Florida good examples of the *porteño* café to sit and chat in. Like the Richmond on Florida 468, for instance, which has always been a meeting-point of intellectuals (a *peña* or literary get-together). The popular poet and retired rural doctor Baldomero Fernández Moreno met his cronies there in "sweet Richmond with leather chairs." In another poem he recalls how "the Richmond will smoke out our meetings / Oh, its edifying lemon teas!" Elsewhere, he tells how he hid behind a pillar to write while people smoked, dishes clattered and an orchestra played blues and tangos: "above my head / a ventilator spun / like a star." There was so much cigarette smoke that "Twenty pillars sink / their capitals / in thick clouds of blue and white smoke" (like the Argentine flag). When the young rebel and future communist Estela Canto was being courted by Borges, she recalled not being allowed, as a woman, into this same Richmond. Victoria Ocampo complained that cafés were "a man's world"; the vain, arrogant men in Silvina Bullrich's *Calles de Buenos Aires* drop in to the Richmond to gossip about their sexual conquests. This male preserve has changed, although in the 1970s you could depend on seeing every Saturday a men-only group including the poet Alberto Girri. The Richmond, with its "English" feel, hunting prints, bronze chandeliers, *boiserie* and ceiling mirrors, was a good place to spy on the smart and chic who patrolled Florida. Dr. Plarr in Graham Greene's *The Honorary Consul* met his mother in the Richmond for tea, annoyed at its Babel of chattering, overdressed society ladies. The popular writer, poet and lyricist María Elena Walsh (1930-) met Borges in the Richmond in 1948. She recalled his "uncomfortable pauses," his "boneless handshake" and delight in eating cakes.

Another grand calle Florida project delayed in time are the impressive glassed-in Galerías Pacífico, referring to the railway company Ferrocarril de Buenos Aires al Pacífico that requisitioned them at the turn of the century. This is an entire block built in 1889 along the lines of Milan's Vittorio Emmanuelle II Gallery or as the Buenos Aires equivalent of the French Bon Marché, but only finally put to its original commercial use in 1992. The vaulted ceilings over the indoor fountains were finished in 1945 with murals by Antonio Berni, Demetrio Urruchúa, the Spaniard Manuel Colmeiro, Juan Carlos Castagnino and Lino Spilimbergo, all socially-conscious artists influenced by the Mexican muralists Diego Rivera, Orozco and Siqueiros. Berni restored the murals in 1968. The Ateneo club moved to these *Galerías* when decadent poet Rubén Darío joined it in 1896, introducing the then socialist poet Leopoldo Lugones, and seeing himself as a "vandal" in relation to the conservative values of the members. Darío remembered: "We younger ones stirred up the atmosphere with proclamations of mental freedom." For a while the Museo de Bellas Artes was also installed there.

The critic Ezequiel Martínez Estrada contrasted calle Florida with calle Boedo, a working-class street (see Part Five) and began a way of categorizing Argentine literature according to its social origins (a system that doesn't tell the real story). For him, calle Florida is "history, religion, psychology, if not a way of facing life... a state of mind." Because of the cosmopolitan nature of the street, Florida was also the name given to a group of like-minded literary experimenters, grouped around the nationalistic-sounding and popular (it sold up to 20,000 copies) magazine *Martín Fierro*, which was directed by Evar Méndez and backed by rich writers like Ricardo Güiraldes and Oliverio Girondo. They and others including Borges met at its offices on calle Florida. They tried out avant-garde tactics like shocking the public, wrote polemical manifestos and mocked the pompous elders through epigrams. Borges denied that there was any importance in the differences between the Florida and Boedo groups, claiming such alleged antagonism to be a "journalistic trick." Basically, he insisted, these young men spent "memorable nights" discussing "largely aesthetic matters." One of their meeting places was on calle Viamonte, in Dr. Maglione's studio. They held lavish dinners in places like the Rural off Plaza Italia, to celebrate Güiraldes' publication of his rural novel about becoming a man and a landowner, *Don Segundo Sombra* (1926), or to honor the Italian futurist F. T. Marinetti on June 14, 1926 in the Príncipe restaurant on Corrientes 642. Many of the group worked for the magazine *Crítica*. Güiraldes' death, and Girondo's departure to Europe, ended the group's encounters in 1927.

Estela Canto elaborated on Martínez Estrada's socially analytical view of calle Florida in the 1940s when she first met Borges and summarized Florida as the great shop Gath & Chaves; the pasaje Güemes, with its restaurant on the fourteenth floor, "the highest point in the city from where you could see the river and the Uruguayan coast," the Confitería L'Aiglon, with its roller-skating ring, and, on the corner of Florida and the Diagonal Norte, la Loba Romana, breast-feeding Romulus and Remus, later transferred to Parque Lezama. Estela Canto broke Florida up into class segments:

> The spirit of the first few blocks up to calle Corrientes was lively and happy, but beyond Corrientes there was another state of mind, with the Bar Richmond and the imposing facade of the Jockey Club. The social tone rose after crossing calle Córdoba. Here stood the Centro Naval, Harrods, the Plaza Hotel and the plaza San Martín. Here voices were lowered, women more soberly elegant and nobody shouted.

Further literary echoes on calle Florida are conveyed in Manuel Mujica Lainez's *La casa* [The house], a novel strangely narrated by a grand house itself on Florida 556 (demolished in 1956) and covering seventy-eight years of patrician Argentine history in decline. Another detail concerns the corner of Florida and Corrientes, where a plaque commemorates Ana Díaz, one of twelve Spanish women who arrived from Asunción, Paraguay, with Juan de Garay. She lived on this corner, then undeveloped countryside called the Esquina del Recuerdo, and can be considered the "mother" of Buenos Aires, once figuring at Garay's side on a 100-*peso* note. She also dared to marry a *mestizo* called Juan Martín in the days when one didn't marry men of mixed blood. In the nineteenth century, on 273 Florida (at that time called calle Unquera), lived Mariquita Sánchez de Thompson (commemorated by a bronze plaque) in whose literary salon "Listen O Mortals!," the Argentine national anthem (words by Vicente López y Planes and music by the Catalan Blas Parera, arranged later by Esnaola), was supposedly first sung.

Despite calle Florida's symbolic importance in the city's cultural network, Victoria Ocampo found it "narrow" and "ugly" on her return from living in France. Novelist Luis Pascarella also denigrated it as "a transformed slum." The British journalist Jimmy Burns "came to despise the way it merely aped Europe without ever quite managing to better it" and concluded that the real Argentina had nought to do with this street that "did not really exist. It was an imitation of something else." But Burns cannot deny Delfín Leocadio Garasa's assertion about Florida: "On calle Florida all historical periods are superimposed, which preserves its existence."

Calle San Martín

Another typical *porteño* street, parallel to Florida, is calle San Martín. It begins in the banking district, but it too has its literary cafés like the celebrated literary-political café Helvética, on the corner of Corrientes and San Martín, which was founded in 1844 and rebuilt several times. It was first patronized by Bartolomé Mitre and since then by journalists from his newspaper *La Nación*, including Rubén Darío and later Eduardo Mallea, the novelist who edited the cultural supplement. Destroyed by tank-fire when Perón was deposed in 1955, it was forced to close and was then rebuilt. The novelist Ernesto Sabato evoked its gloomy charm: "It was a dark place, with a wooden bar top and old *boiserie*. Stained, imperfect mirrors magnified and obscurely repeated the mystery and melancholy of that surviving corner." He labeled it "a *Mitrista* cavern."

The Mitre Museo y Biblioteca on San Martín 336 was Mitre's residence and now holds the Bartolomé Mitre archives, with over 80,000 books and a public reading room. "Don Bartolo," as Mitre was known, was brought up in exile from the dictator Rosas mainly in Montevideo, became a soldier and led the *porteños* to victory in Pavón against Urquiza. He went on to become the first president of the re-united Argentina in 1862, began writing his historical biographies, translated Dante in verse and founded the great newspaper *La Nación* (the *Argentina* was soon dropped) in 1870, which he edited for fifteen years. The paper still remains in the Mitre family (the current editor is also called Bartolomé Mitre; you can peruse this paper on http://www.la nacion.com). The great traveler and translator Richard Burton met Mitre in 1868: "as a bibliophile he astonished me by his knowledge of books, not only of the inside but of the outside; and he has a collection of rare and classical works... unequalled on this continent." In Lucio V. López's *La gran aldea* [The great village, 1884] a character alludes to

Mitre's books: "Few men have more books or papers than he; one day I had the honor of seeing him in his home, I left dazzled by the size of his library."

A typical grand house located half way down calle San Martín was the Gallic palace belonging to Montifiori in this same novel. López evokes the luxury, the tropical plants, the great staircase of carved oak, all dominated by "despotic fashion." This house epitomized fashion; in it "reigned an intimate cult of the century of upholstery and *bibelotaje*... all the mural luxuries of the Renaissance illuminated the walls... bronze and marble statues on columns and in niches; exotic flowers in Japanese and Saxe vases; china from pagodas and from Germany; all the anachronisms of modern taste." An equivalent to a Rubén Darío poem or to today's Museo de Arte Decorativo palace. Most impressive was the "great Louis XIV drawing room with its carved, gilded furniture, covered in gold Genovese velvet," with paintings on the walls, including a fake Rubens ("a naked woman, with reddish flesh and copious bosom"). The narrator comments caustically: "plenty of incongruity there" and "all centuries were there, all periods, all the customs, in a suspicious synchronism if you like." This so-called Buenos Aires aristocracy of the day "did not really appreciate art."

Another characteristic but rather more sober house has been reconstructed by historian-turned-novelist Félix Luna in *Soy Roca* [I am Roca, 1989]. President Roca lived on San Martín 577 from 1885 on and walked to work (though he had an escape tunnel built under his house). His home had a glassed-in patio, a telephone (number 2008), a *bidet* and library, and two palm trees in its garden. For him it was a "good barrio" to live in, before commerce drove people toward the Recoleta.

Also on calle San Martín stands the convent of Santa Catalina de Siena behind high walls, with its tall palm trees. The current building was opened in 1745. Masses are still held there to celebrate the retreat of the English in 1807 who had holed up in this convent. The poet Carlos Alberto Débole wrote: "On the narrow side walk / of the Santa Catalina monastery, / that impassive time chips away /—the past speaks on its walls, / reaches its erect and transitory blue, / and its palm tree." Opposite this church/monastery is a corner of the restored Galerías Pacífico called the Centro Borges, with a café (named Baldomero after the much-quoted city poet), bookshop and auditorium. Nearby is the Teatro Payró, with a plaque stating it to be the oldest independent theatre in Buenos Aires. It was named after the writer Roberto Payró (1867-1928), a novelist-dramatist with anarchist leanings, who was an early contributor to Buenos Aires becoming, in Jean Franco's words, "one of the first cities in Latin America to develop a genuinely popular theatre."

Calle Viamonte

A very literary street is Viamonte, at right angles off Florida. At 494, piso 8, Victoria Ocampo's cosmopolitan literary magazine *Sur* had its offices. It was run by her from 1931 to 1971, with help from the Ocampo fortune, and had as its secretaries eminent writers and critics, beginning with the Spanish poet and critic Guillermo de Torre (Borges' brother-in-law). He was followed by Eduardo Mallea, the novelist who also edited the cultural supplement for *La Nación*, then Pepe Bianco (also an excellent novelist), and finally Enrique Pezzoni. In 1932 *Sur* set up its publishing side; its first book was Federico García Lorca's popular *Romancero gitano* [Gypsy ballads]. Victoria Ocampo paid Lorca an advance of 3,000 *pesos*, which allowed him to become, for the first time in his life, financially independent from his father. The offices, then on Viamonte 548, were sacked by Peronist police in 1953 and Victoria Ocampo spent some three weeks in the El Buen Pastor prison (see El Sur) accused of plotting to bomb the Plaza de Mayo. Victoria Ocampo was born in Viamonte 482, on the corner of San Martín in 1890. Ironically, as noted in her autobiography, Viamonte was originally called Ocampo, and San Martín, Victoria. On Viamonte there was also the French bookshop, an umbilical cord back to France, long Argentina's cultural mentor, and the Facultad de Filosofía y Letras of the Universidad de Buenos Aires, founded in 1896. This grand building gave calle Viamonte its characteristic of intellectual busy-ness (I once worked fruitfully in its library dedicated to Argentine literature), but the Facultad de Filosofía y Letras has now moved to the barrio of Caballito, on calle Puán 480 (it can be visited on http://www.filo.uba.ar). The building today houses the Rectorado. In her lifetime Victoria Ocampo grumpily thought that her calle Viamonte had lost the grace lent by the church and convent: "Now it's one of the many ugly streets, without character, victim of the ignorance of some and adorned by the political propaganda of students who violate the virginal walls of the city." Sebreli also lamented the rise of the new left-wing intellectuals found on calle Viamonte, in its bars Florida and Cotto, and studying in the Facultad de Filosofía y Letras. He labeled them in 1964 as "impotent rebels," rejecting Argentine party politics with idealistic eyes stuck on Cuba, for the lure of the Cuban revolution in the 1960s and 1970s was tremendous.

It was on Viamonte 349 that the poet Alberto Girri (1919-1991) lived in a book-packed flat; a plaque now marks the site. For me, Alberto Girri incarnated a special kind of *porteño* intellectual. Although the city is never an explicit topic in his poems, his attitude to culture prolongs that of the *Sur* group to which he belonged and contributed. His poems work against excessive culture, like exorcisms, a clearing of the mind. As a man, Girri embodied the tango male—aesthetic and ascetic—always smartly dressed, hair slicked down, meeting buddies in local bars, alert to "spiritual" matters. He knew everybody and was one of the few *porteños* who lived from being a poet. Jorge Glusberg's (currently director of the Museo de Bellas Artes) avant-garde gallery and centre, CAYC (Centro de Arte y Comunicación), was also temporarily there.

The chronicler Fray Mocho (José Alvarez) evoked an earlier (1894) literary meeting point, the "cantina dil 20 settembro," a "cave" on Viamonte and Calle de Las Artes that grouped "the cream of our bohemians"—poets, painters, musicians, including himself, at the turn of the century. So perhaps things did not change that much, at least until the mid-1980s.

Plaza San Martín

Calle Florida ends on the Plaza San Martín with a statue of the early socialist poet Esteban Echeverría, inscribed with his verse. At first this epicentre of the city was called the Plaza de Marte and was used as a parade ground by the nearby garrison. In 1878 it was renamed after the great liberator, General José de San Martín (1778-1850). San Martín plotted in London with Miranda and others for the downfall of the Spanish colonies (there's a plaque on his house near Baker Street and a statue in Belgrave Square). He collected an army in 1812 (Argentina was already liberated), crossed the Andes, took Santiago in Chile from the Spaniards, was defeated at Cancha Rayada but regrouped and defeated the Spanish at Maipú. He then occupied Lima and met Simón Bolívar for a famous interview in Guayaquil, Ecuador. In 1824, a widower, he left for France with his daughter, survived in dignified poverty, and died in his town house on the hill in Boulogne-sur-Mer (now a museum, with the Argentine flag flying outside). There is an imitation of his Paris house, the Grand Bourg, in Palermo Chico, Buenos Aires. His embalmed body returned to Buenos Aires in 1880 and lies in a special mausoleum abutting the Cathedral because his freemasonry precluded a tomb inside. The equestrian statue sculpted by Joseph Daumas (1801-1887) of San Martín pointing the way across the Andes was erected in the plaza in 1862, and raised on a plinth by Gustavo Eberlein (1847-1926) with pompous decorations of his deeds in 1900. The statue is a ceremonial centre. The avant-garde Sergio Piñero's mocking poem "Plaza San Martín" evokes San Martín's statue: "Tight sashes of gravel / tie the plaza down / so that the Liberator's statue /—with its heroic FINGER—/ emerges more spontaneously."

The square has inspired quite a lot more poetry besides. Borges' poem dedicated to the plaza has the poet sitting up on this hill (once the river bank) watching the sun setting under jacaranda (*jacaranda mimosifolia*) and acacia trees, with the port itself below longing for distant places. He writes that the peace of this "deep plaza equalizes all souls." In summer it can be shady and cool. The Andalusian poet Rafael Alberti also praised this plaza: "Although it's hard to find a bench without / those lovers who sweeten the Plaza San Martín, / now that I am relaxing—listen, city—I'll tell you / you have the best plaza in the anthology / I'm off to where your palo borrachos make "s" shapes / stared at by the red Torre de los Ingleses." Baldomero Fernández Moreno summarizes this plaza's place in the *porteño* imaginary world by addressing it intimately in the "thou" form, as a woman: "At the sonorous tip of calle Florida / you open up black, profound, damp. / Halt here, walker: / you will not find a more reclusive garden, / a wiser shade, a more discrete wind, nor mist as blue, as elegant." At the moment, the plaza is well tended and grassy (many plazas in the city are sponsored by companies) but it was not always the case, as Vicente Quesada sadly observed in 1889: "That place is no English park, not even a garden. It's a tasteless mixture of all kinds of badly kept, abandoned trees, with two broken fountains that never knew jets of water. You could call this an abandoned place."

Known originally as the Retiro, it was the slave quarter between 1718 and 1739 (in 1791 the slave market was relocated nearby, until slavery was abolished in 1812), then a bullring, holding 12,000 people. Although women did not watch the bullfights, they went to the plaza "to see and be seen," in José Antonio Wilde's phrase. Bullfighting took place every Sunday during summer, from 1801 until banned in 1819, thus creating a significant and unusual cultural gulf between Argentina and the Spanish motherland, for in other ex-colonies like Mexico, Peru, and Colombia bullfighting continues today. The plaza was also the site of the defeat of the English troops under Whitelocke. President Sarmiento made it into a public plaza. At the foot of the rising hill of the plaza is the Monument to the Fallen in the *gesta* (heroic deed) of the 1982 Malvinas invasion, with every name of those killed there movingly carved into the black marble. Quite deliberately, this monument faces *la torre de los ingleses* (see p.153).

Around the Plaza San Martín are some of the grandest private houses ever built in Buenos Aires. The ex-Palacio Paz was designed in 1902 by the architect Louis Sortais for the owner of the once-great newspaper *La Prensa* (founded in 1869) and is now the Círculo Militar. It is, according to the *Guía Pirelli*, the largest private house built in Argentina, modeled, typically enough, on the Louvre facade. Across the plaza is the 120-room ex-Palacio Anchorena, occupying a whole block, built in 1905 and today the ceremonial centre of the Argentine Foreign Office (Cancillería del Ministerio de Relaciones Exteriores). The Anchorena family epitomized the "millionaire" image of the Argentine oligarchy and gave origin to a set phrase "has more money than an Anchorena" and a book by Sebreli. The wonderfully florid and exotic Pabellón Argentino, designed with iron girders by Albert Ballú and erected next to the Eiffel Tower in Paris in 1889, was dismantled and brought to Buenos Aires via Liverpool in 1890 and re-erected in the Plaza San Martín as a *confitería*. From 1910 to 1932 it became the Museo de Bellas Artes. It was then taken apart once more and stored away in a government warehouse in Palermo, to be rediscovered only in 1998.

At the top of the plaza lies the Plaza Hotel (recently bought by the Marriott chain), the most traditional and elegant hotel in Buenos Aires, built by the architect Alfredo Zucker in 1909, where the writer Robert Cunninghame Graham died in 1936. Victoria Ocampo put up her illustrious intellectual visitors like Tagore and Count Keyersling in the Plaza. The French traveler Jules Huret picked out this hotel in 1910: "From the docks one building attracts your eyes to the city and it is the recently built Plaza Hotel, seven floors high, its whiteness standing out against the blue of the sky." José Vasconcelos perversely complained in the 1920s about the "hundred unbearable irritations" of this modern hotel, including too many servants, telephones by the bed and too many lifts. It was in the grill room that great ballet dancers Nijinsky and Pavlova met by chance in 1917. In 1933 Federico García Lorca and Pablo Neruda gave a joint talk at a PEN Club reception in the Plaza Hotel extolling the poet Rubén Darío. Jacobo Timerman was editor of the fine, liberal newspaper *La opinión*, founded in 1971 and shut down in 1977 when he was illegally arrested, and tortured for being a Jew and knowing terrorists. In his account *Prisoner Without a Name, Cell Without a Number* (1982), he recalled weekly lunches with those in power in the Plaza Hotel: "In Buenos Aires there's a place that we habitués had converted into a private club—the basement bar and restaurant of the Plaza Hotel. The wood paneling, tables, chairs, china, décor, all had a pleasantly Art Nouveau look." It was from the roof of the Plaza that Radio Cultura began the first radio transmission in Argentina. The last notable building off the plaza is the stunning art-deco-ish Kavanagh tower, built in 1936 by the architects Sánchez, Lagos and de la Torre and long a landmark, thirty floors high (or more precisely 120.35 meters), commissioned by Corina Kavanagh.

In 1977 the dandy novelist Manuel Mujica Lainez found Buenos Aires more and more alien to his historical sensibility: "I do not recognize this city, apart from here around this Plaza San Martín, because still standing are the four palaces bought by the government and the Plaza Hotel." In Beatriz Guido's *El incendio y las vísperas*, the art-loving upper-class Pradere walks fatefully towards his Jockey Club and also appreciates this older, snobbier city: "he turns down Santa Fe until he reaches Florida. He doesn't take a short cut; he loves that curve where Santa Fe, impregnated by the Plaza San Martín, becomes pregnant. Like a balm, the scent of the magnolias, the lime tree, the jacarandas and palm trees; and the grand iron gates of the Círculo Militar allows him to see the vast patio, with small, graceful fountains, alabaster flower pots and green iron amphora. Only a shameless puti pees into the fountain on that serene autumn night."

Gordon Meyer described the peculiar mood of the Plaza San Martín as the heart of the city:

The Plaza San Martín, late afternoon. Under the green vaults of the tipas, always the last to lose their foliage, the people sit on the benches, idling, drowsing, gossiping, love-making. Only the children show movement. The wide plaza overhangs the river, and marks the end of something; as if from there one could begin something of importance: a long journey, a new way of life, a decision—something, anyway.

But to those in the secret there is nothing to be begun. We know it, watching the purple foliage of the palos borrachos falling noiselessly to the ground. These, not the clocks, mark the passing of time. There reigns a gentle tempo not encountered in northern Europe. No compulsion, no conscience. The people are waiting. Not for something: that is the European error. They are just waiting.

That the Plaza San Martín can be more than its trees and statues is evident in Marco Denevi's (1922-1998) spinster heroine's perceptions in the novella "Secret Ceremony" when she crosses the plaza: "To cross the plaza brought up two problems. The first: that couple. How can they feel like hugging and kissing each other in a plaza at eight in the morning? She passed by this sad spectacle, pretending not to see them... The second: the boys. In the whole universe of galaxies there's nothing worse than a horde of lads... you have to be a woman and cross that mine field to know the jeering and humiliation of her sex. You had better believe Miss Leonides." However, despite these varying perceptions of this historic plaza, the city's sense of its own history is not always great, as Delfín Leocadio Garasa realized when affirming that Rafael Obligado, poet of *Santos Vega*, a *gaucho*esque mock-epic, lived "somewhere" around this plaza: "The lack of concern that Buenos Aires has about its cultural patrimony ensures that we cannot point out in which house facing this plaza Rafael Obligado lived."

La Recoleta

The patrician cemetery is a necropolis of grand marble mausoleums—traveler Thomas Hutchinson called them "gorgeous monuments of marble" in 1865—in shady streets in a variety of fancy styles. It was known as the Cementerio General del Norte until 1949. Rivadavia decided on this cemetery's location, had the land blessed on November 17, 1822, and ejected the Franciscan *padres recoletos*, monks who left their name, meaning "secluded," for the cemetery. V. S. Naipaul called it "a mimic city"; Juan José Sebreli mocked it as "the last *surprise-party* of a dying class"; Florencio Escardó called it a "cyst" in the city; Ezequiel Martínez Estrada more simply, in a poem, called it "the miniature city." The Argentine novelist Martín Cullen more exactly evoked "a Palladian miniature of the city, with illusional vistas."

Buried here are the great patrician families; Albino Dieguez Videla likened walking down the alleyways to reviewing an Argentine Gotha, with tombs from families like the Alvear, the Estrada, the Balcarce, the Paz, the Alzaga... But there are also *parvenus* like Evita Perón. "I recall," wrote novelist Tomás Eloy Martínez in his faction about Evita's embalmed corpse, "the site: the bottom of a crypt in the Recoleta cemetery, under three, ten-centimeter steel beams, behind steel grilles, bullet-proof doors, marble lions." All this to prevent fans peeping at her embalmed body. Wilting flowers piled up when we last visited her family vault. According to Borges, the Recoleta adds dignity to death, especially "the little squares as fresh as patios," the marble, the shade, the quiet, the historical echoes. In a later poem of the same title, death becomes "honorable," the "demure *porteño* death" (though Borges decided to die in Geneva). He points out its double-rowed Doric-columned "portico" (designed in 1886 by Juan Buschiazzo, with the chapel off it), facing the Biela café and the *conventillos* (slum houses where families lived cooped up around a patio) to its north. He also evokes the high cemetery walls, where the dictator Rosas executed his victims and later in the 1970s the Triple A paramilitary assassins dumped their victims. In his *Mis memorias* [My reminiscences, 1904], Lucio Mansilla, Rosas' nephew, remembered how the Recoleta was associated with death-squad activity: "We followed along the corrales, or slaughter house, that lay behind the Recoleta, So many crows! The horses got scared and refused to budge. They did not want to go forward. It was useless egging them on, beating them... What is this? The driver answered without hesitation, 'some dead men with their throats slit.'" In his poem on the Recoleta, Borges also mentions an enigmatic María de los Dolores Maciel, a young girl from Uruguay who was the first person buried in the Recoleta in 1822 (the first grave digger was English). Later, Borges confided to the US poet and translator Willis Barnstone: "La Recoleta. What a terrible, morbid place! All that baroque marble pomposity is an awful aspect of our military past." Another American poet, Robert Lowell, strode (in a poem) its sunlit cypress walks in 1962, past "hundreds of one-room Roman temples," past commemorative busts, past marble goddesses, and found relief "by cupping a soft palm to each hard breast." On the north wall there is a naked, life-size, breast-feeding mother, covered in ivy—probably the owner of the marble breasts that Lowell fondled.

Lucio V. López (himself buried in the cemetery) described the burial of the terrible aunt in his novel *La gran aldea*. The cortege began in calle Florida and ended at the vault in the Recoleta. The protagonist mused: "I got lost in the cemetery's alleys. Such vain ostentation! How easy to take stock there, surrounded by such gaudy [*mamarrachos*] Creole marble works, of human stupidity and pride! There was the pompous tomb of an estancia owner... Leagues and leagues of land, thousands of cattle; leather and wool have built that mausoleum... " At that time, you could still see the river from the Recoleta.

Strangely, nobody is buried there in the literal sense of earth being dug up. All lie in coffins in underground vaults. In the Recoleta are historical figures like Juan Facundo Quiroga, "the tiger of the plains," the source of Domingo Sarmiento's 1845 biographical diatribe *Civilización o barbarie: la vida de Facundo Quiroga* [*Life in the Argentine Republic in the Days of the Tyrants*, 1868], one of the most influential texts in Latin American literature. Facundo's tomb at the entrance to the cemetery has a hooded La Dolorosa by Tantardini on top, in reality a likeness of Facundo's wife. Interestingly, Facundo was buried standing up. Near the vertical Facundo lies Sarmiento, his enemy, above whom a giant bronze condor on a tall pyramid, designed by Sarmiento himself and sculpted by Víctor de Pol, is about to take flight. Also there lies the populist twice-president Hipólito Yrigoyen who died in 1933, aged eighty-one. General Lavalle is there with a life-size bronze grenadier, sword on shoulder guarding his tomb, as well as the man he had executed, General Dorrego, thus proving, in Horacio Vázquez Rial's words, that "irreconcilables" sleep together in cemeteries. The famous boxer Luis Angel Firpo (1895-1960) also stands life-sized in his dressing-gown in bronze outside his vault (he almost knocked Dempsey out in 1923). Rosas, the dictator who died in exile in Southampton, was brought back to the Recoleta in 1989 by President Menem, and the iron grilles on his tomb were appropriately entwined with roses. Although he killed himself, poet Leopoldo Lugones has his mausoleum there (though I couldn't locate it). Another celebrated resident of the Recoleta is José Hernández, the author of *Martín Fierro* (1872), the populist poem about the mistreatment of the nomadic *gauchos* that became the national song (Borges called it a novel in verse) for many Argentines. Partially written in a now demolished hotel (the Hotel Argentino) on the Plaza de Mayo, the long poem celebrated the mystique of the *pampa* in a romantic construction of Argentine identity. The "fierro" of the title refers to "hierro," the "iron" of a knife, the long *facón* that gauchos (in effect today's *peones*) still wear, and "fiero" meaning wild, or lawless. Lucio V. López, author of *La gran aldea*, died of wounds from a duel at the age of forty-six and is buried in the Recoleta with a statue of Falquière's *La protesta* above his tomb. Also there is the tomb of Argentina's first lady of letters, Mariquita Sánchez (1786-1868), and that of a young girl, killed in a car accident, with a greening bronze dog by her side. Borges' poem "Elvira de Alvear" is reproduced on a bronze plaque on the Alvear family mausoleum.

In 1947 the poet G. S. Fraser walked through the Recoleta's Doric portico and down its cypress-lined avenue:

> *every possible style of architecture is represented; there are little pyramids, little banks, little war memorials; sometimes you can see a coffin through a side door; other vaults are arranged like sets of pigeon-holes, with the*

coffins slipped in, their ends visible... Paved and orderly side streets lead off this main avenue at right angles... fashionably dressed men and women walk slowly bearing wreaths for their dead.

President Mitre's family mausoleum (Cecilia Molinari)

This sort of funereal fashion parade was noted by Fray Mocho in 1894, when he wrote that both the Recoleta and Chacarita "were bursting with Sunday-best crowds who, with the pretext of remembering their dear and beloved, were really spying on how they were dressed, the grace of their bodies, the quality of the cloth, according to the tastes and sex of each person." This, of course, is a typical *porteño* trait, but today you'll mainly see tourists and cats.

The Chilean writer María Luisa Bombal, who lived in Buenos Aires from 1933 to 1941 (and who later in Chile tried to shoot her lover), successfully evoked the Recoleta in her story "New Islands" (1935):

> *The same serene twilight suffusing the pampa washes over Buenos Aires, inundating in steel blue the stones and the air and the mist-covered trees in Recoleta Square. Juan Manuel's mother walks confidently through a labyrinth of narrow streets. Never has she lost her way in this intricate city, for as a child her parents taught her how to find her bearings in any quarter. And here is their dwelling—the small cold crypt where parents, grandparents, and so many ancestors rest. So many in such a narrow chamber!... Then, before the altar, she makes the sign of the cross and checks that the candelabra are well polished, that the white altar cloth is well starched. She sighs and descends into the crypt, holding nervously on to the bronze railing. An oil lamp hangs from the low ceiling, its flame mirrored in the black marble floor and shining on the bronze rings of the various compartments arranged sequentially by date. Here all is order and solemn indifference.*

Next to the Recoleta is the Pilar church, dedicated to Nuestra Señora del Pilar who stands on the baroque altar piece. It is the second oldest church in Buenos Aires, begun in 1716 and completed in 1732 by Jesuit architects. In 1932 it was decided to restore the church's original eighteenth-century features by using watercolors painted by Carlos Pellegrini to get the facade right again. Inside, the church is white and simple, with small baroque, gilded side chapels. The ochre and white of this church strike any walker approaching from Avenida Quintana.

Abutting the church is the Centro Cultural Recoleta (also known as the Centro Cultural Ciudad de Buenos Aires, on calle Junín 1930), converted from the original monastery of the "reclusive fathers." Built in 1716, it became a school after the expulsion of the monks in 1822, then an asylum for beggars, and lastly from 1944 to 1978 an old people's home. In 1978 the architect Jacques Bedel and painter-architects Luis Benedit and Clorindo Testa altered the building to make a grand arts centre, with inner patios, cloister-like ways and a large terrace, part of which is the Astor Piazzolla amphitheatre, with a bust of the modernizing tango player and composer by Blas Gurruieri. Below, restaurants and shops look on to the *bajo*. Tall, rattling palm trees and an odd, pinkish chapel designed by Buschiazzo and turned into a theatre called the "Aleph" after Borges, gave me the sense of the whole being like a film set, temporary and lively. Within a few days I recently saw a show of Raquel Forner's large works, a fashion display by Clara Ibargurren, and a collective show by Argentine women artists. There is also a small bookshop, and a Café Literario.

Eduardo Mallea's novel dissecting a high-society fiesta during a hot November, *Fiesta en noviembre* [*Fiesta in November*, 1941], mentions "the old, nearby spire of the Pilar church that seemed somewhat anachronistic, with its rudimentary dome, its simple arches and naive colonial belfry." Outside the Recoleta's entry gates are some huge *gomero* trees (*Ficus macrophylla*), imported from Australia and planted in 1878. Sabato, a character in his own novel *Abaddón, el exterminador* [*The Angel of Darkness*, 1974], "sat down on the circular bench that surrounds the roots of the great gomero tree. The park was getting dark with the afternoon shadows. He shut his eyes and began to meditate on his whole life... " This *gomero* remains a good place to meditate. In her poem "La Recolata" Silvina Ocampo mentions the *gomeros*, rivers of cars, lovers, onanists, dogs – she lived nearby.

Opposite the Doric columns of the Recoleta's entrance stands the most fashionable café of the last thirty years, La Biela [the "connecting rod"], so named because racing car enthusiasts used to gather there in the 1940s and brushed by the overhanging branches of a huge *gomero* tree. The café is expensive, packed with aspiring starlets, models and would-be celebrities, waiting to be recognized. Guerrilla groups often bombed this café in the 1970s as the well-heeled congregated here. Adolfo Bioy Casares (1914-1999) lunched in its now closed restaurant regularly. Bioy Casares, Borges' collaborator, and his writer wife Silvina Ocampo (Victoria Ocampo's youngest sister) lived nearby on calle Posadas 1650 in a writerly union, for they each pursued their own amorous ideals. Borges would often dine there on the fifth floor and after an early 8 P.M. dinner, he and Bioy would sit at a typewriter and concoct their mock detective stories.

Silvina Bullrich deemed the Biela in 1958 to be one of the few places in Buenos Aires where "people knew they would meet each other." Sabato's character Sabato in *Abaddón, el exterminador* regularly sits in the Biela: "but one goes on living and returning to LA BIELA, especially now that one is famous... he would always walk around there crossing the park, drinking a coffee in LA BIELA." Miranda France mocked it (though she was often there): "The terrace of La Biela café was already full of wealthy divorcees, reflecting one another in their sunglasses." But it is easy to be ironic, and more fun to watch the diverse, attractive crowd sitting there, especially in the spring sun.

Borges and Bioy Casares, shortly before Borges' death (Alberto Casares)

There are many other outdoor restaurants and cafés nearby. Walking west alongside these expensive, touristic eateries like the Munich Recoleta or Clark's, you come across the new Plaza Manuel Mujica Lainez (on calles Junín and Vicente López on the site of a demolished market). The square, alas, is covered in graffiti, with a pyramid that is missing its tiles, a waterless fountain, and the plaque commemorating the writer's love for his city defaced (in August 1998, just after walking around this plaza I read an angry letter in *La Nación* complaining of this situation).

Nearby on calle Posadas 1500, the Peróns lived next to each other in separate, but communicating flats. On Avenida Quintana 520, there is a bust, and a plaque stating that the Spanish philosopher José Ortega y Gasset lived there. However, near this smart Recoleta *barrio* there were once slums, the *conventillos* that Alicia Dellepiane Rawson remarked on in a poem: "Opposite the Recoleta / I broadcast this to the most famous living and dead / that I cannot bear the absurd angels / standing on tiptoe above the tombs / to stare at the slums."

By the cemetery's high walls are several tall blocks containing *hoteles de alojamiento* or *albergues transitorios*, where lovers rent rooms by the hour and fornicate clandestinely overlooking the dead. These are not "brothels" as imagined by V. S. Naipaul, for such hotels are common all over the city as many young people still live with their families and cannot bring lovers home. Most *porteños* have tried these hotels out, so they are integrated into the ritual of adultery and couple exchange. Eloy Martínez's revolutionary lovers Nun and Diana in his *La novela de Perón* [*The Perón Novel*, 1985] meet in such a copulatory hotel:

> She was the one who overnight, after resisting weeks of siege, called him by phone and invited him to a hotel alojamiento for the simple thrill of testing that presumptuous body. The room that luck handed them reeked of sex, although it was impossible for anyone to have been rash enough to fall in love there. The bed was adorned with stucco angels threatening to fall down. Under the patched sheets you could see the humiliating plastic cover protecting the mattress. Through the windows disguised by decrepit velvet curtains you could spot the funerary monuments in the Recoleta.

The poet and novelist Fernando Sánchez Sorondo (1943-), one time director of the Fondo Nacional de las Artes, speech-writer for President Menem, author of a scandalous novel about his drug-taking (*Ampolla*, 1984) and now a follower of Sai Baba, wrote a poem about his mother, who died giving birth to him. It links the patrician cemetery with these love-nests: "My mother is buried in a coffin / in a neighborhood of albergues transitorios / and expensive, disgustingly luxurious restaurants, / in the vicinity of a childhood / with gomero trees like circus tents." His mother "flees the Recoleta / and encourages the illegal lovers / in the albergues."

The new Biblioteca Nacional Mariano Moreno, named in honor of the founder of the first Biblioteca Pública in 1810, was finally completed in 1992 near the Recoleta (though Jorge Luis Borges laid the foundation stone back in 1971) nearly thirty years after the architects Alicia Cazzaniga, Francisco Bullrich and Clorindo Testa (also a well known painter) won the competition to design it in 1962. The building, on calle Austria, is located on the site of a razed house—the Unzué family *quinta*—that Perón and Evita had lived in in the last years of their marriage. The house was demolished by the military as part of the proscription of Peronism, the cynical cleansing of the historical slate just as Rosas' mansion was also demolished in Palermo). A plaque on the new Biblioteca commemorates Evita: "Here lived and died she who in life was the flag leader of the humble—*compañera* Eva Perón." Evita died on this site at 8:25 P.M. on July 26, 1952. This portentous moment became the title of Mario Szichman's novel *A las 20:25, la señora entró en la inmortalidad* [At 20:25 the lady entered immortality, 1981], in which a Jewish woman, who had to be buried within twenty-four hours, couldn't be because of the national hullabaloo over Evita's death. The new building perches, top-heavy, on concrete walls, with a windy Rubén Darío esplanade (exploited at one time by skate-boarders). Below the building is a bust of the writer Manuel Mujica Lainez. Héctor Yánover (1929-), a poet and bookseller (his bookshop, El Norte, is on Las Heras) was the first director, resigning in 1996. The library publishes a monthly bulletin, with a program of events from folk music to poetry recitals (one by the socialist Paraguayan poet Elvio Romero when I was last there). The *Hemeroteca* is named after Hugo Wast (1883-1962, real name Gustavo Martínez Zuviría), a best-selling novelist, nationalist director of the National Library under Perón's government, and in 1943 the Minister of Justice. The library is a copyright library with over 1,300,000 volumes and exhibits its rarest acquisitions, from the Gutenberg Bible of 1455 to the first edition of the *Quijote* and Borges' writing desk. There is a lecture hall named after Borges, an exhibition room on the first floor named after Leopoldo Marechal, a *Mapoteca*, and the main reading room, the Sala Mariano Moreno on the fifth floor, with a marble bust of Moreno. The library, open all year, has relaunched the magazine *La Biblioteca*, edited first by Paul Groussac (1848-1929), then Borges, and publishes books (visit the website on http://www.bibnal.edu.ar).

Below the National Library is the Plaza Rubén Darío, celebrating the Nicaraguan poet's six-year stay in Buenos Aires. Opposite, across the busy Avenida Libertador, is José Fioravanti's (1896-1970) statue of Darío sitting pensively, an open folio book on lap, but lacking the clear indigenous features ascribed to him. Behind the concrete plinth you can read these lines from Darío: "Buenos Aires, beloved city," followed by lines from the national anthem about freedom. Behind the library, facing on to Avenida Las Heras there is a new garden, an open-air reading room, called the Plaza del Lector [Reader's Square], with white benches, a high railing, lock-up gates, and a white marble bust of writer José Mármol, whose name fittingly means marble.

East of the Recoleta cemetery, on Avenida Libertador, is the huge reddish mass of the Museo Nacional de Bellas Artes. The original building was a factory for water pumps (Casa de Bombas) for the municipal Obras Sanitarias that was redesigned by the architect Alejandro Bustillo in 1930 as a museum and opened in 1934. On the ground floor is a permanent collection of art works from El Greco and Goya to impressionists Manet, Monet, Degas, plus work by Klee, Picasso and Rodin, and single, impressive pictures from most mainstream modernists, including Pollock. On the first floor is the Argentine art collection (with notable works by Prilidiano Pueyrredón and Cándido López) and twentieth-century foreign art. There is also a library of over 30,000 volumes. It is a unique, surprising museum, with excellent special exhibitions (I "discovered" the British painter Alan

Davie there once, and under Jorge Glusberg's directorship, August 1998 saw a range of shows from Bourdelle's sculptures to the Venezuelan kinetic artist Soto). A character in a short story by Gloria Arcushin daydreams in a bar about this museum: "She thought of Balzac's head, modeled by Rodin, which had seduced her that afternoon in the Museo de Bellas Artes. She felt in the presence of a great, metallic lion, full of creative power... She wanted to see a recent acquisition by Van Gogh, a windmill with little flag, sky-blue and light, and fantasized about stealing it, but in the end, you always get caught."

Next to the museum is the Confitería de las Artes, where law-students gather. A short stroll away over a streamlined concrete bridge with traffic roaring below is the bulky, neo-classical, fourteen-Doric-columned Facultad de Derecho [Law Faculty]. Finished in 1949, it was described by Horacio Vázquez Rial as "a prototype of Fascist architecture, mastodon-like and threatening, from a film about Romans, designed to intimidate those who worked there." Behind this is the vast warehouse now called the Centro Cultural General San Martín, used for exhibitions like the annual Feria del Libro [Book Fair and literary festival] held in April (the 25th in 1999 dedicated to Jorge Luis Borges' centenary was opened by President Menem with a speech denouncing "photocopying terrorists"). There is also a statue by Antoine Bourdelle called "The Wounded Centaur," referring to Quirón, a key figure in Darío's long poem "Coloquio de los centauros," written in Buenos Aires.

Lastly, there are attractive green gardens and plazas along the *barrancas* between the Recoleta and the National Library, like the Plaza Francia with its baroque monument celebrating French influence. The filmmaker María Luisa Bemberg lived in a flat with a fine collection of modern Argentine painting, later donated to the Museo de Bellas Artes, overlooking the tall trees of this little plaza on calle Ricardo Levene. By the tangled gardens of the residence of the British Embassy, is Albert Lagos' (1885-1961) bronze, greening statue of witty Englishman George Canning, book in hand. The statue was moved here from the Torre de los Ingleses after the Malvinas war. Canning was briefly British Prime Minister in 1827, but as Foreign Minister in 1823 was crucial in recognizing South American independence from Spain. From here you can look up to the huge statue of Bartolomé Mitre, hat in hand and on horse, surrounded by white allegorical figures and the typical city dog-walkers at rest, and always the deafening grind of traffic from Libertador.

Avenida Alvear

A stroll down Avenida Alvear, named after General Carlos María de Alvear, grandfather of the Intendente who transformed Buenos Aires, begins in the small Plaza Carlos Pellegrini. Named after an ex-President and founder of the Jockey Club, who in 1914 was honored with a statue by Jules Coutan (1848-1938), the square contains further relics of the vast cattle wealth of the *pampas*. Ezequiel Martínez Estrada's poem "Buenos Aires," published in 1927, summed up this area as "sumptuous palaces and palaces / even more sumptuous. Outside, / don Carlos Pellegrini's statue / wrapped in a seat and flag." Here is the Parisian dream incarnate, expressed by Rubén Darío who prayed to God to let him visit Paris before he died. The authors of the *Guía de la arquitecura de Buenos Aires* [Architectural guide to Buenos Aires] claim that here is the "centre of a zone that sought to be the living mirror of a Country envied by *porteños*." A prime example of French influence is the palacio of the Pereda family, now the Brazilian Embassy, designed by Julio Dormal (1846-1924) but only finished in 1936, in a dated style modeled on a museum in Paris (the Jacquemart-André), and Fontainebleau with the proverbial Mansard roofs and domes. The Catalan painter José María Sert (1876-1945) painted stunningly gaudy ceilings. Also in the plaza is the new Jockey Club, once the private residence of the Unzué Casares family and designed by Juan Buschiazzo (born in Italy, 1846-1917), the architect appointed by mayor Torcuato de Alvear to dignify, perhaps modernize, Buenos Aires. The club moved there after its relocated building next to the French Embassy was demolished to make way for the widening of Avenida 9 de Julio. Jutting into the wide avenue is the protected French Embassy, once the palace of the Ortiz Basualdo family, designed in 1914 by another French architect, Paul Pater. This is where the Prince of Wales stayed in his famous visit to Buenos Aires in 1925. Another Plaza Carlos Pellegrini landmark is the ex-Palacio Atucha, designed in 1924 by French architect René Sergent (who never set foot in Argentina), now flats. All these ornate, academic buildings pompously rejected the modern style—art nouveau—of the day, reflecting Buenos Aires' dream of being a second Paris. It is ironic that it is thanks to foreign embassies that many of these private "palaces" are still preserved. Just off the Plaza Carlos Pellegrini, down the slope on calle Cerrito is the Residencia Alzaga, built by Roberto Prentice for Félix de Alzaga between 1916 and 1919 in the Loire château style and now part of the Hyatt hotel. Not that this archaic Gallic style was universally popular. Baldomero Fernández Moreno once picked his own best poem as the oft-anthologized "Seventy Balconies and Not One Flower," a protest against such architecture, about a building on the Paseo de Julio (now the Avenida Leandro Alem) whose "naked stone overwhelms me with sadness."

The novelist Julián Martel described his protagonist-speculator Luis Glow's palace on Avenida Alvear (created in 1885), with a vast hall in the Alhambra style, a mosaic floor and a marble staircase. He has a servant light up a room, with its Aubusson tapestry, its walls of red silk, its curtains and its ceiling "on which the brush of a true artist had traced some love affairs to which Madame Du Barry would have willingly opened the wings of her best drawing room." The palatial house also contains stained glass, bronze statues and huge mirrors; the only comparison is with a fable from the Arabian Nights. Once Avenida Alvear was lined with these private palaces, but now, despite Manuel Mujica Lainez's assertion that "little had changed since the 1930s," these vast buildings are mostly institutional. The papal embassy, the Nunciatura Apostólica, built by French-born Eduardo Le Monnier (1873-1931) for the Fernández Anchorena family is where President Marcelo T. de Alvear lived from 1922 to 1928. It has more recently accommodated Pope Pío XII during his 1934 visit to Buenos Aires, and later Pope John Paul II during his two visits to Argentina. Next door on the same impressive block stand the Palacio Duhau built in 1932 by French architect Léon Dourse (1890-1969), the contiguous Palacio Hume, built around 1890, under the huge *gomero*, surrounded by ornate railings and with huge gardens falling down the old river bank slope to calle Posadas. These two palaces are relics of the *belle époque*, of the conspicuous wealth hoarded by the oligarchy. Also on Alvear is the Casa de la Cultura of the Secretaría de Cultura de la Nación (the old

Olmos palace built around 1900 as a guesthouse). Opposite this building is the Casa de las Academias Nacionales (mainly scientific academies), originally designed in 1925 by Alejandro Bustillo (1889-1982) as flats to fit in with the character of the avenue. Bustillo fought to preserve this building in 1980, for so many of his buildings had been demolished to make tower blocks that he'd moaned: "They have shot a quantity of living beings that are my works." Bustillo is renowned for the monumental Casino in Mar del Plata and the recently re-opened Hotel Llao-Llao in Bariloche. The rest of the avenue consists of modern blocks of flats and a grand Hotel Alvear (built in 1928 and where Spanish Nobel laureate poet, Juan Ramón Jiménez, stayed in 1948), now mainly private rooms. Alvear finishes in the Recoleta.

Albert Londres, in his quest to make the sex-slave scandal known worldwide, walked down Avenida Alvear, one of the city's smartest streets. He noticed the statue of "General" Alvear by Bourdelle (at the end of the avenue, looking on to the Recoleta), but when he stopped to contemplate it ("a little mild art criticism"), he was made to walk on by a policeman (*vigilante*). He sat on a bench and looked up at the statue, and was again asked to move on. He wondered: "Perhaps no one had a right to look at the statue," so he left. Later he discovered that the president was about to pass by. The statue of General Carlos María de Alvear by Antoine Bourdelle (1861-1929) was erected in 1926. Twelve years in the making, it is set on red granite with four bronze allegories representing Alvear's reputed qualities: strength, eloquence, liberty and victory. Alvear rides above, one hand up in the air. Just by the statue of Alvear is what is called the Palais de Glace, on calle Posadas 1725, first built as a circular skating ring in French château style with Mansard roof and grand steps. It then turned into a tango dance hall when tango at last became respectable, until in 1931 architect Bustillo redesigned it as an art exhibition centre.

This grand avenue following the crest of the *barranca* has a double effect on me. It sends me back to what the authors of the *Guía de la arquitectura de Buenos Aires* call "an atemporal classicism," in which the self-consciously anachronistic buildings give a sense of being outside time and history (as opposed to modernity's stressing of novelty and mutation). The avenue also depresses me with its ostentatious mausoleums.

Avenida Las Heras

The exiled Andalusian poet Rafael Alberti once lived at the north end of this long avenue, recalling especially its trees: "I sing a perspective of shady trees, / the frizzy araucarias brandished as wild beasts / serpents / and the tipas [the yellow-flowering *tipuana tipu*] of my street Las Heras." The rise of this avenue to become one of the *barrio norte*'s most prosperous was noted in Horacio Vázquez Rial's novel *Frontera sur* [Frontier south, 1994], where the author comments on the removal of the city's national penitentiary: "The old Penitenciaría of calle Las Heras fulfilled its function for decades, before a government respecting the interests of the governing classes considered that an institution of that kind could not continue to illustrate a barrio which had become one of the richest in Buenos Aires, and so it was demolished to make a park." Before the penitentiary was knocked down in 1962, "its bulk reminded you of a castle in which evil dwelt." It was built in 1877 by Ernesto Bunge (1838-1903). In 1931, during a brief period under military rule when the death penalty was reinstated, the anarchist Severino di Giovanni was executed there. Earlier, the area around the junction Las Heras and Pueyrredón was known as "la tierra del fuego" [the land of fire]. Jorge Luis Borges saw it as an early version of a shanty town: "Rubble of the beginning, street corners of aggression and solitude, furtive men calling each by whistles and who suddenly disappeared in the lateral night of the alleys. The barrio was the final street corner."

My own favorite café was El Blasón on the corner of Pueyrredón and Las Heras when in 1975 I exchanged my London house for Oscar Masotta's flat on Pueyrredón for a year. Masotta epitomized *porteño* flair; he initiated happenings at the Instituto di Tella, wrote on cartoons and the writer Roberto Arlt, was an intellectual improviser, a dandy, and introduced Lacan to Buenos Aires. He confessed that he chose to live in London because he loved the restaurant The London Grill (Reconquista 435). On calle Paraguay 2650 is the Escuela Freudiana de Buenos Aires, founded by Masotta. The bar Masotta used to sit in, and which he recommended to me, was El Blasón, and I still see the waiter in his white jacket with frayed cuffs, welcoming me with my *café con leche* and *media lunas* as I watched the traffic hurtle past, and scanned the papers for news. I had no idea that Borges had once lived on this corner, on the fifth floor of Pueyrredón 2190. The café was an oasis of idleness in a sea of assassinations and kidnaps culminating in the coup of 1975. Sadly, it is now a bank.

In her novel *Calles de Buenos Aires* Silvina Bullrich has her street-wandering character Gloria explore what she felt was unique to Las Heras: "Without meaning to she entered calle Las Heras. It was a strange street, with an air of avenue and isolated alley. Perhaps, despite its width, its two way traffic and its houses, that street remained sad because it was interrupted by a prison and had to bear the fatal proximity of a cemetery [i.e. the Recoleta] but no other street could boast of such diversity. Nothing was missing, not shops, not a church, not a plaza, not a jail, not a university." The site of the demolished prison is now the Parque Las Heras. The university alluded to is the mock Gothic Faculty of Engineering, with a huge hall, stained-glass windows and a poor Museo de Ciencia y Técnica – Borges called it "the ogival faculty". Also on Las Heras and Pueyrredón is the excellent bookshop El Norte, owned by the poet and one-time director of the National Library, Héctor Yánover. Las Heras meets Plaza Italia by the Botanical Gardens.

Calle Suipacha

This street is named after the first defeat of the Spanish in 1810 at Suipacha, in today's Bolivia. It ends in the *barrio norte*, but begins near the Avenida de Mayo where, backing on to Plaza Robero Arlt, is the San Miguel church founded in 1727 and used as a hospital, with the first cemetery for the poor nearby. Inside are gloomy ceiling paintings. Ramola Nijinsky recalls marrying the great Russian ballet dancer Nijinsky (1890-1959) in that church in 1913: "At the entrance of the Iglesia St. Miguel, M. and Mme. Baton, Nijinsky, and the others of the wedding party were waiting for us. I was taken up the aisle to the strains of the wedding march from *Lohengrin*... The ceremony was long. The clergy, greatly ornate, officiated. I was rather nervous. Would I know when to say 'Yes'? I was strangely fascinated by the heavily gilded wings of the baroque angels. The altar was the most atrocious sculpture one could imagine, and I could not take my eyes off it." Just opposite this church on calle Suipacha 78, surrounded by shops and still close to the

Avenida de Mayo, stood the old house in Marco Denevi's novella "Secret Ceremony." This story won the *Life* magazine prize in 1960 and was filmed by Joseph Losey with Liz Taylor playing the old spinster who is taken for the mother of the damaged young girl Cecilia who lives orphaned in the house (played by Mia Farrow). A Poe-ish tale of enchantment and curse, it ends with a revenge murder. Both the old maid and the young girl live a strange idyll inside the house, which Denevi describes in anthropomorphic terms:

> It has two barred windows on the ground floor, a doorway with two doors, and two funerary bronze knockers; on the top floor a large, project- ing balcony, and nothing else, apart from an enormous crack crossing it like an ill-fated scar... On its left a shop, on its right another shop, oppo- site the wall of San Angel Arcángel, the large house does all it can not to be noticed, as if ashamed of its ugly face and its old age... So the house is there as if it shouldn't be; absent, like a fissure between two buildings beginning to surface, rubble from the colonial city, the one buried under skyscrapers and tower blocks. It would be enough for the shop on the left and the one on the right to squeeze it out like tweezers a pimple.

A little further up this street, you come across one of the city's jewels of a café, the Ideal on Suipacha 384, echoing the art-nouveau style that once epitomized prosperous Buenos Aires, with Doric columns, chandeliers, large mirrors in the manner of London's Café Royal, and an organist playing tangos and waltzes, while over-made up women and stiff, paunched men drink thick hot chocolate. It is far from fashionable, somehow striving to be true to its fading values. Upstairs there used to be an orchestra, and *thés-dansants* and today there are tango classes, as tango dancing is back in fashion. Miranda France described its "gossiping women with hair dyed gold... murmuring their scandals like a litany." Ramón Gómez de la Serna praised this *confitería* with a quip: "In El Ideal there's a floating stage orchestra of young ladies dressed in dance clothes, with a great admiring public staring at them, as blessed souls in purgatory might stare up at heaven."

Strolling further up Suipacha you will find Alberto Casares' bookshop on 521. Casares specializes in Argentiniana, especially travel, literature and history, with wonderful rare books. He also published a limited facsimile edition of Borges' poems, *Fervor de Buenos Aires*, in which he rediscovers his city after years in Europe. Continuing northwards, the walker sees a new Plazoleta Suipacha on Suipacha and Viamonte with a statue of Manuel Dorrego, "paladin and martyr," sculpted on horseback by Rogelio Yrurtia, with railings, lampposts and young trees. Just before Suipacha hits Santa Fe, on 1051 was the bookshop El Dragón, owned by doctor and surrealist poet Aldo Pellegrini, the centre of all surrealist information and activity in Buenos Aires. For decades this was a meeting-place presided over by the generous Pellegrini himself, and where in 1970, over espresso coffees I met poets Alberto Girri, Mario Satz, José Viñals and painters like Rómulo Macció, and many others who dropped into this welcoming shop.

On Juncal and Suipacha stands the Socorro church. It was in the chapel on which the later, current church stands that Camila O'Gorman (born 1828) met and fell in love with a young priest from Tucumán called Ladislao Gutiérrez in 1847. The surrealist poet Enrique Molina's bitter, erotic novel *Una sombra donde sueña Camila O'Gorman* [A shadow from where Camila O'Gorman dreams, 1973] sets this dramatic love affair within the violent context of mid-nineteenth-century Argentine history, with its compulsive throat slitting (*degüellos*), severed heads on pikes, packs of wild dogs and depressing civil wars. For Molina, Camila is "the most exalted and resplendent heroine of this country," but no public statues honor her. At age nineteen, Camila ran off with her twenty-three-year-old lover-priest under false names; they set up a school in Goya on the River Paraná, lived as man and wife for five months, were betrayed, brought back by the dictator Rosas' officers and executed on August 17, 1848 in the Crujías de Santos Lugares, a military garrison (today a suburb of the city). Camila was pregnant. The priest was accused of "having stolen a woman" and Rosas personally gave the order to shoot them to put an end to the "shocking scandal." In 1849 Domingo Sarmiento, later president of Argentina, wrote: "A young lady, a priest and an unborn child shot are not easily erased from one's memory." Rosas' nephew Lucio Mansilla recognized this incident as the "stigma" of Rosas' dictatorship. Sir Horace Rumbold, British chargé d'affaires, concurred. In 1887 he called Camila's execution "the blackest of all crimes, greatly hastening Rosas' downfall."

Camila was in the choir of the old Socorro church situated in what Molina described as "a barrio in formation. Nearby abound quintas with cactus hedges; some foreigners, mainly English, were already living there. The well-born lived on the other side of the Plaza Mayor, the south side." The church was then, as now, painted "a kind of pink, color of a woman's flesh." Molina described the main altar-piece in sensual, baroque, Bosch-esque (and invented) detail, an allegory of the contradictions of Catholicism:

> Opposite, surging out of the darkness, a cliff of lights, an incandescent block inside which you could see treasures bathed in wine, dead covered in mercury, like in mirrors, like encrustations of pearls, lined in red silk, cornucopias of blood, embalmed hippopotamus heads, mouths open, molars substituted by lit candles, serpents with diamond eyes, coiling in and out of the orifices and around the pillars and candelabra, white faces, from whose lips dripped honey-colored saliva, coffins with one arm inside, a fragment of a leg, views of the jungle, scorpions and cherubims fighting, glass balloons, moonscapes, claws, the Gulf stream flowing lazily with sharks, skulls...

Argentina's great film-director María Luisa Bemberg made her film *Camila* (1985) around this same tragic, Romeo and Juliet-ish love-story, but without reference to Molina's earlier novel, and highlighting feminist issues of free choice, a woman's education, and patriarchal control.

The parish of the Socorro was created in 1873 where a small chapel had been built in 1781 on the current church site. It was rebuilt in 1855 with three naves and squat, out-of-proportion columns; the sacristy collapsed in 1875. Today's church was completed in 1896. There are rumors of a tunnel from this church to the Recoleta cemetery. Just down from the Socorro on Suipacha 1333 is the new British Arts Centre, a glass box outside the Asociación Argentina de Cultura Inglesa, with a theatre, video room and art shows (Juan Astica showed there last August when I passed by). At the intersection of Suipacha and Arroyo you can see the gaping hole left by the bombing of the Israeli Embassy in 1992, an atrocity that left thirty dead and provided evidence of continuing anti-Zionism in the city. The offices of the Asociación Mutual Israelita Argentina (AMIA) were also bombed in July 1994—again by unknown and certainly uncaught anti-Semitic terrorists, with the cost of eighty-nine lives. The building has recently been reopened on the same site, Pasteur 633 in the Once *barrio*.

Where Suipacha slopes down to the *bajo*, where once the river ran, lived a typical *barrio norte* poet and leader of the Florida group based around the magazine *Martín Fierro*, the rebel Oliverio Girondo (1891-1967), who was married to the experimental writer, of Norwegian extraction Norah Lange (1906-1972). They lived on Suipacha 1444 from 1933 to his death in 1967. They were generous hosts, running a fortnightly *tertulia*. In the hall stood the Académico, the huge scarecrow that Girondo pulled about in a funeral cart to sell copies of his poem *Espantapájaros* [Scarecrow, 1932]. He sold 5,000 copies. The figure now lies in the Museo de la Ciudad. In 1970 the house was donated to the Museo Fernández Blanco next door on calle Suipacha after the sale of Girondo's books and paintings by his widow. It is now in ruins, but about to be refurbished. Alicia Jurado recalled this "grand house on calle Suipacha" as "a strange house, where valuable objects were mixed with junk, like the gigantic scarecrow... The decoration of the dining room consisted of stained glass from France, fitted into the walls, inside each one a scene from daily life acted out by embalmed frogs." She also recorded Norah Lange's study with its collection of musical boxes and shelves crowded with "trivial objects that she hoarded like a magpie," while Girondo kept his collection of pornographic Peruvian *huacos* [clay figures] under lock and key. At the regular *tertulias* in this house Jurado met Olga Orozco, another of the city's surrealist poets. Next door, the Museo de Arte Hispanoamericano Isaac Fernández Blanco on Suipacha 1422 has a beautifully lighted and presented collection of Latin American religious art, sculpture and silver. In the chapel, an exhibition outlined the history of chocolate, tea and *mate*. There is a cool Spanish garden with tall *tipa* trees, an outdoor theatre and a bar. Architect Martín Noel (1888-1963) built his own Palacio Noel in the 1920s and donated it to the nation in 1936. Its style is eclectic and neo-colonial, with Andalusian and Peruvian Arequipan features. When I was last there I had the museum and shaded garden all to myself.

Calle Lavalle

Cinema-going is a *porteño* passion (in Borges' time cinemas were called *biógrafos*); Buenos Aires is a city of "cinephiles," though video and multiscreen cinemas are changing habits. The writer Ernesto Schoo recently lamented the possible demise of the Shangri-La style cinema, the Gran Teatro Opera on calle Corrientes, "unique in Latin America," built in 1936 with a grand starry ceiling. But like everywhere, cinemas are shutting their doors. Of the 129 cinemas in Buenos Aires in the 1950s there were only 33 left in 1996. One of the streets associated with cinemas today is the traffic-free Lavalle. It is there that the spinster and the orphan go to see films in Denevi's "Secret Ceremony," a title which does not allude to the thrill of cinema-going: "they entered the cinemas of calle Lavalle, they followed those images always rushing too fast, they left drunk, chatted all day about what they had seen": a succinct description of the cinema ritual. Baldomero Fernández Moreno reworded this same pleasure: "Oh sweet drowsiness / of the cinemas / To shut one's eyes a bit / in the stalls and doze."

Although Perón forbade foreign films, and military dictators like General Onganía imposed censorship, since the restoration of democracy in 1983 and without censorship, the city has offered a range of films unequalled in, say, London. The first film, or magic lantern, was shown in the Methodist church on calle Corrientes in 1896. A great cinema is the Gran Rex on calle Corrientes, designed by Alberto Prebisch in 1937 as "one of the most important buildings of the decade," according to Ernesto Katzenstein. A large Travertine marble facade with a three-floor high hall and a huge plate glass window make this sober building a prime example of 1930s rationalism. Julio Cortázar's short story "The Band" tells the story of an intellectual's sudden flight from Peronist Buenos Aires in 1947. Lucio Medina leaves work at streets Sarmiento and Florida and walks to the Gran Cine Opera, with its "star-studded ceiling," despite the sultry February heat, to see an Anatole Litvak film. Instead, he watches a Peronist female band from the Alpargatas [Espadrilles] factory play badly (a famous Peronist anti-intellectual slogan was "Alpargatas yes, books, no"). Lucio buys a program (part of the Argentine cinema ritual is a cheap program and tip to the usher/ette) and begins to realize that the public dresses differently "with what passes as elegant in Villa Crespo or Parque Lezama" (i.e. Peronist suburbs). The shock of this unexpected change in program sends Lucio flying abroad into exile, like Cortázar himself.

The Argentine film industry is also in decline. In 1940 Argentina produced fifty films (compared to Mexico's twenty-nine and Spain's twenty-four), but an innate snobbery despises local films (I know people who refuse to see Argentine films on principle). The few acceptable ones return from abroad as successes, like Luis Puenzo's Oscar-winning *La historia oficial* [*The Official Story*], or Bemberg's Oscar-nominated *Camila.*

Avenida Córdoba

Avenida Córdoba, a busy one-way street, starts in the *bajo.* Walking up the slope (once the river bank) you pass on Córdoba 405 the Lancaster Hotel, where Graham Greene stayed and which he mentioned in his novel *The Honorary Consul.* Strolling on, you will come across the Café St. James on Córdoba and Maipú, where Borges began giving his classes on Anglo-Saxon literature to a dedicated group of students, learning the language as he taught it to his devotees (one of his students became his second wife and current literary executor, María Kodama). Where Callao crosses Córdoba, on Callao 982, you can find the unique bookshop/restaurant, Clásica y Moderna, the first in Buenos Aires to combine food and books, founded some sixty years ago by the Poblets and still run by the family. This is where the late Ana Calabrese launched her book of poems with a jazz band and where, in 1998, the disturbing fashion of holding up entire restaurants continued to hit the headlines (in one restaurant the thieves ate their meal and instead of asking for the bill drew their pistols and took off with a sackful of wallets, with the result that nobody else could pay their bills). The newspaper *La Nación* (September 23, 1998) claimed that Clásica y Moderna was the city's "favorite restaurant for writers, poets and politicians." A plaque was installed recognizing the place as of "cultural interest," and writer Juan José Sebreli, guest of honor at the ceremony, declared himself pleased that Buenos Aires had begun to become conscious of its "cultural landmarks."

A little further up is what Florencio Escardó picked as Buenos Aires' most beautiful building, the Obras Sanitarias palace, a whole block on Córdoba, Río Bamba and Viamonte designed in 1877 by the Swedish engineer A. B. Nyströmer, but not finished until 1894. Inside it has huge tanks containing the city's drinking water. This water-pumping station apparently pumps 72,700 liters of water per day. Its fantastically deceptive outside is entirely made with porcelain wall tiles in pinks, greens, caramels, "a harmonious jubilation," all Royal Doulton imported from Britain. It has a metal Mansard roof, escutcheons representing the capital and the fourteen provinces, thick, baroque "railings" painted green, and outside well-kept palm trees, shrubs and grass. Apart from two caryatids, there is a bust (created by another Nordic, a Norwegian sculptor called Olaf Boys), to Ingeniero Villanueva, first director of Obras Sanitarias, and the building is officially named after him. Ramón Gómez de la Serna compared it to an "opera house that reveals the ancestry of the water works," while the Spanish popular novelist Vicente Blasco Ibañez wrote: "This palace is not a palace. It has arches, great doors and windows, but all is fake." Nothing on the outside predicts what is inside. When it rains it shines like a "gigantic toy." Horacio Vázquez Rial claimed it was copied from a palace in Brussels and that Borges nicknamed it the Palace of Running Water. According to Tomás Eloy Martínez, Evita's embalmed corpse was due to be hidden there for a while before travelling to Italy in 1954. A witness told the novelist, a character in his own novel, about this plan: "He said to me that when he passed the palace of the Obras Sanitarias, he remembered that in the south-eastern corner there were two sealed and empty rooms, originally built for the guards. It's a monstrosity in ceramics, with nothing but galleries of water." But it is not alone among such utilitarian structures in pretending to be something else, for a water-pumping station, the Sans Souci in Potsdam, Germany, was built in 1841–2 to look like a Turkish mosque. There is a little museum inside, open in the mornings. Opposite this extraordinary building is a historical monument, the grand Escuela Normal Saénz Peña, also taking up a whole block.

Further along Córdoba was the Hospital de Clínicas, where the aspiring doctor-poet Baldomero Fernández Moreno touched his first corpse: "we squeezed through the wide door, bumped into the statue of Pirovano, who seemed to invite us in, crossed the gardens and entered the small anatomy theatre where a clean, polished, marmoreal corpse lay on a table." Fernández Moreno wrote about being a doctor-poet in his memoirs *Yo, médico, yo catedrático* (Me, the doctor, me the professor] and often wrote poems on his prescription pad. Many famous doctors passed through this now demolished hospital and medical faculty rebuilt in 1895 on Córdoba, including Juan B. Justo, founder of the Socialist

Baldomero Fernández Moreno, doctor-poet (Editorial Universitaria de Buenos Aires)

Party, and the philosopher José Ingenieros. A new plaza was laid in its place in 1976, named the Plaza Dr. Bernardo Houssay (one of four Argentines to win Nobel prizes), with an arts and craft fair and a small chapel built in 1879. In this plaza is a monument to Ignacio Pirovano (1844-1895), the doctor mentioned by Baldomero Fernández and South America's first surgeon. In the current medical faculty on calle Juncal and Córdoba, the Museo Domínguez is a pharmacological museum with a section on poisons, where I worked on the Aimé Bonpland archives. Opposite the plaza is the grand wedding-cake of the Facultad de Ciencias Económicas, and a little further down Córdoba, before calle Larrea, the Hispanic-styled Conservatorio Nacional de Música Carlos López Buchardo. So many university faculties make this street and plaza teeming and lively. On Córdoba 1536 is the Instituto Histórico de la Ciudad, next door to the Biblioteca Manuel Gálvez.

Plaza Lavalle

Avenida Córdoba passes alongside Plaza Lavalle, originally a Botanical Garden founded by Rivadavia in 1827, and then in 1857 the place where 30,000 people watched the first train on metal rails leave El Parque station (demolished to build the Colón opera house). It now has eminent buildings surrounding it, including the Colón, the Teatro Cervantes, several cafés like the Petit Colón and nearby the Edelweiss restaurant, frequented by actors, on Libertad between Corrientes and Lavalle. The strange *poètesse maudite* Alejandra Pizarnik was a regular and celebrated her Primer Premio Municipal de Poesía there in 1966. But what gives the plaza its meaning—and *subte* stop—is "Tribunales," the local name for the Palacio de Justicia, an eclectic monument by French architect Norbert Maillart, built between 1904 and 1942 with "Egyptian reminiscences," according to Archibaldo Lanús, in its facade's pillars. There is a fine Patio Central and on the seventh floor a library of more than 70,000 volumes specializing in law. On the fourth floor is an imposing Hall of Honor in Carrara marble. Essayist Juan José Sebreli reminded his readers (in 1957, and based on his own experience of imprisonment there) that the prime function of this building was to condemn people to prison: "At half past five in the afternoon, the most relaxed time of the day in Buenos Aires, tea-time, men and women leave their work and seek fun, completely ignorant that in a place nearby, in a basement on the Plaza Lavalle, for the strange inhabitants of the 'lion's den' it was the hour of anguish. Smiling bourgeois strolled under the trees of Plaza Lavalle, deaf to the existence of that subterranean humanity." Opposite the Tribunales is a monument to lawyers who disappeared during the *guerra sucia*. On Avenida Córdoba stands a statue of President Hipólito Yrigoyen by Pedro Ferrari. Nearby on the plaza with Lavalle's statue are permanent stalls selling second-hand books. Just off Plaza Lavalle is SADAIC (Sociedad Argentina de Autores y Compositores), opened in 1940, containing on the first floor a Museo Vicente López y Planes on the history of music in Argentina, with a statue of Gardel at the entrance.

Teatro Colón

On the plaza stands the famous Opera House. On first arriving in 1939, Witold Gombrowicz described a concert held in this grandiose establishment, expecting a Proustian world of the rich and aristocratic who dress up in their boxes not to listen to music, but to show themselves off. Instead, he found people unable to appreciate music, unsure of their opinions, clapping madly because others clapped and because the pianist playing Brahms was from Europe. The Colón (named after Christopher Columbus, Colón in Spanish) was first designed by the French-born portrait painter Carlos Pellegrini (1800-1875) in 1857 with many parts shipped over from England, was then abandoned and finally demolished in 1888 (its original site on the Plaza de Mayo is now the Banco de la Nación). Traveler Richard Burton disapprovingly described this first version in 1868 as a "huge pile whose red-painted roof gives a fine view of the city... its shape is claret chest, its order is of the railway station style of art... The inside is dingy and badly lighted." Ana María Cabrera in her novelized biography of Felicitas Guerrero contradicts Burton's scornful account, recalling the first night of *La Traviata* on April 25, 1857, with a huge gas-lit chandelier, containing no fewer than 450 gas lights, called the Lucerna. Lucio V. López also evoked a gala evening there with *Semiramis* produced, the boxes packed with attractive women, and the *cazuela* (meaning "stew" or pit) the source of all the city's gossip: "in the stew nobody's reputation was safe: haven for spinsters and young maidens, here all reputations passed through the sieve." Thomas Hutchinson in his *Buenos Ayres and Argentine Gleanings* (1865) arrived by boat and immediately noted the opera house's "glaring red roof."

The Colón was finally rebuilt and opened in its present site occupying a whole block in 1908 with Verdi's *Aida,* but has decayed from its original splendor, despite the plush velvet seats, the chandelier in the main hall and the dome, with its mural by Argentine painter Raúl Soldi. Alicia Jurado (1925-) recreates her first visit to the Colón as a child: "the Colón seemed to me to come from a fairy story and I remember the allegorical figures on the dome that later wore away, covered with white paint for years until substituted by Soldi's paintings." Its horseshoe shape fits 2,487 people sitting (with standing room for another 1,000). Musically, the huge opera house has welcomed Maria Callas, Caruso, Toscanini etc, and continues to be a place to be seen. It was bombed by anarchists in 1910 as a symbol of what they most loathed about elite *porteño* society. Georges Clemenceau was there during this bombing, but still saw the Colón as the most beautiful opera house in the world: "the seats peopled by young women in gala dress, the most brilliant spectacle I have ever seen inside a theatre." Roberto Arlt evoked the Colón in his novel *El amor brujo* as having an "ash color," with a "facade of fine lines." His protagonist awaits his teenage beloved at the Conservatorio Nacional, next door to the Colón, with its "Greek masks crowning the balustrade every twenty or so meters," on its "friezes, groups of young lovers" who "sketch out a garrulous Latin feast."

The French traveler Paul Morand found in 1930 that the Colón was really a theatre of social meetings, a "marriage fair" where high society would meet in its "stalls" and discuss marriages between the right families or membership of the Jockey Club. Victoria Ocampo, already badly married, fell in love with Julián Martínez when she saw him in a "stall" at the Colón. In 1967 Gordon Meyer wrote that "my life was constructed round the opera. The Colón in Buenos Aires, modeled on the Scala, is more splendid; it is bigger, the seats are plusher, the boxes larger, more comfortable, the service perfection; and it is crowded with beautifully dressed pretty women. Nobody dresses badly; it would be unthinkable." In an uncollected story called "The Lesson," Meyer returned to the ritual of the Colón:

> A box at the opera has about it a glamour that belongs more properly to an age upon whose internment the last shovelfuls are now being thrown. Even the moment of entrance quickens the senses, especially if one has been for some time unable to afford such an expensive seat. Coming forward from the dark-curtained recess at the rear, I was momentarily stunned. The horseshoe-shaped interior blazed with light from a hundred bronze clusters, and the great "rosette" at the zenith of the painted dome illuminated the panels on the ceiling, each with the gilded name of a composer. From the oval-backed, red-plush seats, glittering with their polished brass cabezales, arose an odour of wood polish, vaguely excitant. The red carpets, and curtains, the multi-coloration of the audience provided by the women's dresses gave an overpowering impression of movement, light and colour—a kind of polychromatic liquid mosaic.

But Philip Guedalla dissented from Meyer's admiring version of the Opera House, in these scathing terms: "There is the Opera, of course, where visitors may be regaled on solid European fare exported in large packing cases from Milan, Vienna, and Covent Garden, But there is nothing Argentine at the Colón except the chatter in the *foyer*; and one had not come six thousand miles in order to enjoy an entertainment that could be taken just as well in Bow Street."

An interesting detail concerning the Colón informs us how *porteños* dealt with Catholic rituals such as mourning; it had eight boxes with metal grilles and a separate exit for those in mourning who shouldn't be seen in public or recognized, but who nonetheless had to go to the opera.

At the side of the Opera House is a Museo de Historia del Teatro, a Museo de Instrumentos Antiguos and a Public Library, specializing in opera. As stated, the main entrance is on Plaza Lavalle; however, since the widening of the Avenida 9 de Julio, the back of the Colón now appears to be its front and is what most people see as they hurtle along the 9 de Julio. This relatively new perspective was noted by some characters on their way to the Opera in Julio Cortázar's posthumous novel *El examen* [The examination, 1986]: "Señor Funes, on seeing that the taxi was taking them along the 9 de Julio on what used to be calle

Cerrito, was shocked to see the back facade of the Colón, which the authorities had covered with a marquee. 'But there used to be a café,' he said. 'Used to be,' Clara agreed. 'A café where musicians used to meet. Extraordinary. How everything has changed in so little time.'"

Nearby on the Plaza Lavalle is a famous café called El Petit Colón, which apparently has nothing to do with the Colón Opera House, as Gloria Arcuschin noted in a short story, describing this area as if for a foreigner: "The front of the Teatro Colón gives on to calle Libertad, it's called 'the first Coliseo,' which indicates that it's the place where the most talented ballet dancers and world-best singers in international opera meet. El Petit Colón is not a small branch of the latter, but a bar on the corner of Lavalle y Libertad, facing the large plaza, with its historical tree, a gigantic gomero, its fountain and monument to ballet-dancers. Opposite is the building with a roof of silvery tiles called Tribunales."

The Colón also houses a ballet school, and puts on ballets. Nijinsky danced there in 1913, and, behind Diaghalev's back, married Romola de Pulszky at the San Miguel Arcángel church on calle Suipacha. Nijinsky returned in 1917 to dance and met Ana Pavlova staying in the same hotel (the Plaza).

Opera in Buenos Aires has not always been a politics-free event. Argentine composer Alberto Ginastera's opera, based on Manuel Mujica Lainez's historical novel *Bomarzo* (1962), was to open in the Colón, but was banned by General Onganía in 1967 for being "immoral" and going against "Christian Argentine values." It finally opened in 1972. Another example of political interference appears in Manuel Puig's novel *Pubis angelical* (1979), where the dying, exiled, middle-class Argentine heroine, Ana, recalls a lover who worked in the Colón in 1973, when President Cámpora's Peronist government released all political prisoners and Argentina drifted toward a secret civil war:

> *During a showing of Rigoletto, in the interval, some thirty or forty thugs entered by a corridor and began to sing bits of the national anthem, shouting. The public, like every time the anthem is sung in public, stood up, in a mixture of respect and fear that made me sick. Respect for the anthem and fear for the thugs. How had they got in? Somebody in the management was in the conspiracy. After singing they began to shout together*

that the Teatro Colón was for Argentine artists only, and out with foreigners. It was a group of nationalists, who hate all foreigners and wanted to force us to employ Argentine singers only.

Teatro Coliseo and Teatro Nacional Cervantes

For many years the Coliseo rivaled the Colón, and Buenos Aires was for a time a city with two grand opera houses. It was built on Charcas 1125 for spectacles, even a circus, designed by the architect Nordman, with room for 2,500 spectators. In 1907 it opened with *Tosca*; in 1909 it gave the world's first performance of Massa's *Zoraide*. By the 1930s, it was in decline, its art nouveau facade demolished. After many years of use as offices it was refurbished and opened in 1962.

On the corner of Córdoba and the Plaza Lavalle stands the Plateresque Teatro Nacional Cervantes. In 1928 Raúl González Tuñón dedicated a sentimental and humorous poem to "the little virgin on the Teatro Cervantes." He defined himself as being "a blend of saint and bandit" and having the "soul of an evangelist, blood of an adventurer." He goes on to describe the virgin's "minuscule greatness" and "humble little light," to claim: "In your cross-road converge all the perspectives / and you are the immense light of Buenos Aires in a little lamp." The statue on the theatre's facade thus becomes a symbol of his own working-class city. The facade itself mimics that of the Universidad de Alcalá de Henares in Spain. Designed by Fernando de Mendoza and his wife María Guerrero, both Spanish actors, the theatre opened in 1921 with the prolific Lope de Vega's play *La dama boba* [The silly lady]. Most of the building materials came from Spain, including tiles from Seville, and iron railings (*rejas*) from Toledo. It was modernized in the 1960s. On the ground floor, there is a small, dark Museo Nacional del Teatro, with photos of famous Argentine actors, and manuscripts.

La City

The neighborhood given an Anglicized name, la City (once also known as the *English barrio* and still containing red letter boxes) occupies some forty blocks north of the Plaza de Mayo in what was known as Catedral al Norte. Here are the bankers, stockbrokers and dealers who have made speculation the giddy thrill as well as the curse of countless

Argentines. Julián Martel's novel *La Bolsa* [The stock market, 1891] charts the rise and fall of Dr. Luis Glow in the Buenos Aires stock exchange of 1880 through a moral and patriotic tale, flawed by anti-Semitism and racism. In this novel the imposing Bolsa has large vaulted arches, a café, a large clock, and a central "arena" with a "promiscuity of people and a promiscuity of languages" releasing "a din of voices, a racket of a thousand devils." First published as a serial in the newspaper *La Nación*, this novel captures a feature of the city's life "where in a twinkling of the eye you can multiply your capital." The Bolsa has moved several times, Martel's model being demolished and the institution moving to San Martín 216 until 1885, next to Rivadavia, and then in 1916 occupying the "palace" designed by Alejandro Christophersen on calle Sarmiento between 25 de Mayo and Leandro Alem. This was another grand edifice, its main hall columned and with a dome. The Bolsa finally moved to its present site next door in 1971 in a building designed by Mario Alvarez.

The stock exchange has not always been the preserve of young men with mobile phones, although certain familiar traits, such as arrogance and cunning, seem to have been in evidence for many years. Lucio Mansilla remembers the Bolsa of the 1830s: "the Bolsa, which at the time was called the *Camoatí* stood on calle Victoria, between Chacabuco y Perú. And 'camoatí' being a Guarani word not found in Spanish dictionaries... I will confide to the ignorant that it means *wasps' nest*. Better name would be hard to find." Robert Cunninghame Graham depicted the stock exchange in terms of *porteño* habits: "Horses were commoner than dogs... Before the Stock Exchange dozens, or sometimes hundreds, stood, and stockbrokers felt their way cautiously amongst them with propitiatory words, hissing and chirruping... The upper classes dressed in black broadcloth, and all wore black felt hats which made them look like touts in the Levant. They held themselves the first of humankind... " Lucio V. López's narrator's first job was with Don Eleazar (a pun on *azar*, meaning chance), a speculator who loses everything. The stock exchange, he writes, was the heart of Buenos Aires' wealth and values: "in the stock exchange, everything is allowed. Like in war; to play publicly with booms and crashes; throw a *gato* [cat], issue scandalous news assuring that war with Chile is a fact [Chile remains the traditional enemy, with border disputes pending]... in a word, sow terror without considering patriotism." It is an evaluation that still holds today. The Guatemalan diplomat, poet and close friend of Rubén Darío, Enrique Gómez Carillo, ironically noted the Bolsa's hold over the collective *porteño* psyche: "There's a famous street corner in Buenos Aires to which people rush to watch the spectacle that most interests a people like this. It seems as if this street corner is no different to any other in the centre. Men hurry by. And you, who are not initiated into the secrets of banking and the stock exchange, would not even turn around. But the true citizens of this metropolis, who feel their heart beating avidly for business, will see in each one of the passers-by a fairy-tale hero."

For some observers, the financial district was the realm of Mammon, a place of greed and frenzy. Ernesto Sabato described la City as a "violent bustle, din, indescribable confusion, hurry, the vast crowd." He questioned the sanity of speculation as a "ghostly, magical process" where those who control these operations sleep only with the help of pills and drugs, "pursued by nightmares of financial crashes." Ezequiel Martínez Estrada evoked the area in his mock-epic "Argentina" (1927): "It's a noise of stuffed traffic / and business and banking eagerness, / calle Reconquista vibrates in the eleven o'clock sun / ... / stock brokers rush by / urgent employees, businessmen who pass / with their business inside them / and their creditors behind." In 1939 Silvina Bullrich's *Calles de Buenos Aires* isolated *oro* [gold] and speculation as the country's curse: "those who lived in Buenos Aires wanted to be happy, to be rich. At least, that's what the city owed them. It couldn't give them beauty nor inner life, but it had taught them to worship gold." She concluded: "Today all Buenos Aires lives under this obsession: gold." Things have not changed much since 1939.

But not all is power and loot, for on calle Reconquista the Universidad Católica occupies the old Merced Convent, with patio and cloisters. On the same street (at 455) is the excellent restaurant, the London Grill, where Jorge Luis Borges often ate. Nearby on calle 25 de Mayo is the Facultad de Filosofía y Letras of the Universidad de Buenos Aires (http://www.filo.uba.ar) in a crumbling art nouveau building where US poet Willis Barnstone taught in 1975. It was an "unimposing, rundown building... which my informants swore had the best professors and students of literature in Argentina. Each floor somehow looked like a basement; this rich country is not generous about upkeep of its public universities." Barnstone added: "My students were alert and outgoing and one needed no tricks to get them to talk." Both perceptions were acute, for little money is spent on building maintenance, and Argentine students are undoubtedly talkative and lively. The calle 25 de Mayo was also the centre for louche "cafés cantantes" at the turn of the century (its heyday was around 1900-1920), as in Manuel Gálvez's 1919 description:

> There was a motley crowd on calle 25 de Mayo, packed with ambiguous hotels, taverns and cafés, that Saturday night. Individuals from the most far-flung nations entered into the cafés or strolled the narrow pavements, staring at the dirty, anarchic windows in the bargain shops that abound in that barrio. At every step there was some café with hostesses, from whose doors shameless women with made-up faces, slack bellies, and depraved faces would call out to the sailors dressed in civilian clothes and to those of the underworld who swarmed there. There were German hotels, Turkish shops, and bars with strange names.

Gerald Durrell adored this street, especially Olly's Music Bar: "It was not the sort of street a respectable man would be seen in, but I had long ceased to worry about respectability. With my various friends we had visited most of these tiny, dark, smoky bars, and drunk drinks of minute size and colossal price, and watched the female 'hostesses' at their age-old work."

Within la City is what is today the Avenida Leandro Alem or *bajo*, previously the Paseo de la Alameda and renamed the Paseo de Julio by Rosas. There are also the areas off the Plaza de Mayo, the calle Reconquista and the above-mentioned calle 25 de Mayo, known as a rough zone of brothels and port bars. Fernández Moreno's poem "Seventy Balconies and Not One Flower" referred, in his own words, to "a new house on the Paseo de Julio, about level with the former Parque Japonés, that I counted one hot night, with Pedro Herreros, sitting on a stone bench. Friends, I am but the author of *Seventy Balconies and Not One Flower*" (but this hasn't stopped people attributing the poem to numerous other buildings in the city). The closing poem in Borges' collection *Cuaderno San Martín* (a title referring to a kind of school exercise book) is called "The Paseo de Julio." The bitter first lines are full of urban alienation: "Mutilated harbor without a sea, boxed-in gust of brackish breeze, / dregs stuck to land, Paseo de Julio, / although my memories, so old as to be moving / I never felt you to be part of my homeland." It is a vision diametrically opposed to that of such *barrios* as Palermo which did make him feel at home. Here in the Paseo de Julio all is ugliness and "your night heated by brothels hangs from the city" in a dystopian perception of the city's hell. It was on the Paseo de Julio that one of Borges' few female characters, Emma Zunz, picked up a Swedish sailor in order to claim she was raped and thus kill her father's tormentor. Again, the image is one of sordid low-life: "on the infamous Paseo de Julio she saw herself multiplied in mirrors, made public by lights and stripped naked by hungry eyes... " Manuel Gálvez describes this same street in 1916 through his poet-protagonist Carlos Riga's alcoholic despair:

> *on finding himself in the atmosphere of a Russian novel, in a story by Gorki, that was given to him by the Paseo de Julio, his artist's soul forgot for an instant the penury of his life. Because he found this street fantastic, with its high arcades; its cheap, foul shops; its kaleidoscopes with views of wars and exhibitions of monsters; the dark hotels that rented out dirty beds for occasional lovers; the sinister cellars that stunk of grime and where sailors reeking of booze sang; its whores, who were the dirtiest dregs of society; its vagabonds who slept under the columns of the arches; its sellers of obscene pictures; the nauseating stink of human dirt...*

On this street (the Plaza Roma) you can find a statue to Giuseppe Mazzini, unveiled in 1878, which novelist Eduardo Mallea described in *La bahía de silencio* [*The Bay of Silence*, 1940] as "refined, distinguished on a low pedestal with his tailored frock-coat." Víctor Gálvez thought it ironic that the city's best statue was that of a foreigner. Mazzini (1805-1872), a radical Italian nationalist, accomplice of Garibaldi, author of the influential essay *The Duties of Man* (1860) and exiled for years in London, was an important figure in Argentine liberal nationalism (he was also praised by Gandhi). Despite its reputed squalor, the Paseo de Julio has figured emotively in the literary imagination, as Delfín

Leocadio Garasa claimed: "The Paseo de Julio will always be associated with *porteño* nostalgia."

The City *barrio* has its museums, including the Museo Numismático del Banco Central on San Martín 216, and the Biblioteca Raúl Prebisch in a building opened in 1862 as the Banco de Comercio. The Archivo y Museo Histórico del Banco Provincia Dr. Arturo Jauretche in a modern building on Sarmiento 362 contains examples of coins and bills as well as models of the area. Next to this museum is the Iglesia de Nuestra Señora de la Merced, originally a rustic chapel dating from around 1600. By 1712, Jesuits had built a complex of chapels and convents. During the English invasion, Liniers used the convent and dug in his troops there, and it became successively a hospital and a factory, until restored to the order of the Mercedarios in 1963. It can be visited, an oasis of trees in mid-City. The ex-convent is now the Universidad Católica. Lastly, the Palacio de Correos y Telégrafos, also known as the Correo Central, is on Leandro Alem, opposite the Bolsa. Inaugurated in 1928, it was designed by the French architect Norbert Maillart and modeled on the New York Central Post Office, with four domes and a facade of four columns. The grand entrance to this cathedral to mail is on calle Sarmiento. Inside, on the second floor, the Museo del Correo is named after the historian and erstwhile Ambassador to Britain Dr. Ramón Cárcano. The essayist Ezequiel Martínez Estrada worked in the Correo all his life, and wrote *Radiografía de la pampa* [*X-Ray of the Pampa*, 1933] on Correo letterhead writing-paper. One last detail of literary interest is that Domingo Sarmiento, who arrived in Buenos Aires in 1852, only bought a house there in 1874 on Cuyo 53 (renamed Sarmiento 1251), where he lived until his death in 1888. Restored, it is today the Casa de San Juan (i.e. it represents the province of that name) in Buenos Aires.

Avenida Santa Fe

Avenida Santa Fe has become more glamorous than Florida, as it cuts through the *barrio norte*. Ambulant Gloria in Bullrich's *Calles de Buenos Aires* tried (vainly, I feel) to characterize Santa Fe in the late 1930s: "An avenue that was happy and typical in the morning became insipid when night fell... so many shop windows showed multi-colored clothes off that at first sight Santa Fe seemed to be preparing for a fashion fiesta, rather than a national holiday or carnival. No street looked better in the morning sun in the whole of Buenos Aires." The writer Rubi Rubens called this avenue, named Santa Fe by Rivadavia in 1822, "this great open-air theatre," where everybody acts, likes looking and being seen, "the *porteña* woman's favorite street." Miranda France walked up Buenos Aires' "most elegant avenue" in 1994, past the boutiques, smart cafés and cinemas, overheard typical conversations like: "'He's divine—but he's my analyst!' laughed a woman in a tight suit and dark glasses. 'I''m an ecologist,' a man at another window was saying earnestly, 'and I tell you that *this city is dying*.'" Santa Fe is the logical extension of Florida, as it starts in the Plaza San Martín where Florida ends. A good place to observe this beginning is the traditional and stuffy café, Le Petit Paris, which looks on to the Plaza San Martín, and where in the evenings a man stiffly plays the organ.

Crossing the lethal traffic rush of the wide Avenida 9 de Julio, you come to a dirty but grand building called the Sociedad Científica Argentina on Santa Fe 1145, dating from 1934. It has a grand marble entrance hall, with Doric columns and a bust of Germán Burmeister, who was recommended to work in Argentina by Alexandre von Humboldt. He wrote a thorough study of Argentine fauna and flora, and founded the great natural history museum in La Plata. There is also a bust of Juan María Gutiérrez, a wonderful library on the third floor with leather seats and green lights, a fine lecture theatre named after Florentino Ameghino, and many cultural activities from concerts to art shows and poetry readings. I worked there in the early 1990s on the French botanist Aimé Bonpland, but it was then a tale of woe, all facade and no maintenance, and no budget for the library (the librarian, now retired, was collecting CDs but couldn't afford a CD player). He had a disease from handling damp, rotting paper and refused to enter some of the library's back rooms. I was alone there, and relished the silence and privacy.

Gordon Meyer's novella "Quits" (1963) explores the love affair between a rich dilettante and his astute, artistic mistress. This upper-class, spoiled Argentine male enjoys spending his inherited loot on her:

> *To enter the fashionable avenida Santa Fé from the quiet plaza was to*
> *emerge from a motionless backwater into a broad hurrying river of life.*
> *Lights were springing on all down the street as far as the wide plaza over-*
> *looking the river. It was the hour that so often had hurt her in those eight*
> *months, the soft scented hour of the Rioplatense evening, when perfumes*
> *loitered in arrogant doorways, and the cars rushed by on altogether differ-*
> *ent errands, the hour of the confitería, the emergence from the hair and*
> *beauty salons, the interval of tea and cocktails and chatter—the prelude*
> *to the greater pleasure...*
>
> *She pushed open the door of the Hermes boutique...*

Where Santa Fe meets Callao in a new energy centre buzzing with people, cinemas and restaurants abound. This is *porteño* social life at its most intense. Writer Enrique Amorim quipped: "These cinemas on the calle Santa Fe should be called 'talking cinemas,' 'chatting cinemas,'" so much did (and still do) *porteños* chatter in the cinema. Equally alive is the next important crossroads, Santa Fe and Pueyrredón, with cafés and more crowds (we once lived there, and the traffic noise made us ill). Further up the wide one-way avenue is another crucial node, the vast air-conditioned shopping mall called Alto Palermo that makes *porteños* feel that their city competes with New York. The mall is clean and first-world, and whole families drift around sleep-walking. I've seen the same in the Paseo Alcorta and the Patio Bullrich, my own favorite "shopping" on Libertador 740–750, which artfully adapts the previous Centro de Remate de Ganado, keeping the original facade. But not all is fashion, McDonalds and window-shopping, for Santa Fe also boasts excellent bookshops like the Librería Santa Fe on 2376 and 2582, as well as a Fausto on 1715 and 2077 (visitable on http: //www.fausto.com) and the new, fashionable Losada Libros on Santa Fe 2074, with a café and literary readings. But the most exciting place to visit, just off Santa Fe on Laprida 1212, is the Museo Xul Solar designed by architect Pablo Beitía by refashioning Xul Solar's house and studio. It is the best designed museum in the city, showing Xul Solar's esoteric, colorful, playful and sometimes Klee-like art, with his weird invented objects. In one of his lectures, Borges remembered Xul's library on Laprida 1214 as "perhaps one of the best libraries I've seen in my life" (though it is not open to the public). Borges claimed Xul as "our William Blake," saying that "he was the most extraordinary man I met in my life." Xul was also a character in Leopoldo Marechal's novel *Adán Buenosayres* (as was Borges). The museum has a little section selling mementos, and organizes cultural activities. A short walk from here takes you to the Museo Casa de Ricardo Rojas on Charcas 2837 (parallel to Santa Fe), the patioed house of the nationalist cultural historian under whom in 1913 the first department of Argentine literature was set up in the Universidad de Buenos Aires; his house can be visited and holds the scholar's library.

Self-portrait by Xul Solar, c. 1960

Plaza Italia

Santa Fe leads, against its four lanes of hurtling traffic, to the hectic, traffic-choked Plaza Italia. In the middle of this square stands the greening bronze equestrian statue of Garibaldi. Guiseppe Garibaldi (1807-1882), the red-shirted, bearded, *gaucho*-dressed revolutionary, who escaped Italy in 1834 and found himself in Brazil, fighting as a republican against the Emperor. He was caught by a pro-Rosas gang and tortured, but escaped to Montevideo in 1840. He fought on for six years in Brazil, married a Brazilian, Anita, his revolutionary equal, and was back in besieged Montevideo when he was recalled to Italy by Mazzini to liberate and unify Italy. Garibaldi appears in Conrad's Latin American novel *Nostromo* (1904) as the epitome of the guerrilla fighter, the Che Guevara of his day. Rafael Alberti, a Communist in exile from General Franco's Spain, roamed this plaza in a poem: "My latent popular nostalgias repose / in the Plaza Italia, its cinemas and bars / and more than ever the wind of freedom, the wind / that gave Garibaldi's monument to the city."

Off the plaza is the Sociedad Rural Argentina ("la Rural"), founded in 1866 to promote agriculture, which hosts the annual exhibition of livestock and farming—a show that includes a speech from the President and equestrian displays, demonstrating that land remains the basis of much of Argentina's wealth. Martín Cullen compared this show's social prestige to the Chelsea Flower Show in London and joked about Argentina's "Bull Epoque." In 1932 Philip Guedalla witnessed this high point in the cattle breeders' calendar, and ironically claimed that the prize bull at the Rural became "a national figure." The Rural, he wrote, combined "the social eminence of Ascot with the technical excitements of the Motor Show." The judges were shipped out from England, while the "crowds wander down the alleys, lingering to stare at the competing monsters," with the largest crowd peeking at the prize bull "embedded in an enormous cube of fodder." Guedalla contrasted this "small locomotive"-sized bull and its price with the "huddled masses round the docks [who] would be better for a little of the same care." I have been several times, wandering the stables with prize bulls, sheep and cattle, staring at the bull-necked cattlemen, and beautiful women behind the tractor stands, tasting the delicious snacks. The horse shows, *gaucho* skills, in fact, remind us from the middle of this very urban city just how crucial the land was and is to Argentine identity. The year 1998 saw the 112th show and the last in the current buildings, for the site has been sold to be modernized, though the grand restaurant will be preserved. The plaza is also home to second-hand bookstalls.

Palermo

"Palermo was rushing towards silliness: sinister 'art nouveau' buildings sprouted like swollen flowers." Borges

Straight north from Plaza Italia you reach Palermo, a *barrio* and the site of a large, popular park, Buenos Aires' *Bois de Boulogne*. It derives from a proper name, a Sicilian from Palermo who owned a slaughter-house and a farm (*chacra*) in the early seventeenth century, although some historians link Palermo with San Benito, the black saint from Palermo, Sicily, who had a chapel dedicated to him there. This is where in 1838 Rosas built his *estancia* called La Quinta, where he lived his last four years in power, as a large rectangle, with inner patios and towers on each corner, surrounded by arcades echoing the Spanish colonial style. Borges called Rosas the "mythological father of Palermo," and more critically in a poem titled "Temptation," "the remote spider of Palermo." Rosas's own letterhead combined both possible origins: "Palermo de San Benito." William MacCann expected to see a country house, surrounded by woods and lawns, but saw instead "an extended plain, with a young plantation along the river, and a foreground of mud huts, with plantations of canes, and a waste covered with gigantic thistles." The Chilean writer B. Vicuña Mackenna, on the other hand, called Rosas' mansion a "creole Versailles." Rosas was forced out into exile in England in 1852 (where he died in his "poor shacks" near Southampton in 1877), and his grand Palermo house was finally demolished by dynamite in 1899.

In 1985 excavations revealed some red adobe bricks from this house that have been placed on a plinth with a plaque, the sole remains of the hated (and loved) Rosas. During his presidency Domingo Sarmiento cleared and drained the land, dug lakes, planted trees (one of his maxims was: "Don't be barbarians, plant trees") and renamed the Rosas estate the Tres de Febrero [Third of February] park, commemorating Rosas' defeat at the battle of Monte Caseros in 1852. It was opened in 1875 by President Avellaneda, who planted a magnolia that still stands with a plaque (which I couldn't find). An "aromo" tree near the Monument to Sarmiento was supposedly planted by Rosas' daughter Manuelita, and under its branches Rosas often pardoned his enemies so that it was nicknamed the "Aromo of the Pardon" (a new tree has replaced it, railed in, without a sign). Urquiza, Rosas' victor, lived in this same palace before retiring to (and being murdered in) his splendid palace San José in Entre Ríos. An English visitor in 1852 remarked: "Urquiza's residence at Palermo is only one room high, and is surrounded with a lot of porticoes. It was built by the wretch Rosas, and lies on a flat plain close to the river, with a grove of miserable-looking trees between it and the water."

The large and popular park that was previously Rosas' estate has several statues, a rose-garden, a planetarium, a restored, colorfully tiled "Andalusian patio" (dating from 1929, a gift to "opulent Buenos Aires" from Seville), and a rehabilitated "lake pergola"—with another statue to Sarmiento, dedicated to "the great thinker of América." You can also see an abandoned, silted-up pond named after the writer Victoria Ocampo (a road-sign explains that she was a "writer who promoted culture, a valiant defender of woman's condition"), a busy, noisy boating lake, and a well-kept Japanese garden. The crushed red-brick paths and jetting fountains of the Poet's Garden link a series of statues, including that of Alfonsina Storni by Argentine sculptor Nila Toledo Guma, which has a casket of Alfonsina's native Swiss earth buried underneath. The statuary also features a caricature of a bust of Borges by Carlos Estévez, images of Paul Groussac and Enrique Larreta, and statues of many Spanish poets including Miguel Hernández, Lorca and Antonio Machado. Among the busts of Latin American writers are Alfonso Reyes (1889-1953), friend and equal to Borges in ironic erudition and Mexican Ambassador in Buenos Aires from 1927 to 1930, and the Maya-faced Miguel Angel Asturias. Asturias, the Guatemalan Nobel-Prize winning novelist, married an Argentine and was a diplomat in Buenos Aires from 1948 to 1952, where he wrote his masterpiece *Hombres de maíz* [*Men of Maize*, 1949]. He made friends with Oliverio Girondo and Norah Lange, loved calle Corrientes and called Buenos Aires "a song to future humanity" (Xul Solar also painted his portrait). Also scattered around are statues of Dante, Shakespeare, Leopardi, etc. On the lake is Pablo Grasq's statue "The Kiss" (or Leander and Hero), made of white Carrara marble. Manuel Gálvez tells the story of a Romantic poet who fell in love with this statue in 1910: "the poet lost his mind over a marble statue next to one of Palermo's avenues who had revealed her adolescent nakedness to him. And every evening the poet went to Palermo, and there, in the lonely mystery of that hour, under a conspiratorial sky, mumbled tender words to his marble beloved." Near the Japanese garden is one of Argentina's first sculptor's works: "The Slave" by Francisco Cafferata (1861). Underneath the brick railway arches on Paseo de la Infanta are outdoor bars and restaurants, a Pumper-Nic (the local version of McDonalds) and an art gallery, and nearby, close to the bridge in the rose-garden on Avenida de la Infanta Isabel 555, the restored and recently opened Museo de Artes Plásticas Eduardo Sívori, with both a permanent collection and special shows. On Sundays the park is packed with smart joggers, roller-bladers, dog-walkers, picnickers and cyclists, while parakeets screech in the trees.

The *barrio* of Palermo, to the south-west of the park, was made famous by Borges on his return from seven years in Europe in 1921 (he returned to Europe again until 1924). His first book of poems, *Fervor de Buenos Aires* (1923), saw Palermo as epitomizing the real, quiet city that his foreigner's eyes created as he meandered around its streets. His family built a two-floored house with a patio and a palm tree on calle Serrano 2135 (the street has been renamed Jorge Luis Borges), which he claimed was "one of the few two-storied houses on the street." He wrote an idiosyncratic biography, his first book, of the local *Palermitano* poet Evaristo Carriego (1883-1912) who lived on calle Honduras 84 (today 3784), a friend of his father's and who reinvented the mood of the *barrios* through his verse. Carriego's modest, green-fronted house-museum can be visited; it serves as a local library. A plaque states that Carriego is "the poet who ennobled the pain of humble folk." Borges called him "the first spectator of the suburbs" and confessed that "he helped me form a real image of Buenos Aires." Carriego wrote wistful songs about deserted streets, with organ-players, street-corner toughs, dreamy lovers, and irrecuperable pasts, close to the nostalgia of tangos. He died young, aged twenty-nine, with one book of poems, *Misia hereje* [Heretical mass], to his name. His tomb in the Chacarita is to be moved to the section entitled "Site of Personalities" as a posthumous honor, while a small plaza off calle Coronel Díaz nearby has been named after him. Another plaza, adjoining calle Jorge Luis Borges, newly named after a writer in Palermo Viejo is the Plazoleta Cortázar (once Plaza Racedo), suitably a children's playground in memory of the author of *Hopscotch*. It is surrounded by fashionable bars, one called "Macondo".

Born in Buenos Aires on August 24, 1899 at calle Tucumán 840, Borges was educated abroad in Switzerland, Mallorca and Spain, returning with his parents and sister Norah (later a painter) in 1921 to live in the still quiet Palermo. Ths return, he said in 1974, was the most important event in his life. Today, the area appears to writers as if conditioned by Carriego and then by Borges himself. Poet, Borges-biographer and tango expert Horacio Salas was brought up in "Palermo's unending siesta" and recalls his grandfather "slowly strolling round Palermo." The poet's grandfather "smiled in front of the little street organ / and heard in the distance / that someone was whistling / a Villoldo tango in a patio. / Without knowing it, his eyes crossed many times / with those of Carriego / perhaps they were friends." It is as if Palermo is more past than present.

Off Plaza Italia are the Botanical Gardens. The tall trees with Latin tags make strolling the paths during the hot seasons a relief. The Gardens, created in 1897 by French-born Charles Thays (1849-1934), Argentina's greatest landscape architect, are rife with wild cats living in the drains and were once likened to a "silent shipyard with trees, fatherland of all the capital's walks" by Borges. Rafael Alberti, who lived nearby on Las Heras in the 1950s, often wandered their pathways with his dog, eulogizing the landscape and singling out "the round *victorias regias*, sleeping beauties / of the waters." Manuel Mujica Lainez thought that the Botanical Gardens' brick-built castle, with crenellations and towers and palm trees, looked like the residence of an English governor in a tropical colony, "ideal to develop a story by Somerset Maugham."

Looking on to the *Botánico* is "Villa Freud," a zone once packed with psychoanalysts of every persuasion, from Freudians to Lacanians, for Buenos Aires is the city of more shrinks per head than anywhere else— even New York. Therapy is no luxury, for everyone indulges in talking-cures and couch confessions. Julio Cortázar once boasted that he was the only Argentine he knew who had never been analyzed. Even Borges went to analysis (Estela Canto named his analyst, Dr. Cohen-Miller, and the reasons for his visits: it still astounds me that Borges would confide in a therapist).

When I first arrived in Buenos Aires in 1970, I was often the only person in a group who had not seen a shrink (I have since). Someone calculated that there are some 15,000 therapists, of every persuasion, from Lacanians to Kleinians, Freudians and Jungians, at work in the city. The Asociación Psicoanalítica Argentina was founded in 1942. The reasons for so many making a living from hearing psycho-babble and talking-cures are various: from a large Jewish element to the obvious urban angst arising from immigrant rootlessness. Therapeutic slang sprinkles everyday talk, with words like "repressed," "phobia," and "omnipotence" common currency; but fashions change, and if you still hear the parting remark "I'm off to therapy", new fads are replacing the five sessions-a-week couch intensity.

The main gates of the zoo face Plaza Italia. It was finally opened to the public in 1888, but was founded by Sarmiento in 1874 as part of his "civilizing mission." The zoo's first director was Eduardo Holmberg (1852-1937), a scientist who traveled around Argentina, writing a long study on the zoology and botany of the Sierra de Tandil, and who was also a poet and short story writer of science-based "fantastic tales." A later director (from 1904-1914), Clemente Onelli, wrote sketches about the zoo called *Aguafuertes del Zoológico* [Zoo watercolors]. Haroldo Conti's poor boy hero Milo regularly visits the zoo, first the famous animals, then the forgotten ones; he befriends a mongoose, tries to liberate it and is caught. Conti evokes the sordid attraction of this zoo during a hot summer: "After the lake, green and thick like a lentil stew, with two or three dusty swans, more or less at the level of the cage with the polar bear with a lame paw, boiling with heat, there was a side path leading into trees that ended at a low, smelly cage leaning against the side of Acevedo street. After waving at the wolves, at the nervous, striped jackals who stunk even more, and imitating the cross-eyed swan," the old man and boy came across this "canine mongoose," trapped in his cage, like them in their lives in Buenos Aires. Against the lovable squalor of Conti's story, the British poet and critic G. S. Fraser visited the "cheerful" zoo in spring 1947, finding the animals amorous. Fraser was struck by the existential quality of one species: "I saw that afternoon for the first time in my life a warthog, and wondered at the mysteries of the creation. It is at once horrible and pathetic, and its wide-set tiny gray-pink eyes seem to be angrily aware of its own absurdity." Estela Canto remembered how Borges was only interested in the zoo's "magnificent Bengal tiger," and that it smelled of "urine, rotten horse meat, martyred animal."

The zoo has lakes named after Charles Darwin and Germán Burmeister, an elephant house called a "palace" and built in 1904 which copied a temple to the goddess Nimaschi in Bombay, a Hindustani Temple from Bombay dated 1901, genuine Byzantine ruined columns on an island and a Parrot Pavilion, donated by Spain in 1899, with attractive tiling. The whole zoo is dotted with sculptures. On Avenida Sarmiento, running alongside the zoo, is an Italianate villa restaurant, *No se lo digas a nadie* [Don't tell anybody].

At the end of Avenida Sarmiento, at the junction with Libertador and opposite the Monument to the Spaniards, is Rodin's 1899 bronze statue of a grumpy, determined-looking President Sarmiento, unveiled in 1911. Rodin also designed the plinth and shield. The Mexican essayist José Vasconcelos found this statue "more than ugly" and said that Sarmiento looks "hunched over like a monkey," adding "if Sarmiento is very ugly, the sculptor should have skipped doing his portrait and just made a monument." He accused Rodin of being "mercenary" when any Argentine sculptor "could have made a better statue of Sarmiento, the saint, than Rodin's." It has been claimed that the site of Rosas' house lies exactly under this statue to his enemy and victor Domingo Sarmiento. Nearby is the sumptuous art-nouveau Monument to the Spaniards in the middle of Libertador and Sarmiento, made in white marble and decorated profusely with allegories about the Discovery and Conquest, with an angel on the top representing the Argentine nation. Vasconcelos thought it seemed made of "sugar." Avenida Sarmiento was the route of the famous "Corso" at the turn of the century when the well-to-do cruised in their carriages on Thursdays and Sundays, eyeing and envying each other. Julián Martel evoked this social procession in his topical novel *La bolsa:* "Buenos Aires society rushes in a triumphal march along the banks of the Recoleta toward Palermo. It is a stunning parade, a superb spectacle." The show was watched by those on foot who also visited Palermo park with its trees and lakes, "ecstatic before the waterfall streaking the artificial rocks silver," but that was in 1891. When Sarmiento planted his palm trees along this "Corso" avenue they were nicknamed "Sarmiento's brooms."

Also in Palermo is the Racecourse (Hipódromo). Owned by the Jockey Club and founded in 1882 by Carlos Pellegrini, it opened in style with a grandstand, glassed in boxes and a dome designed by Néstor Paris for its first race in 1882. In 1908 this was expanded, and today, it is a period piece. Around this stand are gardens, bars and *confiterías*, with the famous Salón Oval on the top floor. Isobel Strachey described this racecourse through her English nanny's experiences:

No book-makers were allowed on the Palermo race course. Tote figures appeared in white letters on a black indicator opposite the jockey club enclosure which overlooked the end of the sandy course and the judges' glass-covered box. A high kidney-shaped pavilion in the enclosure contained an elegant restaurant... As it was summer the restaurant was not very full and most of the people lunching there were men in smart light-colored suits and tiny brightly polished shoes, all busily talking and gesticulating with smooth, carefully tended hands, their hair sometimes brushed close to their heads with a lustrous gum called "gomina." ... They were easily amused... but if their patriotism, their honor, their manhood or their families were mentioned they would immediately flare up with the most conventional and genuine emotion.

Philip Guedalla's day at the races at Palermo was the high point of his month stay in Buenos Aires: "that was, I think, the crown and zenith of all luxury in Argentina, where respectful servitors stood waiting at your elbow to collect your bets and, if you won, your winnings were delivered on a salver—no scramble in the Ring, no queue at a barred window, but your winnings gravely presented on a salver at your imperial seat, from which you could command the whole length of the course. Beyond that point there is no luxury of which the human mind is capable." Such, he concluded, is the "sober luxury of the Jockey Club stand at Palermo." Manuel Gálvez described a day at the races in his novel *La pampa y su pasión* [The pampa and its passion]. Crowds arrive from all over the city "like lines of ants." The protagonist shows his friend the Escuela de Hipología [school of hippology], with its skeletons of famous race horses like Botafogo and Old Man; after eating at the restaurant they go to the popular section called the "dog pound." Such passion for horse racing in the city "is nothing but the form that the urban passion takes from the absorbing, secular pampas cult of the horse." Juan Villalba and Hermido Braga's tango runs: "Cursed Palermo / ... I spend at the bookie's / all I earn at work for a month." Horse racing was the natural sport for the flat pampas and thriving horses. In 1817 the English sailor-painter Emeric Vidal (1791-1861) sketched a horse race on the sands below the city fort, with a priest, a carter and *gauchos* watching (and betting).

Walking south down Libertador, you pass the Museo de Motivos Argentinos José Hernández on Libertador 2373, a museum explaining the *gaucho* and *campo* culture. It recently exhibited a history of the national drink *mate*. Apart from different editions of *Martín Fierro*, this rather uninteresting museum has little to cast light on the author of the protest poem that helped shape an aspect of Argentine identity at the turn of the century. A little further down the Avenida, you enter the *barrio* of Palermo Chico, created by Charles Thays in 1912, home to many embassies among its curving, tree-lined avenues, and the one-third larger-than-life replica of San Martín's Paris home, the Grand Bourg, housing his archives and a library, built in 1946. The essayist Victoria Ocampo, owner of *Sur*, had a town house built to her plans in 1929 by the architect Alejandro Bustillo (1889-1982) in calle Rufino de Elizalde opposite the Grand Bourg, though Bustillo refused to put his name to the design (which was quite at odds with his usual anachronistic style). She lived twelve years in this Cubist "manifesto" house of austere, rationalist, Le Corbusieran lines and geometric forms, with a total absence of decoration. In 1929 Le Corbusier visited Buenos Aires and admired this house. Ocampo had a mural painted by Norah Borges and tapestries designed by Picasso and Léger. Alejandro Moreno, who refurbished the house recently, told me that the view onto the green Plaza Chile opposite is stunning. Nearby is a typical Bustillo 1930 design, the ex-Palacio Tornquist, now the Belgian embassy. A single Bustillo statement characterizes his academic style: "When I designed [the casino at] Mar del Plata, I thought of the Place Vendôme."

Across the urban runway of Avenida del Libertador stands the imposing Errázuriz Alvear palace, built by René Sergent over the years from 1911 to 1917, and since 1937 the National Museum of Decorative Art (as well as a smaller Museo de Arte Oriental upstairs). This

Mansarded palace with four huge Corinthian columns and statues imitating Vissau's "Le Bonheur Publique," is an impressive anthology of styles: *boiserie* from the Hotel Le Tellier in Paris; music room after the Hôtel de Soubise in Paris; dining room after the Petit Trianon in Versailles. The huge Renaissance hall is hung with paintings by Cranach, El Greco, Corot, Delacroix, Fragonard and Manet, with a sculpture by Rodin and panels painted by the Catalan José María Sert. When I was there last an exhibition of pre-Inca erotic pieces from Lima attracted tittering crowds. Located at the back of the Palace is the Academia Argentina de Letras on Sánchez de Bustamante 2663 (current president Raúl Castagnino), which functions as the less grand Argentine equivalent of the Parisian Académie Française or Madrid's Academia Real. The Academia publishes books, displays rare editions, has a good library and is a meeting-place for its members (I once interviewed the poet Roberto Juarroz there in a somber study with leather sofas). As far as I know, only the poet Olga Orozco refused to become a member. In the same building is the Academia Nacional de Bellas Artes. In the château-style gate house of the Palace, *Museo* is an excellent restaurant, with tables outside. It is said that the owner of this solid palace, Matías Errázuriz, so liked looking at Victoria Ocampo's ultra-modern house opposite, that he had Le Corbusier design a seaside house for him. While he still lived in the palace, many visiting artists performed: Lorca recited his poems in the Renaissance hall, Arthur Rubinstein played the piano, and Ana Pavlova danced.

Nearby was the most famous of the tango restaurants, now demolished, called Armenoville, on what is today Libertador and Tagle. Carlos Gardel began there; his co-singer José Razzano recalled "the vague scent of magnolias from Palermo" while playing tangos. The Armenoville figures in Adolfo Bioy Casares' novel *El sueño de los héroes* [*The Dream of Heroes*, 1954], as it does in Vazquez Rial's already-cited *Frontera sur*.

The Retiro Station

This train station (originally three different stations) is another of the city's epicentres, a starting point in these imaginary excursions. The train lines here run north. The oldest of the three, the Pacífico, dates from 1886, the Belgrano station from 1913. The current building was

The former Englishmen's Tower (Nick Caistor)

designed by an English architect, Ambrose Pointer, in 1915, with cathedral-like iron girders vaulting the ceiling (made in Liverpool) and chandeliered cafés and restaurants, with mosaic floors, galleries, Doulton faience walls and English-style, restored, ticket booths.

Opposite the grandiose facade, on the Plaza de la Fuerza Aérea, is what was once called La Torre de los Ingleses [the Englishmen's Tower], a smaller Jacobean version (200 feet high) of the neo-Gothic Big Ben. Brought over in its entirety from England in 1916 as a gift from the Anglo-Argentine community, this clock tower was renamed La Torre Monumental after the Malvinas war. The ever-sarcastic poet Leopoldo Lugones mocked it with a rhyme: "that nearby Tower of the English cries / nostalgic for Westminster, four times a day striking the hours." Clara, the naive provincial whore in Luisa Valenzuela's first novel *Hay que sonreír* [*Clara*, 1966] waits impatiently here for one of her lovers (being on time is not a national virtue): "The tall Torre de los Ingleses, with its brick body and its clock face lighted-up, did not allow her to forget passing time." Baldomero Fernández Moreno observed this clock tower from the Plaza San Martín: "In the distance the red Tower of the English, / little balconies of ink, gilded filigree." There are plans afoot to put in a lift, open the *mirador*, restore it and set up a museum.

The ostentatious Retiro station teems with life, for it is here that Bolivians and Paraguayans arrive and set up markets and their *villas miseria* (shantytowns) on the tracks behind. This is where indigenous South American culture invades Europeanized Buenos Aires. Gordon Meyer compared the station to Milan's. For the Polish exiled novelist Witold Gombrowicz, the once grand Retiro station was the heart of the city, and he would hunt among its young crowds, recreated in his novel *Transatlantic*. Paul Theroux arrived there from La Quiaca on the Bolivia/Argentina border and described the station as having "a high, curved roof supported by girders forged in a Liverpool iron-works, and marble pillars and floors, ornately carved canopies, shafts of sunlight emphasizing its height and, indeed, everything of a cathedral but altars and pews."

Roberto Arlt's modern anti-bourgeois engineer Balder in *El amor brujo* picks up a sixteen-year-old schoolgirl at the Retiro station; the narrator remarks on its:

high walls which as they disappeared above led to tiled, steel arches. At a certain point the glass vault began and light was filtered by the dirty glass, as if stained by nicotine and by the soot of the trains. From all over the station dissonant sounds rose up. An invisible bomb moved ceaselessly about the place. The dull thuds of packages rolling along the platforms... and among the black dome of an iron wood, the light blocked by the numerous girders gave off a faint mustard color.

Eduardo Mallea's cool, theatre-designer Christina (from *La ciudad junto al rio inmóvil*) surveys Retiro from her flat through a mist: "ghosts, the trees of the Plaza de Retiro; ghosts, the tall modern buildings; ghosts the vast, moored station, with its arched dome like the back of some enormous animal."

Near where the station now stands there stood the infamous Immigrants' Hotel, first built in 1857 and remodeled in 1911 into a three-floored hotel, catering for up to 150,000 third-class immigrants per year, who could spend five days free there on arrival—the equivalent to Ellis Island in New York. Writer Francis Korn quotes a newspaper from 1930: "all the regions of the world meet in that first cosmopolitan home." When the German battleship *Graf Spee* was sunk in 1939 in what was known as the Battle of the River Plate, more than one thousand of the crew spent their first nights in Argentina in the Immigrants' Hotel.

Belgrano

The trains from Retiro take you to Belgrano by the tree-covered *barrancas* (turned into a park in 1871, which poet Rafael Alberti found ideal for lovers: "Along the Barrancas de Belgrano / two lovers, hand in hand.") With their tall trees, the *barrancas* were landscaped into a delightful park by Charles Thays in 1892. Or they can also take you to the other Belgrano station, Belgrano R, on Plaza Castelli. The *barrio* was named after Manuel Belgrano (1770-1820), a leader in the popular uprising of May 1810, soldier and inventor of the blue and white Argentine flag in 1812 (the colors reflect the wide dome of the sky on the *pampas*). In 1910 W. A. Hirst found this suburb "extremely untidy." But earlier in 1880 the British chargé d'affaires, Sir Horace Rumbold, rented a house with a tower, magnolia trees and hummingbirds there on the *barrancas* (where the river used to reach), following those *porteños* who had moved there for the clean air after the yellow fever epidemic of 1871. That year Belgrano became the capital of Argentina for three months. The country was governed from this same *quinta* on the *barrancas*, built around 1860 as the *casona de los Atucha*. Today the house is the painter and sculptor Libero Badii's museum on calle 11 de Septiembre 1990.

Belgrano still gives one the sense of its separateness from Buenos Aires, even being cut off when heavy rain flooded the few roads over the railways until the underpass on Cabildo was completed. Only recently has there been a *subte* connection reaching station (and street) José Hernández of *Martín Fierro* fame, who died at his quinta San José in Belgrano in 1888 (his last words recorded by his brother were: "Buenos Aires, Buenos Aires"). Overground trains reached Belgrano from Retiro by 1862. In 1910 it took Manuel Gálvez's Nacha one hour to reach Belgrano by tram, a haven from the slums she knew and a suburban counterpoint to her urban anxiety: "She got off the tram and sank into the silent shadows of the tree-lined streets. She was almost running. Elegant chalets, with gardens and magnificent trees passed by. In some streets the trees formed a roof. From the parks and gardens you could smell flowers. Nothing but a few people walking broke the silence of the neighborhood. All was sweetness and calm. But not for Nacha." Most commentators agree that Belgrano is leafy. Delfín Leocadio Garasa commented that fiction accentuated "this nostalgic touch of an arcadian, patrician Belgrano." Nydia Lamarque's poem naming calle Sucre in Belgrano evokes "the station made sad by the amputated branches of its trees / but consoled by the murmuring casuarinas and poplars and a magnolia bending its head." "Leafy" Belgrano was also captured by Eduardo Mallea: "That taciturn suburb, Belgrano… with its dark, tree-lined avenues, its busy people, its low, uniform houses, its barrancas." Lugones mocked this suburban peace when he versified the arrival of a powerful manager at work in his fast car from his "magnificent / chalet on Pampa y Crámer engendered by his meat-freezing factory." The object of his ridicule is a man who lives next door to President Alvear in a "serene street," with honeysuckle covering these "quintas de Belgrano."

On the plaza, Juramento 2180, is the building designed by Juan Buschiazzo in 1870 which was the local town hall and today is the Museo Histórico Sarmiento (e-mail: mhs@mcmhs.gov.ar), with six

Doric columns supporting its portico. Upstairs are Domingo Sarmiento's archives and a public library, in the spire a clock, and on top a statue of liberty. There are displays of first editions (the tiny 1845 Chilean edition of Sarmiento's *Facundo*), portraits, letters, uniforms and furniture, especially a writing desk belonging to Sarmiento. His granddaughter Eugenia Belin Sarmiento painted an excellent last portrait, which is on view. Sarmiento called his own *Facundo* "a strange, formless, senseless book," an apt description of his autodidact's mind. If you could pick one representative man for the best in all Argentines, along Ralph Waldo Emerson's criteria, it would be the energetic, stubborn and wise Sarmiento, "the most fascinating character in Argentine history, a key figure," according to the Argentine novelist Mempo Giardinelli in 1998. When I was last in this museum a tango class was being held in one of the display rooms. Next to the museum is a fine Cafetería del Museo. The Plaza General Belgrano the museum looks on to has beautiful jacaranda trees which flower in November. The plaza's church, La Inmaculada Concepción, known locally as the Redonda [the round one] for its 120-feet high dome, was built by the Canale father and son between 1864 and 1916; inside is a copy of da Vinci's "Last Supper." Martín in Sabato's Gothic *Sobre héroes y tumbas* follows the heroine and finds himself "suddenly... in the plaza of the Inmaculada Concepción, in Belgrano. She sat down on one of the benches. Opposite him, the circular church seemed to live the terror of his day. A sinister silence and the dying light, the drizzle, gave to that corner of Buenos Aires an ominous feel: it seemed as if in that old building at a tangent to the church hid some powerful and frightening enigma." Which it does, for he spies Alejandra entering the house, and it is in this "curious corner of Buenos Aires, formed by a row of old, two-storied houses" that Alejandra's incestuous madman of a father goes underground. In 1979 Mario Sabato filmed *El poder de las tinieblas* [The power of darkness], based on his father's novel, in this same location.

Opposite the plaza is the house that the historical novelist and millionaire Enrique Larreta (1875-1964) lived in from 1916 after his return from Paris as Argentine Ambassador. He described it modestly as "simple walls, white as if starched" on the outside. The house was donated by him as a Museo de Arte Español (Juramento 2291) and has a lovely, shady Andalusian garden with Moorish fountains, walks, magnolias, tall palms, a large Ginkgo tree and a huge *ombú* (the only "tree" on the *pampas*, but in fact hollow like a thistle), planted between 1916 and 1930. Inside the house is the Alfonso el Sabio library, with an annex devoted to children's books (but not Larreta's own book collection, which remains in family hands) and a theatre. Its neo-colonial style, designed by Martín Noel, was grafted in 1916 on to a house built in 1882 by Ernesto Bunge. Against the fad for France at the time, Larreta was a Hispanophile, published his historical novel *La gloria de Don Ramiro* [*The Glory of Don Ramiro*, 1908] in Madrid, and designed his grand house, Acelain, in the country near Azul along Moorish/Spanish lines. The museum contains stunning pieces, especially a 1503 altar piece from the San Nicolás church in Burgos Aranda del Duero bought in 1912, and which would be at home in any museum in the world. Larreta had been a professor of medieval history at the Colegio Nacional, and, in his words, "I specialized to the point of madness in that fascinating period of Spain's history." You can see his writing table, his carved-oak lectern, and a photo of him with his drooping moustache. There is a large oil portrait by Zuloaga, with the Spanish city of Avila in the background, where his character Ramiro grew up. Larreta held literary *tertulias* in this splendidly furnished house with friends like Manuel Gálvez, Leopoldo Marechal and Ricardo Rojas, and was visited by Ortega y Gasset. In twelve years Ramón Gómez de la Serna only once went inside this "great mansion in the Argentine-Andalusian style, surrounded by beautiful gardens," but would often wander at night with friends around the outer walls "of this writer's hermitage and guess his dreams and feel how he was master of a feudal estate with cypress trees, and in whose rooms, the virgins and altar pieces brought from Spain saturate the air with incense." Opposite Larreta's Spanish house and garden stood a huge restaurant with a patio where poets and painters like Mastronardi and Xul Solar would meet, and shout abuse at Larreta. The slogan of choice, it seems, was "Down with Zogoibi!," referring to Larreta's novel of that name (one of the worst novels ever written in Spanish, according to Borges).

Turning left down O'Higgins you pass number 2150, where a plaque commemorates Manuel Mujica Lainez who lived there from

1936 to 1970. He was famous for, among other things, his quirky birthday parties, where he served vizcacha stew (*puchero*) wearing his velvet smoking jacket. His real work-of-art of a Spanish mansion is today the Casa Museo Manuel Mujica Lainez called El Paraíso, some fifty miles from Córdoba in Cruz Chica, packed with idiosyncratic historical mementos. Further down the street, another neo-colonial Spanish house can be visited, the Casa de Yrurtia on O'Higgins 2390 which the sculptor Rogelio Yrurtia (1879-1950) designed and had built in 1923 and where he lived. On display are his works, those of his wife the painter Lía Correa Morales (I prefer her work) and a collection, including a Picasso, donated to the nation in 1942. Yrurtia is famed for his *Canto al trabajo* [Song to work], a bronze of 1908, the Rivadavia mausoleum and the statue of Manuel Dorrego, erstwhile governor of Buenos Aires who was summarily executed by Lavalle.

The main street of Belgrano is noisy, traffic-polluted Avenida Cabildo where Buenos Aires merges into other Latin American cities in a frenzy of neon, cheap shops, crowds and advertising (Wayne Bernhardson compares this street in his guide to Buenos Aires to Las Vegas without the casinos). The drug addict narrator of Juan Forn's story "For Gaby, If She Wants" from his collection *Nadar de noche* [To swim at night, 1991] finds himself on Cabildo: "Cabildo was packed with people, full of holes covered rudimentarily by planks and street stalls with fake Tupperware, Brazilian cutlery and scissors from Taiwan... "

Another literary street in Belgrano is calle Tronador, 1746 where the Lange family lived. Norah Lange was the only woman poet and writer associated with the *Martín Fierro* literary gatherings. Borges wrote a prologue to her poems *La calle de la tarde* [The street of the afternoon, 1925], and in 1926 she met and later married poet Oliverio Girondo. As a girl she lived in a house which was "vast, with nine rooms and a garden of 1,000 square meters, with ancient trees," the only house with a telephone in the locality (called Villa Mazzini in the 1920s). Leopoldo Marechal alluded to the Lange sisters in his novel *Adán Buenosayres*, and Borges wrote two poems to Norah's sister Haydée, claiming that their house was where he felt he could really be himself: "those who surround know me well / they know my anguish and my weakness." The Lange sisters held weekly literary and musical meetings, where Norah Borges, Alfonsina Storni and the mad poet Jacobo Fijman were regulars, and where Martínez Estrada first met, and then became close friends with, the great short story writer Horacio Quiroga just before Quiroga committed suicide. Estrada went on to write the best book on Quiroga. The world of the Tronador house and garden is recreated in Norah Lange's quirky novel *Cuadernos de infancia* [Childhood notebook, 1937].

In all, Belgrano has many pleasingly eclectic villas, tree-lined streets, cafés, a thriving private university and further plazas, like the Plaza Castelli where, standing on the balcony of the art deco flat lived in by jazz guitarist Pino Marrone and folk singer Gabriela you look over green trees towards the 1922 Hirsch palace on Conde 2084 (architect J. R. Sutton), and also on to the grey-blue Italianate villa, now KEL on Conde 1990, a chain of bookshops stocking English books. Vázquez Rial argued that Belgrano "possesses a commercial and cultural autonomy... you can spend years without having to go to the centre of Buenos Aires."

Bajo Belgrano is where the racing stables are located. Racing at nearby Palermo is a popular focus and the promise of winning a bet a much hoped-for escape from poverty. Francisco García Jiménez's tango "Bajo Belgrano" evokes the eternal illusions of this area with its wind from the *pampa*, its studs, its hopes: "Bajo Belgrano, each week / your shout reaches the centre /—Program and riders for tomorrow! / And the madness of Sundays / meeting by the track, / shouting the name of a hundred race horses / the twenty barrios of the city." Today there is a large Taiwanese presence, and a small Chinatown (also a Buddhist monastery on Montañeses 2175).

Núñez

The next *barrio* after Belgrano R (R stands for Rosario) is Núñez. The poet Fernando Sánchez Sorondo's evocative tribute to one of his mentors, the fellow poet and novelist Leopoldo Marechal, takes up a childhood memory from 1959:

> When I was fifteen, I lived near the river. Our house was in Núñez, by the river. Then, during the summer, I used to walk down to the river bank, round the Escuela de Mecánica and enter a narrow street called Leopoldo Lugones where I knew a shipyard and a forgotten club: the San

Martín. There I discovered magical scenes from the Arabian Nights: an extremely poor shipyard, a zigzagging path through damp, lush vegetation that led tortuously to the river. It was my refuge. I initiated my friends into it. It was my house, and I shared it with Leopoldo Marechal's spirit. There I learned his sonnets to Sophia by heart.

This *barrio* was named after Florencio Emeterio Núñez who donated land for the railway station named after him in 1873 (the actual station was built by British engineers in 1899, one of the oldest buildings in the *barrio*), and today its axis is the Avenida Cabildo, the ancient *camino real.* Scottish immigrants brought over by President Rivadavia founded a school here in 1838, the San Andrés, which still functions. Núñez is also known for the fanatical supporters of its soccer club (founded in 1905 and actually called the Club Atlético Platense or River Plate), with its huge stadium, the "Monumental," the largest in Argentina and seat of the 1978 World Cup finals. Borges, who execrated football, opens one of his silly stories co-written with Adolfo Bioy Casares, "Esse est percipi" from their *Crónicas de Bustos Domecq* [*Chronicles of Bustos Domecq*, 1967], with the lines: "As an old tourist of Núñez and the places around it, I noticed that the monumental stadium was missing from where it should have been." The tale continues whimsically about soccer becoming virtual, a mental game. In the church Nuestra Señora de Luján del Buen Viaje on calle Grecia is a ceramic mural by Raúl Soldi. Mentioned innocently by Sánchez Sorondo, the infamous Escuela de Mecánica de la Armada was one of the places for torturing and "disappearing" people in the *guerra sucia.* You cannot walk or take the bus past it without feeling sick.

Saavedra

On the train line after Belgrano R comes Saavedra. Marechal's novel about the last days of his poet hero includes a visit to the *barrio* Saavedra, where the Amundsen family have their *tertulias* (and where Adán's secret sweetheart lives). This *barrio*, named after Cornelio Saavedra, first president of Argentina's first governing body, has many tree-lined streets and a "Saavedra Park" filled in above a lake. The neighborhood was set up in 1891 when the Saavedra station started functioning. Its parish church was founded in 1932, its facade a copy of the Universidad de Chuquisaca in Bolivia; inside the church Raúl Soldi made a ceramic mural depicting Christ's birth. The pink Museo Histórico Saavedra, on Crisólogo Larraide 6309, is housed in the original 1870 *estancia* house. Like Villa Crespo, Saavedra represents the real city and its limits, for as the philosopher Tesler says: "I like the landscape of Saavedra, a heart-rending landscape where the city peters out." Marechal gives Saavedra a mythical status in the opening of book three of his novel *Adán Buenosayres*:

> In the city of Trinidad and port of Santa María de los Buenos Aires there exists a frontier region where the city and deserted pampas meet in a combative embrace, like two giants in a special fight. Saavedra is the name that cartographers have given to this mysterious region.
>
> The tourist who turns his back to the city and lets his eyes wander over that landscape will soon feel a vague shock of fear: over there, on a broken-up, chaotic plot of land you can see the last foothills of Buenos Aires, unbaked earth-brick shacks and corrugated iron dens inside which frontier tribes, stuck between the city and the country, move about; there as a promise of the horizon you can see the face of the immense pampas appear... During the day the sunlight and the happy throb of the metropolis conceal the true face of that suburb. But when night falls, when Saavedra is no more than vast desolation, the area strips off its brave profile; and the tourist wandering about there can find himself, suddenly, facing mystery itself. Then, on ground level, you can hear the beating of obscure life.

Only those who live there in their *tapera* [hut], like the "poor *ciruja*" [tramp] in his tin shack, can hear at night the horses of the Indian *malones* [marauders]. Marechal's novel is a long parable about authentic Argentine identity, found only in the obscure *barrios* on the margins of the city.

Vicente López

Continuing along either Cabildo or Libertador you reach Vicente López, outside the city limits established by the Avenida General Paz, named after the writer of the national anthem and once a place of small, rustic houses, called *chalets*, along the riverbank. A cultural attraction is the Museo de la Fundación Rómulo Raggio, on Gaspar Campos 861, a grand, decaying Italianate house, with a tower and a Mansard roof once set in a park (now sold to developers). Still belonging to the Raggio family but donated as a museum in 1961, the house contains collections of modern art including Antonio Berni and Raquel Forner, and a theatre. Raggio (1876-1960) was a founder member of the Mercado de Valores; his opulent weekend palace has a surprising round-domed auditorium, with painted ceilings and special acoustic designs. There is also an art library named after the artist Horacio Ruiz y Pombo.

Ezequiel Martínez Estrada recalled visiting the great short-story writer Horacio Quiroga in 1928 in Vicente López. Quiroga preferred living in San Ignacio in Misiones province, where many of his stories dramatize the struggle of unprepared and vulnerable city-dwellers against an ominous semi-tropical nature, and where the house he built himself is now a museum. Martínez Estrada described Quiroga's Vicente López house:

> The chalet was a kind of broken-down bungalow, with country furniture, and a garage-shed-drawing room was an antique shop where a helicopter and a dinosaur skeleton would not have been out of place.
>
> In the large patio there was the coatí cage, a friendly, sociable animal that Quiroga introduced us to as if a member of his family. In the house lived his children from his first marriage [his first wife had committed suicide, later Quiroga would himself]... The women prepared what could be called lunch while we drank and played with the coatí tied up with a thick chain. When Quiroga let it loose the coatí jumped on him and knocked him over. They played together like two animals.

San Isidro

Next stop north along Libertador, or on the coastal train, is San Isidro, a typical suburb virtually joined to the city, following the steep river bank some twelve miles from the city centre. The most celebrated literary beacon is Victoria Ocampo's colonial mansion Villa Ocampo (built by her father in 1890), donated as a museum to UNESCO in 1973, and today housing a Centro Internacional de Traducciones which you have to contact to arrange a visit. The English poet G. S. Fraser was there in 1947: "The quinta is a lovely place with a great pillared entrance hall rising through two stories, stripped woodwork and curly cornices on the doors." Here he met the communist writer María Rosa Oliver, who compared the old patrician society to the ancient *algarrobo* tree in the garden, dead and hollow inside, which "will fall, my dear, will fall." Victoria Ocampo lodged many of her intellectual guests in this imposing house, including the French essayist and publisher Roger Caillois who stayed there for four years during the Second World War – and was her lover- and managed to run a press and a newspaper (back in France, Caillois was instrumental in getting Borges translated and known). André Malraux, the novelist and later Gaullist Minister of Culture, Federico García Lorca, Graham Greene, Waldo Frank, Denis de Rougement, St. John Perse, Igor Stravinsky, and Jules Supervielle also stayed overnight, while those who lunched there include Pablo Neruda, Walter Gropius, Le Corbusier, Indira Gandhi and Antoine St. Exupéry. During the Peronist period the house was a target of hate when a cross was painted on the front gate, with "dissident oligarch" written across it. Alicia Jurado, in *El mundo de la palabra* [The world of the word, 1990] captured Villa Ocampo's garden with its old trees, fountain and statues, its lovely river view, its sweet-smelling jasmine and Santa Rita creepers, and the blue hydrangeas, typical of countless *porteño* gardens. She takes her reader around the vast house and the great hall hung with portraits of the Ocampos. In winter, wood-burning stoves kept the great house warm. Meetings took place in a room with a bay-window, and a table "covered with portraits of writer and artist friends of the house's owner": Lawrence Olivier, Igor Stravinsky, Paul Valéry and Aldous Huxley. Jurado found it a traditional house but one that accommodated modern tastes, with tapestries by Picasso and paintings by Figari.

When the Bengali Nobel Prize-winning poet Rabindranath Tagore (1861-1941) came to Argentina he fell ill and stayed for seven weeks nearby in a house called Miralrío, rented by Victoria Ocampo (she had had to sell diamonds to pay Tagore's rent). María Esther Vázquez described this rented San Isidro mansion as a "building that copied the Basque mountain houses with white wash and green shutters." In his poem "Guest," written in November 1924, translated by William Radice, Tagore speaks fondly of Victoria Ocampo—"Lady, you have filled these exile days of mine / with sweetness, made a foreign traveler your own"—as he stares out of the window at the "unfamiliar" southern sky.

Nearby on the same barranca is the national monument built in 1790, the Quinta Pueyrredón on Rivera Indarte 48, also known as the "chacra [farm] of the happy wood," which used to belong to General Juan Martín de Pueyrredón (1776-1850). Pueyrredón was one of the leaders, with Liniers, of the repulsion of the English invaders in 1807 and Director Supremo (equivalent to president, but with French revolutionary echoes) of the Provincias Unidas del Rio de la Plata from 1816 to 1820. On display is General Pueyrredón's book *Refutación a una atroz calumnia hecha con demasiado ligereza a un general de la República Argentina por Mr. Alejandro Everett, ministro plenipotenicario de los Estados Unidos* [Refutation of the atrocious slander made with levity about a general of the Argentine Republic by Mr. AE, roving minister of the United States of America, 1829], which sounds all too like a Borges spoof. General Pueyrredón was a friend of General San Martín, and father of Argentina's greatest nineteenth-century portraitist Prilidiano Pueyrredón (1823-1870), some of whose paintings hang in the museum. Pueyrredón fils painted over 140 portraits, including those of Rivadavia, Manuelita Rosas, his own father and the woman who refused to marry him, Magdalena Costa Ituarte, as well as notable landscapes. A note says that his 1865 painting "La Naranjera" [The orange seller] fetched over $150,000 in an auction. Prilidiano used the house's mirador [tower] as his studio, and designed the garden. This painter is a character in César Aira's witty novel *La liebre* [*The Hare*, 1991] about a nineteenth-century English naturalist seeking a rare hare during Rosas' reign. He rides out to meet Prilidiano in San Isidro:

> *Prilidiano's siesta was shorter than usual that afternoon, but it was not without its disturbing phantoms, which was normal, far too normal. It was pure habit, as with children. And this man, so important for Argentine history in his century, had a great deal of the child about him. He was plump, impetuous, imprudent, fearful, a slave to his passions, the plaything of the wildest fantasies. Every day he conjured up this theatre of horror within the confines of his villa at the top end of San Isidro village.*

Prilidiano also died in this house, which has an inner patio, a Doric columned gallery and a stunning view over the river and the Tigre Delta islands. A small library with material on Argentine history and literature, donated by a priest, is being catalogued. In this venerable house's garden stands an *aguaribay* tree planted by Sarmiento, and a 200-year-old collapsing *algarrobo*, under which San Martín and General Pueyrredón plotted the liberation of South America. In 1955 the Polish writer Witold Gombrowicz, exiled in Argentina, strolled through San Isidro on the slope with "the immobile river gleaming in the distance, colored like a lion," and saw the Pueyrredón house in the shade of eucalyptus trees, "white, secular, windows closed, uninhabited since Prilidiano abandoned it... with its neo-classical pillars." For inexplicable reasons, Gombrowicz felt haunted by this house (did it remind him of his aristocratic childhood in a Poland he could not return to?), so it became "a cursed house that burst into my inner world." He could only guess at the cause of such anguish: "my only home is this house, yes, unfortunately, my only home is this house, Pueyrredón's uninhabited white house."

Prilidiano was also an architect, redesigning the Pirámide in the Plaza de Mayo and the garden of the house in Olivos, nearer Buenos Aires, that is now the President of Argentina's summer residence. This official residence, once belonging to Miguel de Azcúenaga, was first used by President Agustín B. Justo in 1936 and was more recently occasionally occupied by President Menem, who lived there with his daughter Zulema. Estranged from his Syrian-born wife, Menem's presidency was marked by constant, mordant gossip.

José Mármol evoked 1840s Olivos in *Amalia*: "Following the road along the Bajo, that leads to Buenos Aires and San Isidro, you find, some three leagues from the city, a stopping place called Los Olivos, and also some forty or fifty trees of this name, the remains of an old wood which gave its name to this place... Los Olivos, on a small rise to the left of the road, gives you a good view of the wide river, the long coast and the cliffs of San Isidro." That was where Amalia converted a ruined house to live in, away from Rosas' spies.

It is well worth walking around San Isidro, a village founded in 1706 by Domingo de Acasusso but first settled by Garay on June 11, 1580, thus making San Isidro older than Buenos Aires. An early view of the village was painted by the English painter Vidal, who was stationed between 1816 and 1818 off Buenos Aires on HMS *Hyacinth*, and painted the first documentary sketches of the city (according to Alejo

González Garaño's research) and its people. A view of the first chapel built by Domingo de Acassuso with one spire at the side of the nave, next to a row of poor flat-roofed adobe houses, painted from Mariquita Sánchez de Thompson's *quinta* – a house later owned by the Beccar Varela family and partially donated to the nation—was published in Vidal's *Picturesque Illustrations of Buenos Aires and Montevideo...* (1820). Acassuso's chapel was demolished and replaced by a twin-towered white colonial church, itself demolished in 1896 and replaced in 1905 by a neo-Gothic cathedral, with a single tall spire built by two French architects. The nearby shady Plaza Mitre, with lime trees and *tipas blancas* and a statue of Mitre, has a Sunday arts and crafts fair on the grand stairs rolling down the *barranca*. Near the 1876 Municipalidad on calle 25 de Mayo is a Biblioteca Popular, dating from 1873, that organizes "paseos literarios" (and where we saw a boater-hatted octogenarian totter out with Shakespeare's *The Tempest* in his hands). By the church is a plaque informing passers-by that the autodidact naturalist Francisco Javier Muñiz (1795-1871) was born there. Sarmiento wrote a book on him, collecting his scientific writings in 1885. Muñiz was a military doctor who excavated fossils in Luján and was famous for discovering the "tiger fossil" (*Smilodon bonaerensis*). He also wrote a book on the pampas rhea, *El ñandú o avestruz americano*

Vidal's painting of San Isidro (Picturesque Illustrations)

(1848). Muñiz corresponded with Charles Darwin who cited him in his works. Aong the banks (*lomas*) are huge mansions like the Sans Souci and the grounds of the Jockey Club, with its racecourse. The coastal train, *el tren de la costa*, has been rehabilitated, begins at Maipú station and passes along the foot of the *barrancas* past a station called Borges - not for once named after the writer Jorge Luis, but an ancestor Colonel Francisco Borges (1833-1874), whose life Borges summarized in a poem: "Because that was your life: a thing dragged along by battles" - as far as Tigre. The old San Isidro station has been artfully renovated, with shops, walkways, and good bars to sit in.

Tigre

This fierce-sounding village is where the coastal railway lines end and where the ubiquitous *colectivo* number 60 stops. For many *porteños* it is the point of contact with sub-tropical South America, a weekend place of rivers, islands (some 3,221 of them) and canals in which to escape the city's fumes and smogs, as well as a quiet place to fish (*boga, dorado, pacú, patí, pejerrey, tararira, surubí* and *bagre*, catfish, the only translatable one of the list). Ricardo Piglia's novel *La ciudad ausente* [The absent city, 1992] ends up on the Santa Marta island in the Tigre Delta. As Junior, the investigator, hires a boat he realizes that the Delta is part of a "lost continent," that entering it is like "crossing a frontier that led to the past"— familiar sensations for any *porteño*.

An early advocate was the bookseller Marcos Sastre who wrote his naturalist's study of the Tigre Delta *El Tempe argentino* in 1856 when it was still uninhabited and the canals were clean. Writing to instruct his fellow countrymen, Sastre explains the word "delta": "The Paraná river mouth is land formed by floods and detritus, called the *delta* for its triangular shape, similar to the Greek letter of that name. The Paraná delta comprises three river branches called the Paraná de las Palmas, Paraná Mini, and the Paraná Guazú, through which the river disembogues into the River Plate in the shape of a huge isosceles triangle." His view of the area set the tone for later representations, including Gordon Meyer's bucolic version: "the island-studded delta mazed by a thousand cinnamon channels and green with the falling tears of a million willows."

Violet Bell, the English nanny, is taken for a picnic to Tigre and the Paraná Delta islands in Isobel Strachey's evocative novel *A Summer in Buenos Aires* (1947), where she describes one of the natural canals: "Boat-houses made of light planks or corrugated iron painted white and deep blue sloped into the brown lapping water, alternating with long banks of hydrangea bushes with great, round, light blue flowers and light green leaves, behind these were little white chalets and bungalows covered with trellis-work and long wooden balconies and verandas." River buses travel down most of the canals, and there are *recreos* to eat or spend the night in, from popular ones to El Tropezón, an old-fashioned hotel where the poet (and later fascist) Leopoldo Lugones poisoned himself with cyanide in room nine on February 18, 1937. The suicide note has been framed in the room; in it he forbids anything being named after him, wants to be buried anonymously in the ground, claims full responsibility for his act, and admits that he just couldn't finish his biography of General Roca—"enough!" he scrawled. Here you can sit and eat on the large terrace, or in winter in the glassed-in restaurant under the corrugated tin roof, as huge cargo boats loom past. This is one of my favorite days out from the city.

At the beginning of the twentieth century there was a grandiose Tigre Hotel where Darío penned his great poem "Divagación" [Digression] which he called a course in erotic geography, collected in *Prosas profanas* (1896). Tigre was known by Anglos as the "Henley" of Buenos Aires, and still displays delightful boat houses like the Tigre Boat Club, founded in 1888, or the Club Canottieri Italiani, founded in 1910 and designed as a Venetian palace. These stately monuments to wealth and leisure are somewhat at odds with what Roberto Arlt called the "putrid smell of stagnant water." But despite this distaste for the Delta's contents, Arlt had his ashes scattered in a Tigre canal.

On the river Luján, near the Los Ciruelos docks, the eccentric and inventive painter Xul Solar (1887-1963) built a house, with a studio where he painted his "Proyecto Fachada Delta" (Project Delta Façade), a series of colorful huts on stilts. Xul Solar died in this Tigre house (as already mentioned, his town house is the best museum in Buenos Aires, on calle Laprida 1214, where Borges would call and discuss Swedenborg and the German mystics). Domingo Sarmiento, ex-President and author of *Facundo,* one of the most influential essays ever written on Latin America, discovered the Tigre Delta in the 1850s and lived in three different places. One was a grand house on land that he cleared and replanted himself on the island La Prócida de Carapachay between the river Abra Ancha and the Reyes stream in a place called La Reculada, where he summered during his presidency of Argentina (1868-1874). Another is today the Museo Sarmiento, where his simple, three-roomed house stood on stilts on what has been re-named the Río Sarmiento. This house was partially destroyed by a bomb in 1964. Inside are the anchor chain from his river boat *Talita,* donated by the British, and a bust by sculptor Luis Perlotti; outside another bust, the only one made during Sarmiento's lifetime, by Víctor de Pol. His first house, bought in 1855 on what is today the Isla Sarmiento, was described by his biographer Leopoldo Lugones as "three huts built with rustic planks, with no luxuries." It did, however, have a coop for his rheas, a vegetable garden and eucalyptus fire wood. By all accounts, he lived like a pioneer. Sarmiento planted new species like the *mimbre amarillo* from Chile, and a plaque records the planting ceremony in 1855. Sarmiento wrote many articles extolling the exuberant nature of the Delta.

Martínez Estrada recalled accompanying Horacio Quiroga on a mock-heroic adventure in a self-made sail boat through the Tigre Delta (Quiroga was a proficient carpenter and built his own house in Misiones): "we left for the island of Ogigia or the Bermudas. After getting round the channels of the Gran Capitán he entered the River Plate. I do not know if it was the water or his use of the rudder that made the boat jolt like a horse, convulsions of a marine nag. Half the boat stuck up in the air, so that you couldn't tell whether we were sailing or flying. I hung on to the side of the canoe, alert to a sudden turn that might throw me into the waters... "

The writer most associated with the Tigre Delta is the "disappeared" Haroldo Conti (1925-1976), who knew the riverways backwards, and set his first novel *Sudeste* [Southeast, 1962] around San Fernando and the river Anguilas. Conti refers to numerous canals, islands, *recreos,* fish and buoys. The novel follows an old man who survives this backwater by rowing and fishing (*bagres, pejerreyes*), sometimes cutting reeds, and meeting up with fellow *vagos* [drifters]. The book opens by evoking this wilderness so close to the city:

Between the Pajarito channel and the open river, curving sharply towards the north, getting narrower and narrower to almost halfway up, then opening and zigzagging until its mouth, the Anguilas stream snakes along, hidden by the first islands. Open river, ruffled by the wind, appears suddenly after the last curve. Despite its immensity the water is very shallow. From the mouth of the San Antonio channel to the outlet of the Luján river it is all sand bank. The Anguilas turns in the middle of the bank, in a flat land of reeds. Depending on how you look, the place is desolate on a gray day, when its windy, and scares anybody.

Far to the left the Santa Mónica island appears dark and silent, like a ship. Far to the right, vanishing in a blueish distance, the coast. On a clear day you can just see, to the south, the grey and white outlines, like stage settings, of Buenos Aires's taller buildings, under the constant oppression of a grey cloud.

One last literary association with the Delta is perhaps worth mentioning; the Guatemalan writer Miguel Angel Asturias finished his classic novel about the degeneration of the Maya Indian, *Hombres de maíz* and wrote the whole of *Mulata de tal* [*Mulata and Mr. Fly*, 1963] in his Tigre hut, Shangrí-la (Isla Blanca) on the Río Sarmiento.

Martín García

My favorite island for a long day trip was named after a sailor buried there from Solis' expedition in 1580. This thickly wooded island of 415 acres is on the oldest geological outcrop in South America, and rises ninety feet high. The French botanist Aimé Bonpland, Humboldt's faithful companion during their five year journey round South America, sailed there in 1817 and discovered the *mate* bushes which led to his passion for "Jesuit green tea" and fourteen years in a Paraguay prison for trying to grow it under the despot Dr. Francia. In 1814 Admiral Brown and his *gaucho* sailors had taken the strategically important island back from José Caparro, who had invaded the year before. In 1825 the Brazilians captured the granitic rock. In 1845 the Italian freedom fighter Garibaldi took it. It was held by the British for four years until 1849 as a bastion from which to blockade the river. In 1850, in his essay *Argirópolis,* Sarmiento thought this small island would make an excellent capital for Argentina. In 1874 Sarmiento more prosaically made the island a quarantine station for arriving boats.

Until relatively recently (1957), the island was mainly a prison, holding presidents Marcelo T. Alvear, Hipólito Yrigoyen (who spent fifteen months there in 1930), Perón (four days) and Frondizi (eleven months) at different moments. A plaque commemorates Rubén Darío's stay there in 1895, where he tried to cure his alcoholism and wrote his public poem "Triumphant March," celebrating May 25th, published first in the newspaper *La Nación*. Now open to the public, the island lies some three hours by boat from San Fernando (Tigre). The island is today a nature reserve with thickly wooded parts, lagoons, old quarries and reeds (I once nearly stepped on a coiled poisonous coral snake). Its amenities include a lighthouse, a landing strip, an abandoned *barrio chino* surrounded by a dense bamboo wood, a gun battery placed there by Sarmiento to control shipping, the house Darío stayed in (today a Centro de Interpretación Ecológica), a Museo Histórico and a twelve-roomed Hostería where visitors can stay overnight.

Latter-day compradito (Harriet Cullen)

PART FOUR

The South

"However much he may have seen and heard, he knows that the inner core of the city has escaped him, that place where a common blood pulsates and which, if discovered, could make the city his too."
José Saramago

El Sur (de la Ciudad) and San Telmo

"Every Argentine knows that the South begins at the other side of Rivadavia." According to Borges, El Sur starts once you cross Rivadavia, where you enter "an older, more solid world." Avenida Rivadavia divides the city in two, and it is where all the north-south streets change their name. Florida becomes Perú, Reconquista turns into Defensa, San Martín is henceforth Bolívar. Alberto Salas called it the "*porteño* axis, veritable plant stock from which the whole city takes its life." Supposedly the longest street in the world (an oft-quoted tourist board boast) it reaches beyond number 20,000. The South was the smart side of town under Rosas until the yellow fever epidemics of 1870 and 1871, which wiped out ten percent of the population and drove the wealthier survivors north to what is today the *barrio norte*. The insalubrious Riachuelo river was thought to be the prime factor in the disease's spread. The move north allowed the richest 200 families to build anew, in the opulent French styles of the day.

The best way to walk back into the past is to take calle Defensa (the old Calle Real del Puerto) from the Plaza de Mayo; it's the direct route on

Sundays to the San Telmo fair on Plaza Dorrego. On the junction with calle Alsina you walk past a Plazoleta de las Estatuas, where you can have your portrait drawn. On this junction is the Estrella pharmacy, built in 1894, which has preserved its *fin-de-siècle* furnishings. Above the chemist is the modest, quirky Museo de la Ciudad (Alsina 412), run by the man who knows more about Buenos Aires than anyone, the architect José María Peña. It organizes changing displays of historical and domestic trivia (I overheard an old woman say: "I recognize so much from my home. I didn't realize that we are history"), and contains a small reference library. Next door on Alsina is a moody art-deco café dating from 1925, the Puerto Rico, with its ceiling fans, brown pillars and delicious snacks. When you reach calle Perú, you are at what in 1821 was baptized the "manzana de las luces" [block of enlightenment], where the old university stands. The institution was originally occupied by the Jesuits from 1633 until their expulsion from the New World by the Spanish crown in 1767 (Rosas allowed them back in 1836 and expelled them again in 1841). The building where the Jesuits used to store their tea, tobacco and other produce from their estates in Guayrá became the University of Buenos Aires in 1822, housing the Department of Exact Sciences in 1865. The facade was designed by the French architect and painter Carlos Pellegrini in 1863, but was partially destroyed in the opening of the Diagonal Sur boulevard in the early years of the twentieth century. Parts, however, are still visible in the inner patio. In her memoirs *Descubrimiento del mundo* [Discovery of the world, 1989], Alicia Jurado describes the Jesuit cloisters as "permanently in repair where you would always see piles of bricks and sand" and recalls that the building was cold, uncomfortable "and eminently anti-functional." Next to these cloisters stands the Iglesia de San Ignacio, the oldest remaining church in Buenos Aires, founded by the Jesuits who arrived in the city in 1608, first built a chapel here in 1675 and constructed the existing church in 1722. From 1822 to 1836 it was the city's cathedral. Inside the church is a virgin, Nuestra Señora de las Nieves, dating from 1611. Underneath are tunnels (which can be visited from calle Perú 222) dug by the Jesuits in case they had to flee persecutors. Poet Enrique Banchs mimicked the church bells "Don—don, from San Ignacio, / tin—tin, from the Monjitas / the bell of the old lady, / the bell of the young maiden"; the bells were cast in 1845 and 1869.

On calle Perú, between Victoria and Alsina, once stood the Club del Progreso, founded in 1852 to celebrate the national reconciliation and become the political and social headquarters of the city's affluent society. In 1900 it moved to an imposing building on the Avenida de Mayo 633, which lay empty for years. Lucio López sets a grand ball in the Perú building in his 1884 novel *La gran aldea*. For the "old-guard *porteños*," the Club was "a dream mansion." López asserts: "It's in the Club del Progreso where one can best study Buenos Aires" social life in thirty-year periods." He describes the entrance, the card-room and the dining room "that we all know." Alas, the place is no longer so familiar to readers, so his advice that "one dines execrably in the Club del Progreso" means little. There was also the library (without books): "In spite of everything anyone would think the people read there... Nothing of the sort! There they talked."

From this long-gone palace we jump to calle Moreno, where the poet and novelist José Mármol lived near the Palladian Colegio Nacional. This establishment provided the setting for Miguel Cané's *Juvenilia* (1882), his memoirs of his boarding-school days there from 1863-1870 and one of the best accounts of growing up in all of Argentine literature. Originally, from 1732, it was a Jesuit College. Under Rivadavia's presidency it became the Colegio de Ciencias Morales, and in 1863 President Mitre turned it into the Colegio Nacional. The current columned building was designed by Norberto Maillart in 1910 and finished in 1938. Albert Einstein was officially received here in 1925 when he arrived to give lectures in Buenos Aires. The poet Baldomero Fernández Moreno lamented the "modernizing" of the Colegio Nacional: "Relentless time wields its pickaxe. / Where is my old Nacional Central? / This grand palace means nothing to me, / there are so many others like it in the city." It has monumental Doric columns, a vast marble staircase, a library and a "flag" room, which you can tour with a guide.

Juan Manuel de Rosas (sometimes spelt Rozas), the rich and well-bred landowner who became dictator of Buenos Aires and ruled with terror, lived on this same calle Moreno. His regime, permeated by what José Mármol called "the disease of fear," lasted seventeen years, aided by his secret police the *Mazorca*. He forced everyone to wear the red federal ribbons to show their support for him, and even moustaches had to be cut in a special, federal way. Rosas drove many of his enemies into exile or death. He had the street named Restaurador in 1836 but it remained known ironically as calle La Biblioteca (the library). There are memorable scenes in Rosas' house in Mármol's novel *Amalia* set in 1840, as well as dialogues between Rosas, then a widower, and his adored daughter Manuelita. Rosas lived frugally, and Mármol described the dictator's centre of operations as being a bare room, with one table, chairs against the wall, a dirty kitchen just off, all around a patio without trees. This house that Rosas shared with his wife Encarnación ("this Lady Macbeth" in biographer Fleur Cowles' words) was painted red, was more a public meeting-place than a home and was certainly the headquarters of all spying activity, run by his astute wife. The naturalist W. H. Hudson's family hung two colored portraits in their drawing room in Quilmes of Rosas, known also as the "Tiger of Palermo," the "Nero of South America" or simply the "Englishman" because he was fair and blue-eyed. His wife's portrait, on the other hand, showed her with black hair piled high and "black unloving eyes [that] gazed straight back into ours." Lucio Mansilla, in *Mis memorias* [My memoirs, 1904], described his uncle Rosas: "My uncle was short, gaunt, agile, methodical, indefatigable while working, at home on a horse, full of manias like all the Rosas, and never tiring of them. He would rather be garroted than admit he was cold or hot or had had enough."

Also on Moreno (350) is the 1880 Museo Etnográfico Juan B. Ambrosetti built by Pedro Benoit and part of the Universidad de Buenos Aires. With its Doric-columned facade and tall palms, it is open to the public and successfully counters the prejudice that Argentina had no pre-Conquest past worthy of curiosity. Then, as we're on Moreno, it takes only a hop to reach the old Quinta de Maza, once the Prefectura de Policía, a whole block between Moreno, Belgrano, Cevallos and Sáenz Peña, inaugurated in 1899. In *News from a Foreign Country* (1991), novelist Alberto Manguel depicted this police station that all returning Argentines from abroad had to visit to renew their passports:

> *The Central Police Headquarters in Buenos Aires has the air of an Italian palazzo seen through distorting lenses. It squats in the centre of the older part of town, too large on the sides and sunken on the top, stained*

with age and crumbling. Long queues of people waiting for papers (documents are issued here) serpent their way around it, and from rickety booths police guards with machine guns survey the doors.

Manguel's character enters this building, climbs the "palatial stairs" which smell of urine and disinfectant, and walks "countless corridors," past women in white pinafores carrying "fat cream-colored folders," into the bureaucratic nightmare of Kafka's Castle. Note in passing that the adjective "Kafka" ("*Qué Kafka!*") is commonly used in Buenos Aires, as bureaucratic red-tape is a minefield, to mix metaphors. Fortunately, the passport procedure has been modernized, and the place for renewals changed to calle Azopardo.

Back to Defensa, you pass the Museo Nacional del Grabado (Defensa 372) and Bernardino Rivadavia's house at Defensa 350 (only its original facade has been preserved, and there is evidence that he never actually lived there, but on Defensa 145) and then cross the lorry-clogged Avenida Belgrano, which links the port via a bridge, passing the Santo Domingo church and convent, founded in 1603, with the current church completed in 1779. One of its towers is incrusted with bullets from the English invasion of 1807 (the lead pellets replaced by wood to make them visible). Inside are framed regimental flags taken from the English. The nautical painter E. Vidal painted this church in 1817, with its blue tiled dome and spire, and its women going to church without hats (the servants wore *rebozos* and the mistresses *mantillas*). All carried fans; one servant clutches a rug for her mistress to kneel on because the church had no pews. Most travelers of the period commented that only the women seemed to like going to church. In 1822, in a republican purge, Rivadavia expelled the Dominican monks from the church named after their order and allowed an astronomical observatory to be installed until Rosas brought the monks back in 1836. There is a 1585 virgin "del Rosario," known, inevitably, as "de la Reconquista y la Defensa," a 1773 San Vicente Ferrer carved in wood, and Manuel Belgrano's mausoleum. The church has one of the oldest libraries in the city.

Where Defensa hits México is the café Almafuerte, named after the popular poet whose real name was Pedro Bonifacio Palacios (1854-1917), of whom Borges said he was "unjustly forgotten." It stands on the corner facing the ornate wedding-cake that was the Antigua Casa de Moneda, or Mint, built between 1879-1881 and now an art gallery. Turning west, you will soon reach the site of the former Biblioteca Nacional on calle México 564. The earliest library, on Perú and Moreno, was mooted by the revolutionary Rivadavia in October 1810, soon after the demonstration in the Plaza de Mayo that confirmed the parting of the ways with Spain. It opened in 1812, with Manuel Moreno in charge and a donation of 3,000 volumes, mainly Jesuit books from Córdoba. By 1825 it had 12,000, but during the Rosas years and suffering a series of crises it was continually out of funds. An early director was Marcos Sastre, then the writer José Mármol (1818-1873), followed by Vicente G. Quesada and José Antonio Wilde.

This second Biblioteca Nacional opened in 1901, having been originally designed in 1896 by an Italian architect, Carlo Morra, as the National Lottery (Borges relished this irony). The French historian and critic Paul Groussac, born in Toulouse like Carlos Gardel, arrived in Buenos Aires in 1866, was director from 1885 to 1929 and oversaw the move. He lived with his family in a flat on top in calle México, and, blind at the end of his life, died there. He was apparently something of a tyrant, and when writing his excellent biographies forbade his family to talk; his nickname was the "ogre." Under Perón, the anti-Semitic and popular novelist Hugo Wast was director from 1931 until Borges, though semi-blind, was nominated in 1955 after Perón's fall. He explained the attraction of the library: "Leaving behind the sounds of the plaza I enter the Library. At once, in an almost physical way, I feel the gravitation of the books... ordered things, the past rescued and magically preserved." The reading room sported busts of writers and a lovely blue-glassed dome. V. S. Naipaul visited Borges there in 1972 and was disheartened:

> *The white and pale blue Argentine flag that hangs out into Mexico Street is dingy with dirt and fumes. And consider this building, perhaps the finest in the area... There is beauty still in the spiked wall, the tall iron gates, the huge wooden doors. But inside, the walls peel; the windows in the central patio are broken; farther in, courtyard opening into court-yard, washing hangs in a corridor, steps are broken, and a metal spiral staircase is blocked with junk.*

Before taking over the Biblioteca Nacional, Borges worked for nine years, following the death of his father in 1938, at the "lugubrious" Biblioteca Municipal Miguel Cané (Carlos Calvo 4319), under his friend the poet Francisco Luis Bernárdez. He was sacked by Perón in 1946 and famously humiliated by being made government inspector of fowl, eggs and rabbits in the capital's markets. In his essay on Buenos Aires, *La cabeza de Goliat* [Goliath's head, 1943], Ezequiel Martínez Estrada praised the silence of the national library: "The Biblioteca Nacional is solemn and severe like the inside of a Parliament. The museum silence falls like heavy pleated curtains from the ceiling, from the bookshelves, in a compact silence of books."

Just before reaching the now abandoned Biblioteca Nacional, you face the building which once accommodated the Sociedad Argentina de Escritores (Argentine Society of Writers), mocked by its acronym SADE, on calle México 524. The association was founded by Leopoldo Lugones in 1925 and located in Victoria Ocampo's old family house. Its first president was the often-quoted-in-this-book-poet Baldomero Fernández Moreno. Borges was elected president under Perón from 1950 to 1953. The critic and biographer María Esther Vázquez described this building as "a large colonial house with a long entrance hall (*zaguán*) and carved iron grilles, a series of rooms lined along the right of patios with black and white marble stones and high ceiling crossed with beams." In the central patio there was a shade-giving *Santa Rita* creeper. Borges also liked the place, calling it one of his favorite "colonial" buildings. Alicia Jurado also recalled this house and its library above the second patio, reached by a narrow staircase which led to the "poets' balcony," where poems were recited in the annual Fiesta de Poesía. In her days SADE had some 1,500 members, but Jurado reckoned that only some fifty were real writers (to join you had to have something, anything, published). Important celebrations were held on June 13, the Day of the Writer, when SADE issued its *fajas* [sashes or slips around books] *de honor*. Jurado became its secretary in 1959, the only woman in the group that ran the place. It has since moved to Uruguay 1371, and the building has been converted into the Casa José Hernández, a Centro Cultural, with a Biblioteca Popular and the inevitable patios named after Borges and Manuel Mujica Lainez (known as "Manucho").

El Sur today draws tourists on Sundays to its antique and junk fair at San Telmo on the Plaza Dorrego, which during the week can be quiet. The square has outdoor cafés, a shady *gomero* tree, restaurants and restored houses, which includes the Fundación Forner-Bigatti, the studio and home of Raquel Forner and her sculptor husband, which can be visited on Bethlen 443. Also on the Plaza Dorrego, a plaque signals the Romantic, socialist poet Esteban Echevarría's (1805-1851) birthplace. A block further south is the Modern Art Museum on Avenida San Juan 350, built in 1915 as the municipal tobacco warehouse, and on calle Humberto the attractive, tiled San Telmo church (officially Nuestra Señora de Belén), founded by the Jesuits in 1734 but not completed until much later, with an image of San Rafael, patron saint of fishermen, inside. Next to it is the 1735 Buen Pastor prison for women, formerly run by nuns, where Victoria Ocampo spent twenty-six days in 1953 and which is now a prison museum. Opposite is the neo-colonial Guillermo Rawson school, shaded by trees, once the Bethlemite monastery, then the medical faculty, and from 1897 a school. Further down calle Humberto 1 is the publishing house Sudamericana, founded by a Spanish exile from Franco to become one of the most prestigious literary publishing houses (*editoriales*) in the New World. Sudamericana published the unknown Colombian Gabriel García Márquez's *Cien años de soledad [One Hundred Years of Solitude]* in 1967.

A parallel street to Defensa, also beginning in the Plaza de Mayo, is calle Balcarce, which runs along the *barrancas*. A stroll down this street leads you past many tango clubs and bars, including El Viejo Almacén and Tango Sur, as well as the sculptor Rogelio Yrurtia's 1907 "Canto al Trabajo" – shiny bronze musclemen dragging a boulder - and the painter Juan Carlos Castagnino's (1908-1972) restored house (it was a post office under Rosas). The novelist Roberto Mariani detailed the "peculiar architecture" of calle Balcarce as a mix of modern warehouses with "ancient patrician houses, with humble facades covered in vines, with iron-barred windows and doors of carved wood, but unfinished, and roofs made of tiles that are so low that you fear one might fall on to you."

A more typical version of the Sur in the late 1930s and 1940s, before tourism found its crumbling buildings picturesque, emerges in Silvina

Bullrich's novel *Calles de Buenos Aires*, where Gloria and her sister wander on foot:

> They set off along the grey streets of the barrio sur. That city did not appear to be the same one that bustled with life on Florida or Corrientes, it was a forgotten corner of old Buenos Aires. Even the way people walked was slower, almost halting. But this place did not inspire calm, on the contrary there was an anguish of things deteriorating. It was the death agony of a provincial city, badly built, insecure.

Around the same period, in his mock epic *Canto a Buenos Aires* [Song to Buenos Aires, 1943], Manuel Mujica Lainez evokes the South and its decadence into a slum. He writes: "of the houses in the Sur with patios and grilles / that hide a vine or an old palm tree / and whose sole ornament, on a naked wall, / is a new plaque with laurel leaves and coat of arms, / against whose inscription: Here Lived... bounces / the insolent football kicked by the boys from the barrio." In its scorn for football, the proletarian activity, you hear a dying class moan through Mujica Lainez's voice. In the mind of the young, vagabond Borges the Sur was dangerous: "Behind its suspicious walls / the Sur keeps a dagger and a guitar." The Sur was where the *saladeros* (salting factories) were located, polluting the air and waters, but giving jobs. At the turn of the century, the abandoned old houses of the rich became *conventillos* (tenements), each room lodging a large immigrant family. Haroldo Conti described such a way of living in his novel *Alrededor de la jaula* [Around the cage, 1967], where the old man Silvestre, who runs a merry-go-round on the Costanera Sur, lives on Independencia and Balcarce:

> on the flat roof [azotea] of a complicated house for rent with two entrances and a labyrinth of corridors and staircases. Every now and then he would bump into a new partition, because it was a house that besides getting old, if it could get any older, changed its shape continuously…the flat roof was spacious… Silvestre had built at one end a shed and a kind of portico out of two pillars of small tin cans, which gave it all a friendly, independent air. The walls of the flat roof were low, but he had raised them with chicken wire, on which he'd grown the creeper dama de noche.

This was in the 1950s, when the area was already changing, with modern blocks dwarfing the remaining old houses like the one just described. The change in attitude to the Sur can be gauged by a cartoon in the newspaper *Clarín* by Crist that reworks the famous lyrics of Homero Manzi's tango "Sur" which opens: "Sur ... / high wall and after / Sur ... / a light at the almacén." In Crist's contemporary version, the old all-purpose shop, the *almacén*, today becomes "a light in the shopping mall…you'll see me relaxed in McDonalds, waiting for you." The Sur for most *porteños* is both a state of nostalgia for a simple, rougher past, and an up-to-date place, avidly welcoming North American fashions—an image of the mutating city itself.

Parque Lezama

Strolling further down either Defensa or Balcarce, you hit the old Parque Lezama, supposedly where Pedro de Mendoza first landed in 1536. Sabato identified the large statue that commemorates this event ("Buenos Aires made him immortal" engraved on the side): "There he stood, imperious and determined, don Pedro de Mendoza, pointing with his sword to the city which he had decided to found here: SANTA MARÍA DE LOS BUENOS AYRES, 1536. What barbarians, was the term he always used." What today is known as calle Martín García was in the 1840s named after an Irish-born Argentine national hero. According to *Amalia*, this "steep slope was named after the fierce admiral who fought a maritime war for the Republic against the Brazilian empire, because the house where he usually lived was nearby." The fierce admiral in question was William Brown (1777-1857), who helped defeat the blockading Brazilian fleet at the Victory of (the Isla) Juncal in 1825. As a sea-dog he had also fought off Peru, and set up the first packet service between Buenos Aires and Colonia in Uruguay in 1814. He lived in what is today a reconstructed square orange house with a tower (the huge Bombonera football stadium in La Boca looms behind it). Ana María Cabrera recounted the popular and tragic story of Brown's daughter Elisa who drowned herself in the Riachuelo in 1827, aged nineteen, after her *novio* (fiancé) had died: "mad with love she walked into the waters wearing her bride's dress. Tellingly, she was called the Ophelia of the River Plate." Lucio Mansilla lamented in 1904 at not being able to return to Brown's house, "our Nelson, old Brown, on whose knees I galloped." The river no longer reaches this *barranca*, just waves of cars and buses and lorries below.

Today's dusty and littered gardens once belonged to a summer house owned by Gregorio Lezama, which is now the fascinating, packed Museo Histórico Nacional, with its railings and square *mirador* (entrance on Defensa 1600). The museum is replete with historical bits and pieces from swords, to suits, medals, letters, writing desks and fascinating documentary paintings that convey Argentine history better than words. Horacio Vázquez Rial claims that the dungeons under the gardens were for African slaves. Outside, lovers stroll, lads play football, revealing ball skills related to cramped spaces, coffee-sellers do business, gangs of roaming kids throw stones at each other, families picnic in the dust. You have to guess how this park might have been. The gardens were bought by the city in 1884. There is an amphitheatre, and several statues, walks, a temple, even a place to play chess. Around the park is the Russian Orthodox Church completed in 1901, the first in South America, with five colorfully mosaiced onion-shaped domes. In 1937 the novelist Eduardo Mallea brought an American girl friend to this park and typically turned it into a heavy-handed symbol of old Argentine identity, when Argentina was really Argentina:

The old colonial park raised its hill in a luxuriant green amongst statues stained by the mud of constant rain... The park's railings had been destroyed; what was authentically old in this old Argentine park had been destroyed; all that remained was the dignified, modest and low house of the little museum with its watch tower [mirador] *that barely stood higher than the badly cut grass. His friend stopped and stared in amazement at the creole resignation of the old, disused park, that dignity that survives the violence of strangers' hands, that solemn simplicity in bad times, that proud severity against all kept women that gave its soul to that Argentine site.*

That the Parque Lezama strikes a symbolic chord in *porteños* can be seen with the novelist Ernesto Sabato who opens his *Sobre héroes y tumbas* with Martín being picked up by the sexy, destructive Alejandra under the statue of Ceres, still there in the park. Later Sabato wrote the words to a tango, with music by Aníbal Troilo, which began: "I have returned to that bench in Parque Lezama / now as then you can hear in the night / the dull siren of a distant boat. / My clouded eyes seek you in vain," as if he, Sabato (now almost blind), was Martín, waiting for "Alejandra" (the title of the tango). Baldomero Fernández Moreno's poem "Parque Lezama," written in 1941, recalls his youth flirting in the garden, "now riddled / by drizzle and lichen and loves, / supple with roots and creepers." It was a place where many like him had sought out "rotten foliage for our living mouths," where he would read Antonio Machado's poems and where "every statue was a throbbing Venus / every palm tree was from the East, / whilst outside the traffic throbbed / its howling wind of cars and people." A magic space outside the urban hell. In 1991 Borges and Maria Kodama brought the Mexican Nobel Prize-winning poet Octavio Paz to the park: "Borges wanted to show us the Russian Orthodox church, I don't know why, but it was closed... we happily walked the little damp paths under trees with large trunks and singing foliage. At the end, we stopped in front of the monument to the Roman She-Wolf and Borges tenderly touched Remo's head with his hands." This Loba Romana was a gift from Rome in 1923, a bronze copy of the one in the Campidoglio.

Borges was once arrested in the Parque Lezama for cuddling with Estela Canto (who had wanted to bed him, but he gentlemanly refused as they were not married); another time he sang a *milonga* to her and the visiting Spanish writer Franciso Ayala. Estela Canto described this park in her memoirs:

> We walked round and round the devastated park, that had little to do with the secret, exuberant and Romantic park of my childhood, with its railings covered in jasmine, its fences with lilies, a rose garden scenting the summer, a pond full of tadpoles, the arbors roofed with honeysuckle, its ravines and rock gardens. In the end, it was still the Parque Lezama, at least, a magic name for the kids of my generation, perhaps for Borges's. We sat down on the steps that look on to calle Brasil, in the ruined amphitheatre that tried to be a Greek theatre and failed. Opposite us was the blue dome, shaped like an onion, of the Russian Orthodox Church.

Perhaps, to answer Paz's question, Borges took Paz and his French wife Marie-José to the Russian Orthodox Church because it reminded him of Estela Canto and his own sexual failures. But in a very urban city like Buenos Aires, this old park was a paradise (a walled garden). As Cádiz-born poet Rafael Alberti wrote, "I drink the green wave raised by Parque Lezama."

La Boca

"*They say it was in the Riachuelo/ but those are lies forged in La Boca.*" Borges

From the river bank heights of the Parque Lezama you can watch the traffic below roar toward La Boca, the flat land reclaimed from the river. In the 1830s La Boca was where Lucio Mansilla went fishing. Immigration changed this rural aspect. The name comes from being the *boca* or mouth of the Riachuelo, where the second discoverer of Buenos Aires, Juan de Garay, first landed when waves still lapped the Parque Lezama. La Boca is the immigrant, essentially Genovese area, associated with tango and *lunfardo*, the dockside, underworld idiom of Buenos Aires. Built on low-lying land, it was often flooded, so the first shacks there were built on stilts and pavements were raised. Manuel Gálvez's well-born drop-out Monsalvat searches for his lost whore Nacha in the seedy and cosmopolitan La Boca of the centenary year 1910:

> He wandered all the barrio. He went to gambling dens, to brothels, to inns. He was in different bars and taverns and in each one they spoke a different language. Here you could hear sentences in English or German, and phrases in Norwegian or Russian or Finnish. He recognized the Balkan languages; there the Arabic dialects of North Africa. He entered a bar of Koreans, a Chinese restaurant. For a month he dealt with all kinds of people. A crowd of freeloaders, pathetic devils and delinquents passed in front of his eyes.

In another of Gálvez's novels, the short *Historia de arrabal* [History of a neighborhood, 1922], a doomed love affair is set completely in a topographically exact La Boca. This lurid story tells of a *frigorífico* [meat freezing plant] worker, Rosalinda, who falls for an anarchist Daniel. She is raped by her step-brother El Chino and made to work as a whore until El Chino's sexual magnetism (a strange scene in the novel) forces her to kill her anarchist love. The novel opens by describing "the walls and roofs of the Frigorífico, whose monumental buildings extended to the Riachuelo like an immense, high and compact white bulk." This grim place gives off a stink from the carcasses and blood. Gálvez picks out "calle Garibaldi as the heart of La Boca, of old Boca with its zinc-roofed and plank-built huts where everyone spoke Genovese dialect." The lovers meet in the Plaza Brown: "It was a poor plaza, an empty plot of land, with grass only at its edges and few trees. Through some branches you could vaguely see the svelte and simple Sáenz Peña shuttle bridge [*transbordador*]. An infinite silence subtly filled the plaza..." The vast metallic, rusting bridge, built in 1914, is now preserved as of cultural interest. They stroll through the Plaza Matheu, the dockside along the Riachuelo, and today's touristic Vuelta de Rocha. You can take the 152 colectivo from Avenida Santa Fe in the *barrio norte* and end up on this bend in the river called the Vuelta de Rocha, named after the first owner of the land, Colonel Juan José Rocha. In this bend in the river ships piled up side by side, a high masted jungle often painted by Quinquela Martín. Off the Vuelta is the atmospheric and popular alley, once a railway siding, called Caminito in 1959 after a tango by Juan de Dios Filiberto (a wonderful name).

In *Frontera sur* [Frontier south, 1994], a novel that matches the history of a family of Spanish immigrants with the development of the city of Buenos Aires, Horacio Vázquez Rial explains the origins of tango: "Barracas al Sur, la Boca, Avellaneda, tango musicians had to pass through these barrios: there you would find all the cafés, the brothels, and other indefinable joints: although tango had begun its rise up the social ladder, this languid song continued to grow in the outskirts [*las orillas*] of the city." So strange was La Boca to Borges that he said it was "the only point in Buenos Aires where nothing seemed like Buenos Aires, the only barrio where tourists came from other barrios." For La Boca remains different architecturally, the "tourist" part of the city, and not just for *porteños* but for foreigners (as illustrated in nearly all the guide books to the city). Apart from La Boca, Borges concluded, "the remaining suburbs of Buenos Aires are more or less the same. A street in Saavedra is like a street in Barracas or Villa Luro." The essayist Martínez Estrada echoed Borges' perception: "We penetrate the streets of La Boca and find ourselves in another country." The *criollo* (or native-born "white") drunk in Gálvez's *Historia del arrabal* refused to live in La Boca "because it is a 'barrio of gringos'"(meaning Italians).

Juan José Sebreli found that La Boca was for years the most dangerous *barrio* of Buenos Aires, mainly because of its brothels, whores and opium dens. One of the most infamous brothels, "El Farol Colorado" [the red lantern], used to be known for its porno films.

Gálvez transformed this part-cinema, part-brothel into "El Farol Rojo" [also the red lantern] in his La Boca-inspired novel. In the 1920s, heyday of this red light district, Buenos Aires was "the primary market for human flesh in the world." The reason was that seventy percent of immigrants between 1857 and 1924 were single young men who urgently wanted, and would pay for a woman. The French investigative reporter Albert Londres noted that "the city swarmed with males" and saw "men, nothing but men." One underworld gang of pimps called itself the Zwi Migdal, dressed as false rabbis and met in a phony synagogue on calle Córdoba; 500 male (if not erect) members controlled over 30,000 women. Zwi Migdal was closed down in 1930. The best account of this white slave trade is Londres' best-selling and sensationalist *The Road to Buenos Aires* (1928). The fearless journalist made friends with pimps and learned their secret language, discovering that a woman brought over from Europe was called "baggage" or one without papers was "underweight." He discussed earnings, systems and markets (how women—*gallinas* [hens]—were bought and sold). All this trade was to make money out of sex; a pimp confessed to Londres: "Our women are penny-in-the-slot-machines." Londres has a chapter titled "La Boca." It starts:

> *La Boca: the mouth—the mouth of Buenos Ayres. Buenos Ayres is the southernmost of the three great harbors of the world. You must go three kilometers further to get to La Boca. Look at the map: you will see that the women there could not very well descend any lower. You have heard of the end of the world. La Boca is the end of the sea… La Boca reminds one of a conscience, which, loaded with all the mortal sins and driven ashore here, survives amid the execrations of the world.*

Not only a port for every kind of ship, but the place where the Polaks reigned with their Jewish whores. He described the brothels: "The real La Boca is the *Casitas*. They are unbelievable… The men, instead of sitting down, are standing up, leaning against the wall. Humble, patient, resigned, like a queue of poor people waiting outside a relief office in the winter." The equally poor, equally resigned, whore could expect to see up to seventy-five men a day (like Cándida Eréndira in García Márquez's story). Vázquez Rial's novel *Frontera sur* quotes from Londres and dramatizes this brothel world and the closing down of the Migdal pimp association. A pimp explains the trade in Jewish women bought in central Europe:

Ruth, let's say, to give her a name, was respectful, humble, thin... They put her on a ship with a creep like me, they disembarked in Buenos Aires, and locked her up in a foul place so that later the brothel [el quilombo] would seem like heaven, and after a week or a fortnight she would be sent to La Boca: a room, a patio, and twenty or thirty men waiting in candle light.

Dancing girls in the heyday of La Boca's brothel culture (Vida Nocturna)

In 1919 Gálvez exposed the vice trade to those Argentines who ignored what was going on under their noses in his novel *Nacha Regules* (translated into English in 1922):

> *Twice he had descended into hell, but never imagined that he would go further down into the deepest circles of the abyss. To search for Nacha in the appalling pit where those who have lost everything lie: their soul, their personality, their body. They do not even own their bodies, which belong to men who sell them like dogs or horses. They cannot run away or kill themselves. They are not even free to be alone, nor to be sad, nor to reject the drunk who dribbles or any stinking wretch. Monsalvat walked about these places and spoke with these miserable women, who had been turned into animals.*

Gálvez blamed men "with deformed consciences" for this rampant prostitution, pointing out that those made rich were protected by the state, society and the police, making Buenos Aires "something horrible, hugely depressing" and "a vast marketplace for human flesh." Leopoldo Lugones had to admit in his book *La grande Argentina* [Great Argentina, 1930] that "nobody ignores the fame that Buenos Aires enjoys as a market place for prostitution." Later, under Peronism, the sordid nightlife of La Boca was severely restricted.

Other reasons for La Boca's fame within the city of Buenos Aires include electing the first socialist deputy, Alfredo Palacios, in 1904. Palacios campaigned against the white slave trade and spoke of his shame that Buenos Aires was infamous in Europe as "the worst of all the centres of immoral commerce in women." In 1882, following a strike, Genoese immigrants had declared the *barrio* "the Independent Republic of La Boca," with its own flag. This flag was personally torn down by the then president of Argentina, General Roca (from 1880-1886), the man responsible for modernizing Argentina by expelling the nomadic Indians from the national territory, which paved the way for the vast *estancias* and later agricultural wealth.

La Boca has also been home to many artists, including Benito Quinquela Martín (1890-1970), who incessantly painted this port *barrio* and whose studio has been transformed into a museum named after him on Avenida Pedro de Mendoza, 1836; also in this museum are works by de la Cárcova, Victorica (1884-1955), Raquel Forner (1902-1987), Antonio Berni (1905-1981), and Sívori. Nearby is the beautifully converted Italianate 1899 warehouse, now a modern gallery, Fundación Pro 9 (Pedro de Mendoza, 1929), which recently exhibited Rómulo Macció (1931-), who works in La Boca. Visit it on www.proa.org, as it is also an art publishing house.

In the 1960s, La Boca became home to fashionable artists and drop-outs. Clara, the ingenuous tart in Luisa Valenzuela's novel *Hay que sonreír* visits the flat of her lover Alejandro in a passage that shows how La Boca meant bohemian squalor to many *porteños*:

Alejandro took Clara to the banks of the Riachuelo and she laughed enthusiastically when she saw the houses painted in colors.

"How pretty, Alejandro, look how pretty!"

"How can you find them pretty! It's garish, kitsch. Come on, let's not waste time around here."

"Do you live in a house painted in colors like these?"

"What do you think! I hate colors."

Clara thought that having been an architecture student obliged him to be severe, and didn't insist.

They reached a house with several floors, with walls covered in corrugated iron. To enter you had to descend thirteen steps; Clara counted them exactly.

In the patio kids were fighting and their mothers shouting to make them come and eat lunch. They climbed up a broken-down staircase reeking with every conceivable smell from kitchens; Clara felt sick and leaned on Alejandro's arm. On the first landing a baby was howling...

Inside, thrown into a corner, the wide bed was unmade, lying on top of a pile of books, and it seemed round and warm like a broody hen. At the side of the window there was a table covered in papers and rulers, and beyond that a washbasin with a worm-eaten mirror...

Alejandro looked at her proudly:

"This is the bohemian way of life," and she believed him.

The painter Macció captured La Boca's charm: "I like this place. In the streets there's a village feeling, despite being seven minutes from the Plaza de Mayo. Dogs bark at night and howl at the full moon." La Boca can also appear exotic to a foreigner. The Hong Kong experimental film-director Wong Kar-Wai located his film *Happy Together* (1998), a subtle study of the fluctuations of love between two male lovers, in the area: "I

liked La Boca because it reminded me of somewhere in Hong Kong—
the smell of it. They told me it was a dangerous place, but I thought, it's
not so dangerous to me." This comment illustrates how a city will
remind a traveler of another city (Buenos Aires / Hong Kong—who
would have made that link?), that travelers bring with them their stock
of urban comparisons.

The smelly Riachuelo is today a cemetery of rusting and rotting
boats, especially on the Vuelta de Rocha. The millionaire novelist
Enrique Larreta evoked the run-down harbor scene in a poem: "I see in
front of me / the hospital of boats. Red, underpinned / boats, boats in
dry-dock, boats with paint pealing, / painted sweetly instead by the
flames of the setting sun." Baldomero Fernández Moreno, whose poems
capture so realistically his city, also noted these ships "stuck to the quay
/ wide, dirty, dormant old boats. / Waters of the Riachuelo, / stinking
waters, / waters streaked with oil."

Rusting ships on the Riachuelo (Harriet Cullen)

La Isla Maciel and Dock Sur

The Maciel Island and South Dock refer to a rough area off La Boca, with *frigoríficos*, shipyards and shantytowns. In Bernardo Kordon's (1915-) story "Sunday on the River" from the patriotically titled *Relatos porteños* [Porteño tales, 1982], we get a description of a lorry load of Sunday day-trippers crossing the Riachuelo over the high Nicolás Avellaneda bridge and looking down on to La Boca. The *barrio* looks like "a colored, dusty tapestry," and the trippers look at the Dock Sur, with the "railway sidings, next to the dark bulk of the Frigorífico Anglo." In Vázquez Rial's *Frontera sur*, about the criminal underworld of pimps and whores in Buenos Aires, one of the petty thugs comes from the Isla Maciel: "No, people like you never reach as far as here. Never go beyond La Boca, the Farol Colorado brothel. If you dare, you might take the boat for a short trip to the Pasatiempo. The island and the Dock are scary. The misery of fear. And that's where you will really find misery."

Yet at the turn of the century, in Manuel Gálvez's novel *El mal metafísico* [The metaphysical sickness, 1916], this same miserable Isla Maciel was a poor man's Tigre, a magnet for Sunday outings:

> He suggested the Isla Maciel. It was similar to the Tigre, and only common folk went there. Anarchists celebrated their picnics... That Sunday jaunt was on a hot day. Riga and Heloísa took a morning tram to La Boca. The Uruguayan woman refused to go by car. They had to act like petit bourgeois or workers. In La Boca they approached the docks on the Riachuelo, to be rowed across. Boats made Riga sad. They were old boats, mostly sailing ones, painted blue, yellow, red... The rowing boat moored by a jetty and they got off. Close by the river there was a wooden hut, and next to it some trees where couples and modest families were having lunch.

Rosalinda, the pretty, abused, factory worker in Gálvez's *Historia del arrabal* lived on this "island," "in that slum of shacks, raised on stilts and built with planks and corrugated zinc. Painted in violent colors, they were now faded and grimy... All were caricaturesque. Their angles twisted, the beams broken, the pillars wobbly, the colors stained, an architectural wasteland." It is the unmistakable image of an early shantytown. When the island flooded, muddy water covered the ground, leaving a stink of "rotten fish." At one time Rosalinda hits rock bottom, and in rags and dirty clothes she is forced to prostitute herself in Dock Sur's calle Facundo Quiroga, "fringed with bars and restaurants of ill-repute and frequented by sailors from around the world." Today Dock Sur has not changed, and people live on the breadline in the shadow of the vast, polluting petro-chemical installations.

Tango

"I find sort of annoying the quasi-religious attitude that Argentinians have toward the tango." John Ashbery, US poet

"The tango is our national anthem." Osvaldo Bayer

The tango craze hit the world in the 1920s through the singer Carlos Gardel. It was a sophisticated and difficult dance that has since remained in fashion, in the wake of films like Bertolucci's *Last Tango in Paris* and Madonna's singing role in the musical *Evita*. Springing from a mood of betrayal and jealousy, it was the melancholic music of the down and out and originated in the 1870s in brothels, possibly in La Boca, where tough men from the underworld—*guapos, compadres, malevos*—danced together waiting for the whores to be free. For *fin-de-siècle* Argentina was an immigrant society of men without women (a sub-theme of Leopoldo Marechal's novel *Adán Buenosayres*, which illustrates pessimistically "the disjunction between the sexes. The great problem of Buenos Aires!") This collective frustration was what Robert Cunninghame Graham saw as the continuation of "antique Spanish or semi-Moorish rules" separating the sexes. Manuel Gálvez made clear the link between tango and his protagonist's sense of isolation and confusion in the Buenos Aires of 1910: "In cabarets and tangos he found, he didn't know why, the same deep sadness that he felt in his soul. Sometimes, when the bandoneón's music surged up from deep inside, that music from the outskirts made him think of crimes and wretched landscapes, it spoke to him of desolation, of despair, of the bitterness of life." In *Historia del arrabal* he develops a more ambiguous description of the music: "it was a sensual, swinish, fringe music, mixing insolence and baseness, voluptuousness and toughness, secular sadness and the coarse happiness of brothels."

Male tango dancers (Triptyque, Canada)

The tango used *lunfardo* (essentially a mix of Italian dialects and *vesre*—reverse slang) in its lyrics. Surprisingly, it began without lyrics, with a *bandoneón*, a small accordion brought out from Hamburg by German sailors, and piano and violin. Then words came with Carlos Gardel, and its popularity spread back to Argentina from Paris, where it was a craze just before the First World War, and again in the 1920s. Cunninghame Graham, the Scottish aristocrat and adventurer, recorded the 1870s tango fashion in a sketch with a Spanish title, "El Tango Argentino": "Those were the days of the first advent of the Tango Argentino, the dance that since has encircled the whole world, as it were, in a movement of the hips. Ladies pronounced it charming as they half closed their eyes and let a little shiver run across their lips. Men said it was the only dance that was worth dancing. It was so Spanish, so unconventional... " He then described Parisian tango in terms that apply still today: "A tall young man, his hair sleek, black and stuck down to his head with a cosmetic, his trousers so immaculately creased they seemed cut out of cardboard, led out a girl dressed in a skirt so tight that

she could not have moved in it had it not been cut open to the knee."
But their dance is compared to the original tango that he had witnessed
on the river Yi in Paraguay, where the rough *gaucho* picked his partner
"round the waist and seemed to push her backwards, with her eyes half-
closed and an expression of beatitude."

Tango's finest lyricist (with Homero Manzi) the great Enrique Santos
Discépolo defined it as a sad thought that is danced. Borges meditated
on its undertones of violence in a poem titled "Tango": "The tango
creates a murky, unreal past / that somehow becomes true, / an
impossible memory of having died / fighting, on a suburban street
corner." Horacio Vázquez Rial thought of it as "a dense lament that
quickly turned into violently carnal words, in proclamations of
imprecise desires," while Philip Guedalla evoked it as "a haunting air
[that] marches unhesitatingly from the sudden drama of its opening bar
to the defiance of its close." Tango, he concluded, is "the voice of a great
city." Ramón Gómez de la Serna turned his definition of the tango into
one of the witticisms he called *greguerías*: "The tango is the grumble of
Buenos Aires and its outsiders, its musical tribulations, its sentimental
death-throe, its neurotic tremor, its sensual snore, its exclusive rainbow."
The painter Tomás in Silvina Bullrich's novel *Calles de Buenos Aires*
linked tango with national identity: "the morbid sensibility of a people
who created tango, a prolonged whine, where all is desperation, deceit,
betrayal. Tango shocked him, and yet despite himself he felt moved: it
was the cry of his land, of his sad city." Perhaps the pithiest summary
comes from Ernesto Sabato: "Hybrid dance of a hybrid people." The
fact is that everybody has an opinion about tango.

Argentina's upper classes were shocked that this brothel dance should
be associated with their country; the writer Enrique Larreta, ambassador
in Paris, wrote: "The tango in Buenos Aires is a dance exclusive to
brothels and bars of the worst kind. It is never danced in the drawing
rooms of the well-born. To Argentine ears tango music stirs up truly
disagreeable ideas." But by 1925 (the date of Gardel's first trip to
Europe) Parisian fashions triumphed and tango became Argentina's
national song, in cabarets, and tango cafés. The word "tango" is
probably African in origin, linked to *tambor*, a drum. Its roots are
Cuban (the *habanera*), while the *milonga* emerges from a separate rural

tradition. Today there is an Academia Nacional del Tango on Avenida de Mayo 833 in what used to be the Palacio Unzui, rebaptized the Palacio Carlos Gardel.

The epitome of tango was Carlos Gardel who rose out of his rough working-class life in El Abasto market to become a smooth crooner and film star. The son of a French washerwoman, born in Toulouse as Gardes in 1887, he had a police record and a mysterious past. When he died in 1935 in a plane crash in Colombia, the myth was completed and Gardel became synonymous with the self-indulgent melancholy and *ennui* of tango. Later poets like Juan Gelman wrote tangos both for collections of poems and to be played (by the Cuarteto Cedrón). Many writers from Borges to Sabato and Horacio Salas have explored tango as a way into Buenos Aires' soul, for many tangos are nostalgic about the city. As Discépolo said: "The character of my tangos is Buenos Aires." Enrique González Tuñón's twenty-two stories called *Tango* deal with characters through the mood of the music: betrayals, murders, prostitution, machismo and its code of honor, proletarian bleakness. The most dissenting view of the tango as metaphor for Argentina came from Ezequiel Martínez Estrada, who called it a "dance without a soul for automatons." It managed, he said, to parody "the seriousness of copulation because it seems to engender without pleasure." It is indeed very gloomy. Borges claimed that tango offered "a disconnected and vast *comédie humaine* of life in Buenos Aires," that it articulated its real social history.

Riachuelo

This is the "little river" that borders the southern limits of the city, draining the *pampas*. It has changed course over the years, but is thought to be the creek Juan de Garay first ventured up. Up until the 1840s it represented the most picturesque sight near the city, as in José Mármol's description, where beyond "the flowery valleys of Barracas you can find the graceful Riachuelo, and to its left the glazed plain of La Boca, one of the most beautiful views around Buenos Aires, seen from the high river banks of Balcarce." Later, however, its pollution became proverbial, as Ezequiel Martínez Estrada remarked with distaste: "the poor Riachuelo drags its secular dregs from the tanneries and salting works, rinsing itself constantly in its own dirt. Blood, organic matter, scraps." Unfortunately, the early leather curing, then the beef salting, and finally the *frigoríficos* and local light industry have sluiced their muck into the river, which today stinks. Baldomero Fernández Moreno wrote in his poem dedicated to the Riachuelo: "Waters from the Riachuelo, / stinking water, / water with stria, / of oil." Enrique Cadícamo's tango "Fog on the Riachuelo" (1937) describes the semi-abandoned dockside: "Murky anchorage where boats stay / forever by the quays. / ... Bridges and rigging through which the wind howls. / Coal-fired ships that will never leave. / Grim cemetery of ships... "

Several bridges cross this fetid river, including the gigantic Puente Avellaneda built in 1939. The *Guía Pirelli* claims that you can see the sun rise over the river from up on this huge bridge. In Gálvez's *Historia del arrabal* the factory workers used the still-standing but abandoned Puente Transbordador, "the black, huge, iron factory of a bridge, taller than the tallest houses, and while the mechanical ferry moved from one bank to the other, packed with people and cars, it let out a frightening noise, vibrating and shaking the foundations of the quays along the Riachuelo." Begun in 1908 and opened in 1914, it could be seen from everywhere, a part of the landscape, with the ships' masts, dominating the *barrios* "like an enormous ill-fated obsession."

9 de Julio

Buenos Aires boasts that the 9 de Julio is the widest avenue in the world. It is hell to cross as a pedestrian, but it does give a post-Haussmann perspective to the city, with the obelisk in the centre and clearer views of the grand back of the Colón Opera House. The Spanish novelist Miguel Delibes visited Buenos Aires for a fortnight in 1955 and found this wide avenue "proof of *porteño* vigor," and certainly it was dynamic in comparison to dull Francoist Madrid. He also noticed the cars: "Night and day, the incessant flow of cars, ten to twelve lanes wide, is really staggering." Commenting on its claim to the world record for width, Juan José Saer wrote "that the avenue is wide is undeniable" but detected "a tendency to boasting about nothings that could arise from the unconscious conviction of a painful absence of really praiseworthy things." What distinguished the avenue for him was not the obelisk but its "palo borracho trees, with their light-green, swollen, spiky trunks." Many buildings, as well as trees, had to be demolished to widen this avenue, as the poet and short story writer Silvina Ocampo (sister to Victoria and wife to Adolfo Bioy Casares) lamented: "Oh cruel city... that axes down the trees of Buenos Aires / to add one meter to the avenue."

The American poet Robert Lowell, on a visit to Buenos Aires in 1962, wrongly placed the obelisk (rather than the Pirámide) in the Plaza de Mayo in his poem "Buenos Aires": "On the main square / a white stone obelisk / rose like a phallus / without flesh or hair." In fact, the *obelisco*, on Corrientes and 9 de Julio, designed by architect Alberto Prebisch (who claimed it symbolized nothing), was erected in 1936 to commemorate the four-hundredth anniversary of the founding of the city. Perhaps the explanation for Lowell's confusion is that he went crazy when in Buenos Aires and had to be flown home in a straightjacket. The obelisk has been the butt of phallic jokes ever since. It was built very quickly to forestall the building of a monument on the same site which had been planned for the populist Hipólito Yrigoyen. It stands 210 feet high. Julio Luqui Lagleyze sees the obelisk as the symbol of modern Buenos Aires. César Fernández Moreno's ironically patriotic poem "Argentine Until Death" identifies the *obelisco* as a focus for the city's imaginary centre: "I'm a porteño / Here I am at the foot of the obelisco looking up." Rafael Alberti sarcastically admired it: "under your Obelisco my mouth halts / its oh! of amazement." Under it lie the foundations of the San Nicolás Church. To have an obelisk equates Buenos Aires with Paris (Place Vendôme), New York and Washington, all with their own obelisks.

Constitución
"The first bridge at Constitución and at my feet/ Clamor of trains weaving labyrinths of iron." Borges

The 9 de Julio leads to Constitución, the name of a *barrio* and a plaza and the site of a grand railway station, Ferrocarril General Roca, once know as "del Sur" and opened in 1865. From inside its huge vaulted ceiling with stone roses you could take the plush train to Mar del Plata or a slow train south to Barriloche and Esquel, an Argentina emptied of nomadic Indians by General Roca's "war of the desert." Horacio Vázquez Rial sees this imposing Victorian station as a cathedral with immense naves raised to celebrate the exploits "of the hero [Roca] by the oligarchy for whom he was the efficient champion." Silvina Ocampo has her boy protagonist in the story "The Impostor" set off for an eerie journey to the *campo* from this station:

> It was suffocatingly hot. I reached Constitución station at four o'clock. My books were tied under leather straps in my case, and the case was very heavy. I stopped to finish a strawberry ice cream next to one of the stone lions that guard the entrance staircase. I climbed the stairs. I had twenty minutes before the train left. I wandered about the station, looking into the shop windows... from the platform the clock's sphere, its perfect circle, reminded me of some beautiful theorems.

Borges' autobiographica, story "The South" (his own favorite story) has a librarian working in a public library on calle Córdoba, who is wounded on his head (like Borges had been in real life, nearly dying of a fever) and recovering from septicemia in a sanatorium on calle Ecuador. He takes a train south from Constitución station to his imaginary death. The story "The Aleph" features Borges himself as a character in his own tale, mocking a bad poet who was the lover of Beatriz Viterbo. Viterbo, who ignored Borges' love for her, lived near Plaza Constitución on calle Garay. When the house was to be demolished, Borges was shown the "Aleph," a point in space that contains all the points, in the cellar under some stairs. He there discovers that Beatriz had had a love affair with the poet-rival he despised. Novelist Tomás Eloy Martínez remembers the station smelling of "disinfectants and recently baked bread." The station is crowded, very South American, a landmark for all *porteños*.

Matadero

The slaughterhouse, the *matadero del Sur,* was originally situated next to today's Plaza Constitución until it was moved west in 1871 to what is now the Parque Patricios and was called then Los Corrales. It was finally relocated on the outskirts of the city in 1901 in what became Nueva Chicago (or Liniers). The libertarian Romantic poet Esteban Echeverría set his allegorical short story about Rosas' viciousness, "The Slaughter

House," written between 1839 and 1840 but published only in 1871, in the abattoir. But literary historians are not sure exactly where this was, since Echeverría wanted a symbolic tone and the *matadero* was a metaphor for Rosas' Buenos Aires. After heavy rains and Lent, cattle are again killed for meat, a bull escapes, and an effeminate opponent of Rosas (a "Unitarian dog") is assaulted, and about to be raped, dies of rage. The slaughterhouse was called "de la Convalecencia," as it was near a hospital in the barrio del Alto in what is today Plaza España. It was a sloping piece of land, bordered by a ditch of rainwater, being a run-off also for all the blood. Echeverría's description was one of chaos and squalor: "In winter those stockyards become mud swamps in which animals sink up to their necks and get stuck, cannot move." He recalls the foul scene of slaughter:

> *The sight of the matadero from a distance was grotesque, full of anima-tion. Forty-nine cows were being dragged along and more than two hundred people stamped over that mud bloodied by so much killing... The most prominent figure in the group was the butcher, knife in hand, arm and chest naked, long, knotted hair, shirt and gaucho trousers [chiripá] and face smeared with blood, followed by hags in rags, dogs fighting over scraps, and kids chucking intestines at each other.*

An early foreigner's description of the *matadero* is Sir Francis (or "Galloping") Head's of 1826 which includes mud, *corrales*, pools of blood, gulls, and a confusion of horses, bullocks "roaring," "hamstrung," some killed, some skinned. Wrote Head: "I was more than once in the middle of this odd scene, and was really sometimes obliged to gallop for my life, without knowing exactly where to go."

Shortly after, in 1833, Charles Darwin found this same slaughterhouse a macabre tourist must:

> *The great corral, where the animals are kept for slaughter to supply food to this beef-eating population, is one of the spectacles best worth seeing... When the bullock has been dragged to the spot where it is to be slaugh-tered, the matador with great caution cuts the hamstrings. Then is given the death bellow; a noise more expressive of fierce agony that any I know: I have often distinguished it from a long distance, and have always known that the struggle was drawing to a close. The whole sight is horrible and revolting: the ground is almost made of bones: and the horses and riders are drenched in blood.*

W. H. Hudson, ill in exile in England and seventy-seven years old, recalled the abattoir as it was when he lived in Argentina, around 1870, in his memoir *Far Away and Long Ago* (1918). The cattle were killed to make *charque* or jerked, dried beef for Brazilian slaves, hides and tallow. The cattle had their hamstrings slit and their throats cut, amid the "awful bellowings of the tortured beasts," with barking pariah dogs and screaming gulls. Hudson described the awful scene: "The blood so abundantly shed from day to day, mixing with the dust, had formed a crust half a foot thick all over the open space." The area was blighted by a "smell of carrion, of putrefying flesh, and of that old and ever-newly moistened crust of dust and coagulated blood... Travelers approaching or leaving the capital by the great south road, which skirted the killing-grounds, would hold their noses and ride a mile or so at a furious gallop until they got out of the abominable stench."

Today the killing takes place at Liniers. I once went there with the Colombian poet Juan Gustavo Cobo Borda. We stopped by a shed with a huge pile of bones, where bare-chested toughs shoveled what felt like sticky sawdust, but was in fact bone meal, sent to China as fertilizer. We stood at dawn above the entrance to the labyrinth of paddocks as a line of throbbing lorries stretching to the horizon, each one with some forty cattle packed inside, waited to open their cage, as the *peones* herded them in. It was mind-boggling. That night over 17,000 cattle were slaughtered.

Pompeya

Newspaper editor Jacobo Timerman, later in the news himself for his exposure of how the military kidnapped and humiliated left-wing Jews, was asked by the British journalist Jimmy Burns where the real Buenos Aires could be located. He sent him to the *barrio* of Nueva Pompeya, "a poor suburb of Buenos Aires, in drab concrete and fading pink, which had nevertheless managed to preserve within its boundaries an image of what the city had once been." Burns focused on Pompeya's bird market, "where men in white overalls haggled over prices and feathers danced and dived amidst the crowds like the remnants of a gigantic pillow fight." This bird market, near the Sáenz station on Avenues Sáenz and Perito Moreno, opens every Sunday morning, and specializes in song birds.

The low-lying area that is now Pompeya, to the west of Constitución, was often flooded from the Riachuelo until filled with ashes from the many local (and often clandestine) slaughterhouses. In the 1890s the main Avenida Sáenz was known as the "road of bones." Around 1920 this *barrio* was where the country began and where, according to Nougés, Borges visited the *pulpería* "La Blanqueada" (a cross between a store and a bar). The neighborhood got its name from its concrete, neo-Gothic church designed by the painter and architect César Ferrari and inaugurated in 1906. In the "patio" of the Virgin, with a bronze Virgen de Rosario, there is a cloister with inscriptions from Virgil and Homer.

In the 1950s Pompeya became the site of many *villas miseria* or slums. It is also recognizable for the Spanish-style bridge over the Riachuelo, rebuilt in 1939 when the iron bridge of 1910 was demolished. It is still known by its old name the Puente Alsina, but officially it is the Teniente General José Félix Uriburu. In the Dr. Antonio Sáenz library, there is a museum with paintings by Carlos Alonso, among others, and manuscripts by Julio de Caro, Homero Manzi, the tango lyricists, and the novelist Manuel Mujica Lainez.

The tango poet and lyricist Homero Manzi (1905-1951) set his songs in *Tango Barrio* (1942) in Nueva Pompeya or Puente Alsina (an alternative name for the *barrio*). It was "a landscape of piles of tin plate, fences of cina-cina, wooden shacks, obscure ponds, nearby embankments, trains crossing the afternoons, but it had its poetry." For tango was born in this sub-urban squalor, this "barrio of tin cans" or "barrio of frogs" (the Riachuelo often flooded), as the sound of immigrants' nostalgia for a lost home. Rosalinda was brought to live here by her violent pimp El Chino in Gálvez's *Historia del arrabal*: "The pimp took her to live in a wretched shack, with two rooms, next to the sinister Suburb of the Frogs. You couldn't call it a house but a stinking pigsty that flooded with rainwater and where enormous rats ran in and out." The change from remote *barrio* to asphalted city district is the theme of Tagle Lara's tango "Puente Alsina" (1927): "Puente Alsina, yesterday you were my comfortable home, / with a swipe of its claw the avenue reached you / Old, solitary and confiding bridge, / you're the brand that progress has left on my forehead." Silvina Ocampo remembered that Borges loved going there: "one of the most dirty and lugubrious places in Buenos Aires... He was happy there."

Villas Miseria

"Barrios of a Buenos Aires ignored in guide books/ for tourists." Raúl González Tunón

Buenos Aires' slum areas are named ironically following the numerous *barrios* beginning with Villa, like Villa Devoto, Villa Urquiza and so on. It was off Palermo that V. S. Naipaul was surprised in 1972 by his first sight of a *villa miseria* with its

> unpaved streets and black runnels of filth, but the buildings were of brick, with sometimes an upper story: a settled place, more than fifteen years old, with shops and signs. Seventy thousand people lived there, nearly all Indians, blank and slightly imbecilic in appearance, from the north and from Bolivia and Paraguay; so that suddenly you were reminded that you were not in Paris or Europe but in South America.

The politicized painter Antonio Berni was stirred by these shantytowns and created paintings using materials found there, and drew on central characters, *villeros*, like Juanito Laguna and Ramona Montiel, who won Berni the Venice Bienale in 1962. The *villas miseria* replaced the *conventillos* or slum tenements of earlier years as the spaces where migrants, often illegal, set up temporary houses. The essayist, and one-time editor of the review *Sur*, José Bianco, claimed that *villas miseria* were "the revenge that Spanish America has taken on Atlantic America, because our politics fomented the wealth of the humid *pampa* at the expense of the country's interior."

Luis Pascarella likened the earlier *conventillos* in 1917 to a "can of worms," resembling stables or prison cells. Some of the old houses in San Telmo contained as many as forty rooms, crowded with immigrants and offering only the most rudimentary sanitation. Living packed into *conventillos* allowed workers to find work in the city centre and avoid expensive transport by tram and train. Cámbaceres described such a slum tenement in his novel *En la sangre* [In the blood, 1886]: "Two rows of rooms with thin partitions and corrugated tin roofs, like niches in a gigantic dove house, surrounded the narrow, long patio. Around about the rubbish on the grimy floor, a fire burned in a brazier, and a stew simmered." The historian José Moya studied the housing figures and contradicted the assumption that the *conventillo* was ubiquitous by claiming that in 1887 only one-quarter of the city lived in such Dickensian conditions, shrinking to nine percent by 1919. However, Horacio Vázquez Rial saw the *conventillo* as part of a dirty business world involving supposedly patrician families:

> ... *the worst conventillos, the meanest and most expensive, with the cruellest landlords, ready to chuck families with kids into the street after two days if they hadn't paid ...*
>
> *"The warm bed ones," continued Frisch.*
>
> *"Those ones were all owned by the same person, one of the worst shits in this city, who personally sent the police in when he wanted to get a bed back from someone dying. And that's something in a place with so many shits. Esnaola, was his name. Juan Pablo Esnaola. The Argentine fatherland thanked him for having shortened the hymn that Parera composed. It's his version that is sung."*

Marco Denevi, a writer with a fine ear for *porteño* slang and satire in a Roald Dahl-esque combination of craft and surprising endings, opens his short story "Journey to Puerto Aventura" (1973) with a woman complaining that people in cars appear to be happy as she sits on the pavement in a summer heat-wave. Her husband borrows an old car and they are soon lost:

> *"Jocito," she whispered. "Where are we? What is this suburb. Stop, for God's sake."*
>
> *I put the brakes on the Lincoln and looked around. We had reached a narrow street that zigzagged like a mountain road, with other narrow streets crossing it any old way. And not a light on the hazardous corners, no lights anywhere. This was a ghetto, the slums of a nightmare Buenos Aires. Wherever we looked we saw a formless bunching of makeshift shacks. This jumble lay in impenetrable darkness, in absolute silence. No moon to soften such doom. Where on earth where we? In some abandoned cemetery; some demolition site? My word, this was a hell without souls, even the devils had flown. It seemed to be a lie that a city could have such hellhole.*

The final twist is that the couple decides to stay on and live in this hideous *villa miseria*.

It is ironic that the *villas* grew like crowded medieval cities, with dangerous, narrow passages between over-crowded buildings, mocking the ordered, grid city around them. The radical poet Raúl González

Tuñón, who fought in the civil war in Spain, evoked these desolate places:

> *Villas, villas miseria, unbelievable and dark*
> *where oblivion blew out the last light,*
> *Villa Garden, Villa Cardboard, Villa Rubbish,*
> *streets traced by the vicissitudes of hunger,*
> *the sudden tide of the dispossessed*
> *and the forcibly unemployed; the dreamers*
> *in a pathetic exodus from distant provinces,*
> *who shame the pale forehead of our fatherland.*
> *Barrios of a Buenos Aires ignored in guide books*
> *for tourists.*

In August 1998 *villeros* opened the luggage hold of a bus leaving the Retiro Bus Station and disappeared with all the suitcases back into the slum that you look on to as you wait for the buses.

Football

"*Football is one of Argentina's most important cultural activities.*" President Carlos Menem, 1999

Soccer is without a doubt the national sport, or even a substitute religion. There have been famous boxers (Firpo's KO of Dempsey ranks highest in Argentine moments of glory), racing-car driver Juan Fangio is a legend, and sultry tennis star Gabriela Sabatini makes male hearts flutter. But soccer-passion rules the hearts of *porteños*. A way of defining your allegiance to Buenos Aires is through support of a football team. A typical supporter would be part of a gang (*barra brava*), meet in the same cafés, go on Sundays to see the same team, though many more watch it all day long on TV. In 1931 Scalabrini Ortiz pointed out the lure of football as an antidote to Sunday blues: "The porteño Sunday is sadly famous for its tedium. Now at least there is professional football."

The fanaticism of football supporters is proverbial, related not only to *barrio* identification, but also to national pride, hero worship and the escape from poverty and the *villas miseria*. The city's clubs are organically linked to the neighborhoods in which they are located, none more so than Boca Juniors, founded in 1905 and national champions first in 1918. With their 65,000 capacity stadium, the giant horseshoe-shaped La Bombonera, built in 1944 near the Avellaneda bridge over the Riachuelo and dwarfing La Boca, they were once supported by the Italian immigrants of La Boca. In fact, Boca Junior supporters used to be called *los xeneixes* (in Genovese dialect meaning the Genovese). César Fernández Moreno fancifully imagined that "their cement stadium La Bombonera, tightly encircled by wavy, corrugated zinc huts, tinges the whole country blue and gold." Maradona's biographer, Jimmy Burns, described the build-up to a match in this stadium:

> *Amid the sweet scent of the jacaranda, heavy drum beats and frenetic flag waving, thousands of football fans are making their way to the Bombonera stadium of Boca Juniors. Bombonera means chocolate box in Spanish, but there is nothing sweet or contained about the scene. The masses shatter the quiet Sunday of Latin America's most sophisticated capital city, like a wild tribe let loose on a tea room. The men—for there are few women or children among them, so intimidating is the sport still—are bare-chested and wave their shirts like broken chains. They move relentlessly as if to war. Their chief, Diego Maradona, looks down on them from the top of a double-decker bus, dark eyes unflinching, hair cropped and dyed in the war paint of the Boca colours... The chorus is provided by a radio reporter whose voice is crackling with hysteria. "Our idol is coming... "*

Young footballers, La Boca (Harriet Cullen)

Maradona, a.k.a. "El Pelusa" (fluffy hair) and a typical *cabeza negra*, was born in 1960 in a suburb of Avellaneda, the eldest son of part Indian and part Italian immigrant parents from Esquina in Corrientes province (where Diego would often escape to fish and rest). He grew up as a *villero*, in a tiny tin shack in Villa Fiorito, a shantytown off the southern suburb of Lanús, with no privacy, but surrounded by a clan-like family. After a youth spent playing football in the street, he precociously attracted the attention of the football hierarchy and signed a contract with Argentinos Juniors in 1973, three years later becoming at fifteen the youngest player ever to play in a premier division. He transferred to Boca Juniors in 1981 and led them to the championship, as he would later lead Argentina to the world title in Mexico in 1986. While rising up the football ladder, Maradona also moved up the social scale, first to Villa del Parque, and then to a mansion in Villa Devoto. But despite national pride, Maradona transferred to Barcelona, then Naples (propelling them to the Italian championship), and began his descent into cocaine addiction, moody rebelliousness and dissolution which ended up with arrests and public scandals, despite his friendship with President Menem. The English novelist and sports writer Brian Glanville summed up Maradona's football skills: "thick-thighed, enormously quick in thought and movement, a superb finisher and a fine tactician." Maradona became as big a national idol as Gardel (and indeed was often equated with Gardel). Jimmy Burns called Maradona "the most naturally talented player ever," undone as a person by his unpredictability, as Burns' biography reveals. Wong Kar-Wai set his film *Happy Together* near the Boca Juniors stadium and told the British film critic Richard Williams: "I'm a big fan of soccer, and we shot one scene in the Boca Juniors stadium, during a match against River Plate. It was just like a carnival, very different from what we see in Hong Kong. Wonderful. We even met Maradona. Actually we made a scene with him, too, but in the end I cut it."

In César Fernández Moreno's words "The national *pathos* accompanies Boca Juniors like no other team." However, their rivals River Plate have their stadium, the Monumental, out on Figueroa Alcorta 7597, where the 1978 World Cup Final was played. Independientes, meanwhile, have their old stadium in Avellaneda.

Buenos Aires has eight first division teams playing within its perimeters. Borges, although an avowed Anglophile, execrated the introduction of football by the English brothers Thomas and James Hogg in 1867. They founded the Buenos Aires Football Club on calle Viamonte 38, playing their first match in June 1867 in Palermo. By 1885, another Briton, Alexander Watson Hutton, had introduced football into schools. By 1893 the Argentina Association Football League was founded.

A riot ensues in Marechal's novel *Adán Buenosayres* in the *barrio* of Villa Crespo when Juancho and Yuyito argue over football in an archetypal city scene:

> *Juancho began praising the Rácing team and their famous forwards; given this, Yuyito, frowning, exalted the eleven from San Lorenzo de Almagro in whose honor he had devoted his life. Words come and go: each one drops praising his champions and begins the dangerous tactic of attacking the other until Juancho thought of saying that San Lorenzo were eleven knock-knees, and reminded the other of the thrashing that Rácing gave them recently. Hearing this insult, Yuyo felt a lump in his throat, recovered his cool and answered with the three goals that San Lorenzo scored against Rácing on the Boca Juniors pitch. Eternal gods! Without more ado Juancho punched Yuyo on the chin...*

Football can be a matter of life and death. In Sabato's novel *Sobre héroes y tumbas*, we overhear a slangy conversation in a bar about football: "'That Sunday was tragic; we lost like cretins. San Lorenzo won, even Tigre won. Tell me, when will all this end?' His voice became hoarse and solemn, and looking into the street, he said bitterly: 'This country can't be fixed.'" In his analysis of myths about Argentina, *El país de las maravaillas: los argentinos en el fin del milenio* [The country of miracles: Argentines at the end of the millennium, 1998], the novelist and critic Mempo Giardinelli reveals that he is scared and wary about going to football matches. He now empties his wallet, and pays for a seat rather than standing, admitting "there are stadiums I would never dare go to." He reports that between 1958 and 1996, seventy-one people were killed in football violence.

Violence notwithstanding, passion and skill are central to the Argentine game. At the national level, Argentina reached the finals of the first World Cup in July 1930, played on home ground in Buenos

Aires, but were defeated by arch rivals Uruguay 4–2. Not until 1978 (the eleventh championship) did Argentina actually win the World Cup, and this was under General Videla's sinister military junta, where football passions were manipulated to conceal the *guerra sucia* being waged under everyone's nose. After seven years in exile, the novelist Osvaldo Soriano was taken to see San Lorenzo football team in 1983 and realized how politics entered football, for the real spectacle was not on the pitch but in the stands. While the players played, 30,000 fans chanted in chorus: "*It's going to end / it's going to end / the military dictatorship*" and continued "*Shoot them, shoot them / the military who sold our nation.*" Soriano saw how rival fans joined together to fight the police and their dogs, observing: "It's been ages since any soldier has dared go to a match to revive the glorious days of Videla, Massera, Agosti and the World Cup of '78. That hollow victory."

Barracas

The *barrio* of Barracas, meaning warehouse, lies west of La Boca and south of Constitución station and is now a poor, rough area of rundown factories. In Sabato's *Sobre héroes y tumbas*, it becomes the focal point of the writer's exploration of Argentine identity. The Olmos family live in a ruined *quinta* on calle Río Cuarto with a surprising *mirador*, their house surrounded by factories and slums, and full of recluses who represent Argentina's living history. (The most famous of the Barracas factories is the espadrille-producing Fábrica Argentina de Alpargatas built in 1885 filling out several blocks on Avenida Regimiento de Patricios.) The ironic Quique questions the character of this *barrio*: "but WHO would live in Barracas? And I, obviously, calmed him down by saying NOBODY lives there. Apart from some four hundred down and outs and as many dogs." The tango "Whistling" evokes down-at-heel Barracas: "A street in south Barracas, / one summer night, / when the sky is blue / and sweeter than the song of an Italian boat / from the Dock, / moaning its languid lament."

Victoria Ocampo told the story of her ancestor Enrique Ocampo's crime of passion, when he shot the rich widow Felicitas Guerrero de Alzaga in the face and then killed himself. In her autobiography Ocampo includes a letter in phonetic spelling in the Spanish from a woman related to Felicitas's *novio*, dated February 13, 1872: "a great catastrophe in the quinta of the Alzaga widow in Barracas," when Ocampo, "well dressed, with diamond buttons" called round, shot Felicitas in the back and himself in the heart; "all society is disgusted." In the face, in the heart: the facts alter, for this story is more an expression of urban myth-making than truth. The poet Carlos Guido y Spano called doña Felicitas "the most beautiful woman in the whole republic." She had married the far older Martín de Alzaga, descended from the man who helped eject the British in 1807, who died while she was still young. She had then fallen for a man whom she met in a storm near her *estancia* on the coast. The Alzaga *quinta* where this crime took place in 1872 no longer stands, but her heirs built a chapel to the woman's memory in 1879 on Plaza Colombia. Called the Iglesia de Santa Felicitas and recalling two saints with the murdered woman's name, it was designed by the architect Ernesto Bunge in red adobe brick with plaster statues and an imitation Lourdes grotto. A Carrara marble statue represents Felicitas with her son; windows were brought from France, the organ from Germany. The two large steeples, facade and rotunda have been restored and look new, although the back of the building reveals severe wear. Taking up a whole block behind the church is the imposing, orange, château-like Colegio de Nuestra Señora de Lourdes Santa Felicitas, built in 1893.

The murder touched a romantic chord in *porteño* urban mythology, a local version of Romeo and Juliet that was soon turned into both gossip and literature. Juana Manuela Gorriti was the first writer to recreate this *crime passionel* in her story "Feliza," with its image of the dead woman's desolate house: "Feliza's dwelling, once so happy and visited, remained empty and silent... grass grew on the paths of her park and the wind groaned in the cypress trees." A recent best-seller by Ana María Cabrera recreated *fin-de-siècle* Barracas, in her view a *barrio* of grand houses and romantic gardens, such as the residence of the Montes de Oca whose entry gate had two marble lions guarding it. At the end of the street was the *quinta* of José Hernández Plata, grandfather of he who penned *Martín Fierro*. Nearby was the crenellated house of the Saénz Valiente, possibly built for the viceroy Sobremonte, but all gone.

Amalia, the widow from Tucumán, lived in Barracas, and hid the wounded *unitario* (or anti-Rosas plotter) who tried to flee to

Montevideo, and barely escaped the dreaded secret police, the *mazorca* in José Mármol's long historically-exact novel about 1840s Buenos Aires.

By 1910, the centennial year in which Manuel Gálvez set his novel *Nacha Regules*, Barracas had become the slummiest and cheapest brothel area. Monsalvat seeks out Nacha along "dark, silent streets" and finds the house of a woman who might help him "in a labyrinth of alleys near the Hospice of the Mercedes." Gálvez creates a deliberately hellish note:

> It was a strange place, in austere colors and lines, and really desolate. Hard to conceive of anything more harsh. A narrow street between two high walls that suddenly twisted and from where you could only see sky and night. From where Monstalvat had entered, only the walls and trees of the women's insane asylum. It was silent like a desert. Monstsalvat's hair stood on end. He turned into an alleyway, which at the end revealed the black rails of a goods yard. Huge dark shapes—sleeping wagons—piled up there.

Barracas, with its high pavements that remind you that it used to flood there and leave the streets muddy, can still be hostile to aimless wanderers.

On calles Vieytes and Suárez stands the Monumento a Don Hipólito Vieytes, a statue with a book in its hand and a reproduction of the city's first printing press, placed there in 1911. Because it was once perceived as a healthy, fresh-air place, many hospitals were built, including the Hospital Británico on calle Perdriel and the Instituto Nacional de Microbiología Dr. Carlos Malbrán, where Argentina's Nobel-Prize winning scientist César Milstein worked. It has its own Museo de Ciencias Naturales de Especialidad Zoológica Médica, and a library. On calle Barracas is the famous Borda or Hospital Nacional Neuropsiquiátrico de Hombres José Borda, with a woman's equivalent hospital, the Braulio Moyano, next door. I once visited the old poet Jacobo Fijman (1898-1970) when he was interned there in the vast patio-ed and decrepit building. Also in the area and a "must," according to the *Guía Pirelli*, is the Antigua Librería Argentina Años Verdes on Patricios 955, for second-hand books and postcards, with a tango bar.

Quilmes

Beyond the city limits lies Quilmes, named after a tribe of repatriated Indians and linked to Buenos Aires by train in 1872. This was where General Beresford landed with his British troops in 1806. There is still a British link in the form of St. George's School, recently celebrating its centenary. Quilmes is also a *balneario* [resort], with a pier. In Bernardo Kordon's story about a group outing, "Sunday on the River," we find a description of this popular river-beach, where all kinds of transport from cars and lorries to delivery bicycles fought to find shade under trees, as if all were escaping a "bombardment." A character comments: "With so many people about this seems like calle Florida brought to the river." The riverside resort area is evoked as "the most diverse huts from stalls that sold everything to smoking barbecues to shooting ranges. Everybody was shouting like madmen, and the loud speakers could not dominate the pandemonium." Quilmes is also the place name for Argentine beer (Cervecería Quilmes, founded in 1890) owned by the Bemberg family who built model workers' housing. The film director María Luisa Bemberg [*Camila, De eso no se habla, Miss Mary* etc.] came from this rich family. The commercial traveler William MacCann passed through Quilmes in 1848 and noted

> *a large brick-built church, with a cemetery attached; this was once enclosed with a wall, which is now quite destroyed; and the cattle entering in search of grass, deface and destroy the tombs. The village consists of one very fine house, and perhaps a dozen of ordinary character; around, in little detached plots of ground, are the usual ranchos, or huts, formed of cane-reeds and mud, which at a distance appear to be smothered in tall rank weed.*

He lamented the disappearance of the Quilmes Indians, repatriated from Catamarca, but extinct. He explained "the wretched poverty and desolation" as caused by the men being obliged to fight in the wars.

Nearby, and a must to visit, is the *rancho* (shack) where W. H. Hudson lived, now a museum called the Parque Ecológico Cultural Guillermo E. Hudson (he is known in the Hispanized form, G. E. Hudson, in Argentina), surrounded by industrial sites and shantytowns. Hudson wrote about his years as a boy in his classic autobiography *Far Away and Long Ago*, by far the best account of *campo* life in the nineteenth century. He wrote in his precise and vivid style:

The house where I was born, on the South American pampas, was quaintly named Los veinte-cinco Ombues, there being just twenty-five of these indigenous trees—gigantic in size and standing wide apart in a row about 400 yards long. The ombú is a very singular tree indeed, and being the only representative of tree-vegetation, natural to the soil, on those great level plains, and having also many curious superstitions connected with it, it is a romance in itself. It belongs to the rare Phytolacca family, and has an immense girth—forty or fifty feet in some cases; at the same time the wood is so soft and spongy that it can be cut with a knife, and is utterly unfit for firewood, for when it is cut up it refuses to dry, but simply rots away like a ripe watermelon.

W. H. Hudson (Archivo General de la Nación)

The house was made of adobe bricks and was long and low; a poor house for his North American immigrant parents and their large family. The isolated rural life of nineteenth-century Quilmes has vanished, alive only in Hudson's wonderfully visual prose. The shack has some photocopies, a few books, some material on Cunninghame Graham and a schoolroom, but is best seen from the outside.

PART FIVE

The West

"I am a citizen of the calle Corrientes"
Carlos Gardel

"Calle Corrientes is a superstition, I would say from Colombia or Peru...
In Buenos Aires nobody thinks of calle Corrientes."
Borges

Avenida (often known as calle) Corrientes

To stroll this crucial and symbolic street is to get to know the heart of popular Buenos Aires. Night and day it is packed with wanderers; it has theatres, cinemas, cafés, second-hand bookshops, pizzerias. It is fitting that the Peronist poet Leopoldo Marechal has written a *Historia de la calle Corrientes*, so called since 1822 when that "great urbanist" Bernardino Rivadavia named it to echo the city and state of Corrientes (meaning "currents," referring to the great Paraná river). In his history, Marechal defined the street atmosphere in 1931, before the street was widened in 1936, with its "night professionals." Here, "the street awaits them with its theatres and cinemas open, with its dazzling cafés, with the frenzy of its lights and sounds." This night and day street, busy with drifting, talking crowds, is evoked by the poet Gustavo Riccio: "Neon signs of the calle Corrientes, / magnificent, bursting with mercurial blood!"

Corrientes divides Buenos Aires in two; it is a source of nostalgia for *porteños* abroad, and stands for the common man, the man of Corrientes and Esmeralda (from Scalabrini Ortiz's essay *El hombre que está solo y espera* [The man who is alone and waits, 1931]), who identifies his soul with tango. And not just "man," for the poet Augusto González Castro, in his poem, "Ballad of the Street Porteña" praises the "women of Buenos Aires, / lovely porteñas / ... dominating and tender / along Corrientes and Esmeralda." Lyricist Celedonio Flores' tango "Corrientes and Esmeraldas" calls that junction *the* "porteño street corner." Homero Expósito's tango "Sad Moments on Calle Corrientes" imagines the long street as a "river without buffers where the city suffers." In his first tour of Buenos Aires, Vázquez Montalbán's detective Pepe Carvalho registered calle Corrientes as an "aging and chaotic set, as if the businesses and buildings fought to disagree aesthetically." In one of his sketches, the chronicler of Buenos Aires low life, Roberto Arlt, deemed that Florencio Sánchez's statue on Garay and Chiclana was in the wrong place. It should have been on Corrrientes, on any corner, by any café, to celebrate his appeal to the common people. For *porteños*, Corrientes is "the most beautiful street in the world."

In the 1930s the long Avenida Corrientes had, according to Arlt, four personalities. From Río de Janeiro to Medrano it was full of "cheese dairies," factories and foundries. From Medrano to Pueyrredón it lost its personality and became "a common street without characteristics" of small businesses. From Pueyrredón to Callao "a miracle happened" in the shape of the zone of cloth and weaving, run by Turks and Jews, with Jewish cafés and synagogues. Corrientes proper started at Callao and ended at Esmeralda. Wrote Arlt: "It's the porteño heart, soul of the city." In this street *porteños* think they're back in the provinces, it's the street where people drift and daydream, the street of nocturnal pleasures, "the street that never sleeps."

The stroller will quickly realize that calle Corrientes is also the tango avenue, for it was here on Corrientes 1553, then on number 1714, around the vaulted art-deco fruit and vegetable Abasto market (built over two blocks in 1893, also known as the *barrio* of Carlos Gardel), that Gardel grew up. This cathedral-like market building was the Covent Garden of Buenos Aires, and has been converted into a vast shopping mall. Gardel once claimed that "I am a citizen of the calle Corrientes"; certainly his favorite cafés, his homes, his friends were all to be found there. When his body was brought back in 1936 from Medellín, Colombia, where he died in an airplane crash on the ground on June 24, 1935, 30,000 people met his coffin at the North Dock. Many thousands more filed past his coffin in Luna Park on Corrientes, where speeches and a concert were held in his honor. Gardel is a character in Horacio Vázquez Rial's novel *Frontera sur*, where he reveals that the real Charles Gardes, born in France, died and was replaced by an Uruguayan from Tacuarembó (there has been much debate about Gardel's supposed Uruguayan roots). The novel chronicles a rich period in social history. We read that Gardel was burned alive, took six months to be brought back to Buenos Aires and that the crowd that lined calle Corrientes as his corpse was taken to the Chacarita cemetery was seven kilometers long.

Silvina Bullrich's jay-walking Gloria leaves her *barrio norte* social perch and enters the uniqueness of the crowded Avenida Corrientes in the late 1930s, looking at "bloodless faces, prematurely aged, badly aged. The street was wide, one of the few well-lit ones in the city. There were several cinemas, shops, restaurants on every block. All was opulence, all spoke about material comfort, a palpable luxury." Over the years the street has become more tacky, more South American, but it still satisfies diverse material appetites.

Leftish writers and literary rebels prefer calle Corrientes with its art cinemas, second-hand bookshops open all night and cheap *boliches*, especially the bar La Paz at Corrientes 1599, opposite the San Martín Cultural Centre, where you could smoke and watch intellectuals arguing under its neon lights. Its renovation has unfortunately made it aseptic. To say someone was a "habitué of the downtown Café La Paz," as was Francisco Sanctis in Humberto Costantini's novel, was to typify him, to explain him. For Osvaldo Soriano, the café La Paz was "where young intellectuals would meet to argue and seduce." Another meeting place for the bookish was the café/bookshop Gandhi, now moved to Corrientes 1551, which opened in 1984 with its large photos of Borges, Cortázar, Marx and Goethe. David Viñas and the late Enrique Molina were habitués of the bookshop, similar to the Gandhi in Mexico City.

This is also the place where the "furtive reader" can waste time in the "grimy second-hand bookshops of calle Corrientes," in Leopoldo Marechal's words. These second-hand bookshops reflect the street and city in their hybrid nature:

In narrow hallways, in mean back rooms and even pretentious salons, you can see all kinds of tomes on shelves, divulging all the sciences, muddled up and disparate like soldiers of a foreign legion: on humble shelves Homer and Ponson du Terrail rub shoulders, a manual of Swedish gym and a metaphysical treatise live happily together.

Such second-hand books are crucial sources of learning when money is short.

It is obvious that ghosts of former cafés define this avenue. In the 1940s the Polish writer Witold or Witoldo Gombrowicz (1904-1969), marooned in Argentina thanks to the outbreak of the Second World War, but who stayed on there until 1963, met two Cuban exiled writers Virgilio Piñera and Humberto Rodríguez Tomeu, with others, at the Café Rex on Corrientes, and they collectively translated Gombrowicz's great novel *Ferdydurke*. Later, Gombrowicz would meet his younger Argentine friends (he was obsessed with "youth") at the café La Fragata also on Corrientes, often playing chess.

In his messy, sprawling essay on Buenos Aires, Ezequiel Martínez Estrada picked on Los Inmortales (the name today refers to a pizza chain) on Corrientes 922 as emblematic of the street's café life: "In its room always crammed with voices, smoke, wide-brimmed hats, people dreamed of fame and money as in no other spiritual ghetto in Buenos Aires." He named Florencio Sánchez and Evaristo Carriego as regulars (the short-story writer Horacio Quiroga and the philosopher José Ingenieros also frequented the place). In this same café writers Roberto Giusti and Alfredo Bianchi held their literary *tertulia*, setting up the magazine *Nosotros*. A would-be poet in Bernardo Verbitsky's novel *El noviazgo* [The courtship, 1956] stares into the café with the large window front: "He longed to be a bohemian as if it was an order of the elect." The name Los Inmortales, according to Jorge Bossio, came from a joke about the writers sitting there being immortal because they never ate anything. Vicente Martínez Cuitiño, a playwright, wrote a history of this café.

Raúl Scalabrini Ortiz's essay *El hombre que está solo y espera* cites the Café Royal Keller (demolished) on Corrientes and Esmeralda as typical of how overheated café life could lead to strife. The Uruguayan poet Ildefonso Pereda Valdés inadvertently insulted Amado Villar in a review. He recounted how he went as usual to the Café Tortoni, met Villar and went on, with all the *martinfierristas* [avant-garde poets], to the Royal Keller on Corrientes to join a group of Peruvian avant-garde poets, led by the Arequipan Alberto Hidalgo (a "Quechuan idol," according to Marechal). Suddenly Villar punched Valdés and a fight broke out. Pereda Valdés was saved unexpectedly by Borges and Mastronardi. In the Café Keller the Italian futurist Marinetti called for all the libraries of the world to be burned; Vicente Huidobro and Pablo Neruda, passing through the city, also frequented the place.

In Manuel Gálvez's satirical novel about bohemia in Buenos Aires in the 1900s, *El mal metafísico*, the Café Brasileña on Maipú and Corrientes is the gathering point for intellectuals and starving writers:

It was a vast square place, packed with tiny tables on which shone sugar bowls and coffee cups. On the walls, awful pictures represented the harbor of Santos, with blacks carrying sacks of coffee, scenes from fazendas, the beach at Guaruyá, with mountains in the background, by the blue ocean, under the Brazilian heat. In all the pictures enchanted islands, tall, wooded peaks...

People from the most opposed intellectual factions met there at night, in small groups. Violent anarchists, persecuted more by hunger than by the police, who venerated Kropotkin, Salvador and Angiolillo and threatened to destroy society with bombs and feeble literature, rubbed shoulders with musicians and theosophists, who were tame and inoffensive who movingly worshipped Wagner or Blavatsky. Close to some anonymous, pontificating café genius, the literatoides argued over the merits of half the literary world, hurling insults, doctrine, paradoxes and quotations at each other. A Nietzsche disciple exasperated the socialists, forgetting about his torn trousers and ascetic pockets with views about Individualism, Pleasure and Pride. Famished reporters from newspapers, actors from the National Theatre. Nobody was missing. Despite the diversity of minds and jobs the clients in La Brasileña: poverty, the vice of daydreaming, a sharp tongue, old dirty clothes, a wide-brimmed hat, long hair, a lavalliere tie.

Horacio Quiroga was another habitué of La Brasileña, as was Baldomero Fernández Moreno who in a poem punned the café's name with Brazilian women ("Brasileñas). The atmosphere with its "great sacks of coffee, / wide palm leaves, / green walls, mirrors" led to fantasies of being a *fazenda* owner "just by drinking coffee / at night with the Brasileñas."

Another famous ghost café on Corrientes, between Florida and Maipú, was Aue's Keller, "the best beer cellar and restaurant of its time" in poet Conrado Nalé Roxlo's memoirs, *Borrador de memorias* [Memory draft]. He was a regular, "faithful to its night-time group," which had earlier included Lugones, Mitre, Martel, etc. Rubén Darío boasted that nearly all the *Prosas profanas*, his provocative poems published in 1896 in Buenos Aires, "were written quickly, either in the offices of *La Nación*, or at café tables like Aue's Keller." The critic Garasa lamented that "when Aue's Keller was demolished [to make way for the Diagonal] it was as if the city died a little." He quotes a poem by Ernesto Palacio: "Now that Aue's Keller is closed, where can we celebrate, / brother poets, our orgies?"

Corrientes is also the theatre street, encompassing the popular, escapist and political. Osvaldo Soriano, on returning to Buenos Aires in 1983, praised a movement called Teatro Abierto [Open Theatre] at the Teatro del Picadero in the Pasaje Rauch (on Corrientes and Callao) as the only cultural resistance to the military repression. A group of actors, writers and directors had joined up and put on free shows that were meant to dispel political apathy, in which "for the first time since the dictatorship began, art could express itself freely, provocatively, without beating around the bush." In revenge, the theatre was burned down in 1980. The *pasaje* was originally a train cutting, expressing "the simple mystery of your curve," in Baldomero Fernández Moreno's words.

A busy cultural centre, the state-owned Teatro Municipal San Martín on Corrientes 1530, has three theatres, a cinema named after the poet Leopoldo Lugones and galleries, including a Museo de Arte Moderno on the ninth floor. It was opened in 1960, an "appealing space" said the sad and suicidal poet Alejandra Pizarnik, but "rather dead." On the next block, a new development, with little bars, trees, passage ways, called the Complejo Plaza, has theatres named after Pablo Neruda and Julio

Cortázar. The last landmark on the avenue is Luna Park, built on Corrrientes 1066 in 1905. After boxing was officially permitted in 1910 (up to then it had been banned), Luna Park became the place for many famous boxing matches. More than 2,500 people paid to hear the famous Dempsey-Firpo match on the radio in 1923. Luna Park moved in 1932 to a nearby lot near the port vacated by the railways on Corrientes and Bouchard; it closed to boxing in 1988.

The Barrios

Before leaving the centre out along Corrientes west, a few words on the *barrio*. In 1930 Borges brilliantly noted that "Buenos Aires' unexpected beauties lie on the outskirts." He mentioned the "miserable majesty" surrounding the goods station La Paternal, dusty streets, the *orillas* of the city, and, of course, the rough area of Palermo, with its *compadritos* and tango—in other words, those part of the city without glamorous European echoes. In "The South" Dahlmann sits in a train that leaves Constitución station and watches how "the city breaks up into suburbs." Julio Cortázar's character Traveler, the protagonist's non-travelling double in his experimental novel *Rayuela* [*Hopscotch*, 1963], compared Buenos Aires to "an enormous belly that shakes slowly under the sky," and to a huge spider with its eight feet sticking out into the suburbs and the "dirty" river.

Yet outside the fashionable and historic areas of the giant spider that is Buenos Aires, the *barrios* can seem monotonous and interchangeable. Most of these *barrios* developed either from railway stations, or from churches. Can a barrio like Flores be confused with another like Avellaneda? Roberto Arlt's picaresque salesman Silvio divides the *barrios* like Caballito, Flores, Vélez Sarsfield and Villa Crespo into zones he would cover week by week. Arlt contrasts the low sordid buildings and the blue dome of the sky: "The low streets of the suburbs were miserable, dirty, flooded by sunlight, with boxes of rubbish in the doors, women with huge bellies, hair uncombed and squalid, chatting from doorways and calling dogs and kids back in, under an arch of clean, diaphanous sky." Silvio particularly recalls a suburban butcher: "A ray of sun shone on to the beasts of reddish, black flesh hanging on hooks and ropes by the tin counters. The floor was littered with sawdust, a smell of lard was in the air, swarms of black flies buzzed on bits of yellow fat and the expressionless butcher sawed the bones while outside the morning sun shone."

Calle Garibaldi, La Boca (Harriet Cullen)

According to Germinal Nogués, there are officially forty-six *barrios*, but a tango sung by Alberto Castillo refers to "more than a hundred barrios." Juan José Sebreli outlined Buenos Aires' historical outskirts, called "shores," in his study of daily life and alienation. From the 1870s to the 1900s, one zone to the north, at the end of Avenida Las Heras was called Tierra del

Fuego. This was where all the thugs and cutthroats hung out, a frontier of fights and murders. In the southeast the dangerous no-man's land was the Matadero del Sur, where tango was born. Novelist Estela Canto found that each *barrio* was a world unto itself, with few travelling outside the invisible limits: "The pale faces that inhabit the little houses suffer specific and local anxieties. Their problems arise from a radius of ten blocks... in the local beehive of their barrio, each one different to the other for subtle, imperceptible reasons, nobody makes contact with the North, and rarely with the Centre of the city." One explanation was that tram fares were high and most people kept to their *barrios* through lack of money. This meant that lives were lived in their entirety in one place, leading to crucial ties and intense loyalties. In this sense, the *barrios* are often beloved, viewed nostalgically, are less Europeanized than the city centre and constitute the bulk of the city. In 1998 novelist Mempo Giardinelli could still claim that the *barrio* "is how the provinces transplanted themselves in the Capital and remained as they are."

Barrios are a kind of *beatus ille*, a salutary counterpoint to the ever-changing, sordid city, as in Salvador Merlino's poem "Memories" evoking Villa Lugano "as a corner far away from the city." The *barrio*, in the poet's eye, was not city nor country, neither poor nor sad: "every now and then a little hut, a fence / along the green earth with white buds. / And sad streets for city feet /—despite the sun, plenty of dust; without the sun, plenty of mud... To say the end of the world was to name my barrio." That people had to leave these *barrios* for the city and suffer urban alienation is the theme of Fermín Estrella Gutiérrez's short poem "San Ireneo Street": "san Ireneo street, narrow and short, / lost in the silence of the suburb; / afternoons become deeper in your peace / and only my anxiety disturbs you."

Villa Crespo

The quickest way into Villa Crespo is by *subte* to Malabia, and then a walk into calle Warnes, where Borges' cunning female character Emma Zunz, having faked a rape, kills her father's mill-owning partner who lived "in the run-down slum" area. Leopoldo Marechal's novel about the love-sick, school-teaching poet, *Adán Buenosayres*, opens in a boarding house on calle Monte Egremont 303 in Villa Crespo, where he has a room next to his bohemian philosopher-friend Samuel Tesler (based on the avant-garde and mentally ill poet Jacobo Fijman). Marechal himself lived for a while here, working as a librarian in the Biblioteca Popular Alberdi. Nearby is the church of San Bernardo with its clock tower "phosphorescent like a cat's eye" at night, striking the hours. On the front is a cement statue of a Cristo de la Mano Rota [Christ of the broken hand]. Building of the Parroquia San Bernardo began in 1896 in the eclectic Roman/Greek style, with a six-feet concrete Christ, whose hands disintegrated in the rain. The statue is known locally as the Christ with a broken hand, even though the hands have since been restored. Marechal describes the bar and shop la Hormiga de Oro, the café Izmir, the quiet calle Warnes, the busy calle Gurruchaga, the "tannery" La Universal with its "dirty-black walls and pestilential carts," the whole building "like a malignant mushroom." This leather-tannery (in reality called La Nacional), along with the Fábrica Nacional de Calzado, formed the industrial base for Villa Crespo, named after the mayor of Buenos Aires don Antonio F. Crespo, who initiated the *barrio*'s development. A street, Murillo, is still packed with leather shops. There is a delightful Plaza Nazar, and the whole *barrio*, with a large Jewish element, is poor and real, giving me a sense of a Buenos Aires that does not merely ape Europe, as it did Marechal fifty years ago.

The first publishing house in Villa Crespo was founded by Manuel Gleizer, who fled Russia in 1908 and set up office on Corrientes 5200, ending up publishing Mallea, Borges, Lugones, Fijman, and, of course, Marechal. His offices became a meeting place for young writers and intellectuals, from the González Tuñón brothers to the socialist Alfredo Palacios. Gleizer is a character in Marechal's novel.

Villa Crespo is where the country meets the city, with low houses and poor people, real *porteños*, according to Marechal, as opposed to those who live in luxury in the *barrio norte*. The *barrio* established itself after the river Maldonado was sunk underground and the flooding stopped. Poor immigrants, especially Italians and Jews, arrived and lived in *conventillos*. The *barrio* was then connected to the city by the metro, or *subte*, line B. The once grand house belonging to Balcarce has been "divided and subdivided into the hundred alveoli of a gigantic tenement," a slum. Villa Crespo is eulogized as the Real by Marechal:

Numens of Villa Crespo, tough, happy fellow-citizens; old harpies gestic-
ulating like gargoyles, because this or because that; gangsters grumbling
tangos or whistling folk songs; infantile devils wrapped in the colors of their
teams River Plate or Boca Juniors... and above all you girls from my
barrio, music of high heels and giggles, suburban muses.

Alberto Vacarezza's tango opens: "¡Villa Crespo!... rough barrio / with
narrow streets / and cheaply built houses / you are pretty because so
ugly."

Museo de Ciencias Naturales Bernardino Rivadavia

Before you reach the Chacarita Cemetery, you pass along the Parque
Centenario – geographically now the central point of Buenos Aires -
where the Museo de Ciencias Naturales named after Bernardino
Rivadavia stands on calle Angel Gallardo 470. Rivadavia had the
original idea (he had many and was an ideas man) to create such a
museum in 1812. It was started in 1823 in the Manzana de las Luces
in San Telmo, in the Convento de Santo Domingo, when Rivadavia
had already invited the celebrated botanist Aimé Bonpland out to
Buenos Aires (in 1817). But Bonpland realized there was no money,
and set off exploring Corrientes and Misiones. By 1827 there was a
small collection of insects, birds and fish, but during Rosas' tyranny the
museum fell apart. Only under Urquiza was it resuscitated when in
1854 it moved to calle Perú 208. The encyclopedic German scientist
Germán Burmeister (1807-1892) was appointed director in 1862.
Burmeister had been recommended by Alexandre von Humboldt to
Mitre and Sarmiento on the basis of his travel book and scientific
survey, or description, of Argentina *Reise Durch die La Plata-Staaten.*
He particularly strengthened the paleontological side of the collection
and left unfinished a five-volume project, illustrated by himself, called
Description Physique de la République Argentine, the first volume
appearing in 1876. There is a statue of Burmeister in the Parque
Centenario in Caballito, unveiled in 1900. Burmeister died in 1892,
followed as director by the Russian scientist Carlos Berg, and then in
1902 by Argentina's great eccentric scientist Florentino Ameghino. The
son of Genoese immigrants and born in La Plata in 1854, Ameghino
was an autodidact. Bruce Chatwin praised his "wonderful powers of

imagination" and his "weakness for colossal names" (such as calling a fossil *Florentino-ameghinea*). Chatwin describes how he took on world opinion by arguing that *"all* hot-blooded mammals began in South America," even man himself "which is why, in some circles, the name of Ameghino is set beside Plato and Newton." This, surely, was science as patriotic duty, and Sarmiento duly wrote of him as "Argentina's sole scientist [*sabio*]." Ameghino's defining book was *La antigüedad del hombre en el Plata* [The antiquity of man in the Plata, 1881], but he was a prolific writer, with more than 20,000 pages to his name. In relation to Chatwin's later quest for the Mylodon down in Patagonia, Ameghino had shocked the world by announcing that this monster was still alive in 1897. Another facet of Ameghino is that he opened bookshops, the first called Glyptodón in Buenos Aires (there's a second-hand bookshop of the same name on Ayacucho 734), the second called Rivadavia in La Plata. He was an evolutionist, collected (with his brother) and donated to the Museo over 28,000 pieces of fossil, to earn the nickname "el loco de los huesos" [the bones loony]. There is a Parque Florentino Ameghino created on top of the old Cementerio del Sur (streets Caseros, Monasterio, Santa Cruz and Uspallata) which overflowed with the yellow fever dead in 1871. Once all the bones were removed to the Chacarita, it was made into a memorial park to the dead.

Ameghino was followed by Angel Gallardo (1867-1934), who has an avenue and *subte* station named after him. A relation was the writer Sara Gallardo. In 1923 Angel Gallardo was followed by Martín Doello Jurado, who remained until 1946 and under whose directorship the new building was opened, the first wing in 1931 and second in 1934.

The Chacarita Cemetery
In Borges' poem "La Chacarita," he explains how the vast cemetery was opened in 1886, beyond the "neighborhood of the 'butchers,'" after the yellow fever epidemic of 1871 when the Cementerio del Sur (today's Parque Ameghino) could not cope with so many dead. Borges calls this people's cemetery "a slum for souls," a "drain for that fatherland that is Buenos Aires." Ramón Gómez de la Serna is less pejorative: "La Chacarita is everybody's cemetery, the ultimate wharf, the last harbor

where the immigrant says goodbye for the last time." An architect friend, Alejandro Moreno, once called it "a supermarket of the dead." Nevertheless, it has a grand six Doric-columned portico. Next to this extensive cemetery are the British and German cemeteries. At one time, the Chacarita was known, in Manuel Gálvez's words, as "the cemetery for the poor," but in this vast necropolis are the mausoleums or tombs of Perón (it was broken into and one of his hands cut off), and of the "creole songbird" [*el zorzal criollo*], Carlos Gardel. The name of this cemetery reminded Gómez de la Serna of "a taste of something fertile and country-ish, as if the bones could grow into pillars with fussy capitals," for *chacra* means "small farm."

Carlos Gardel, the "creole songbird" (private collection)

According to legend, Gardel's bronze statue holds a permanently lit cigarette, although this detail is normally added by passing tourists. The idol, "who sings better and better every day," lived in Buenos Aires from the age of two, on calle Corrientes 1553, then 1714. After a rough youth spent around the Abasto market, he embarked on a singing career as a duo with José Razzano. In 1917 he encountered the tango, and virtually created the sung version. According to Simon Collier, between 1917 and 1921 he recorded seventeen tangos, but in 1923 alone he recorded thirty-three. Gardel cultivated mystery; there was a bullet lodged in him after a street attack, but nobody knew the intimate details of his sex life, and rumors were rife. He falsified his birth details to claim he had been born in Tacuarembó, Uruguay. He hung around the Café de Los Angelitos and once sang tangos to the Prince of Wales at the grand *estancia* Huetel. His last home on calle Jean Jaurés 735 is today a tango bar. Edmundo Guibord wrote: "Carlos Gardel = Buenos Aires," and there is no doubt that Gardel's music crystallizes for many an ideal of Argentine identity associated with the *barrios*, the passing of time, male friendship and the city itself. Gardel, with his famous smile and brilliantined hair, became the stereotypical *porteño*, with his *mate*, his love for gambling and horse-racing, and his allegiance to his male friends, the *barra*. The Spanish novelist Miguel Delibes in his visit to Buenos Aires found the Gardel tomb the most significant monument in Buenos Aires, and reported that Gardel, "the king of tango," was a "national symbol." The morning he went to La Chacarita two women were crying, flowers draped the tomb and statue, while more than twenty plaques lamented and honored Gardel. Delibes concluded that he died twenty years before "but his memory lives as if he had died yesterday." One time we were there we saw a woman cross herself in front of (Saint) Gardel's statue.

Many writers and painters are buried in the Chacarita, including the poet Alfonsina Storni and the La Boca painter Quinquela Martín. Tomás Eloy Martínez described the burial of one of the ersatz Evita corpses in his novel *Santa Evita*:

They entered in a straight line along an avenue that copied the layout of the city. On both sides rose enormous mausoleums, covered in plaques. Behind glass you could see chapels and coffins. At the end of the avenue

*there was open land. On the right a few statues stood out representing a
guitarist, a man thinking and a woman pretending to throw herself down
a hill. On the left, piles of tombstones, some gardens and a few crosses.*

The false Evita is given the name María de Magaldi and is ironically
buried next to the tomb of the singer Magaldi, said by the grave digger
in the novel to have been Evita's first lover.

Horacio Vázquez Rial writes of this same vast Chacarita in his novel
Historia del Triste: "in the porteño cemetery of La Chacarita offerings to
Carlos Gardel and la Madre María were never lacking." A character,
doña Amanda, leaves carnations for this "famous popular saint's holy
shrine" before visiting her late husband in the "gigantic necropolis." He
is buried in one of what Vázquez Rial calls "maximum-use pantheons"
or "sinister lines of identical, anonymous niches piled on top of each
other, and designated by numbers and names on small metallic
plaques." The above-mentioned Madre María (María Salomé Loredo de
Subiza), represented by a life-sized sculpture and always surrounded by
flowers, was a famous faith-healer and spiritualist who mixed
Christianity with a belief in reincarnation. Born in Spain in 1855, she
was arrested in 1914 for illegally practicing medicine. She died in 1928,
but her cult lives on today.

In the Cementerio Británico bordering the Chacarita there is a statue
of William Morris (street 39) and the tomb of the film director
Leopoldo Torre Nilsson (1924-1978). Next to this cemetery lies the
Cementerio Alemán, with swastikas on the tombs of the dead from the
sinking of the battleship *Graf Spee* in 1939.

Once

*"I think of Plaza Once, notorious for its ugliness, and I feel my eyes filling with
tears."* Borges

Another starting-point for an excursion, real or imagined, is the well-
defined *barrio* popularly known as the Once (officially Balvanera),
named thus for being the eleventh electoral zone and because of the
September 11, 1852 battle of Pavón, when the city of Buenos Aires stood
up against Urquiza, the victor over Rosas. It was known from the 1920s
as the "Jewish quarter" or "Russian *barrio*" of Buenos Aires, without ever

being a ghetto. The Once is bisected by calle Corrientes, has a once grandiose railway station on the Plaza Once (Ferrocarril Sarmiento), and today is also the centre for the city's Vietnamese and Korean communities. The Plaza Once is also known as Miserere, a name that refers to the slaughterhouse, the "corrals of Miserere." The guidebook writer Germinal Nogués rightly called this plaza the most South American in Buenos Aires: "Saturday mornings in Buenos Aires the Plaza Once bursts into life, revealing the city's South American soul. There you find the same rhythm, the same noise, the same people, and color in shop windows as you might find in Bogotá, or La Paz or in Lima." In 1941 Baldomero Fernández Moreno claimed that the Once "smells of a large glass of fresh milk," and that from there you could "guess the pampas of berets and sandals [*alpargatas*]," the rural past of Argentina.

On the Plaza Once is the odd, art-deco mausoleum of Bernardino de Rivadavia, the radical, mulatto first president of Argentina in 1826, who died in exile in Cádiz, Spain. Rivadavia created the university, the public library, invited scientists like Aimé Bonpland out to Argentina, introduced *habeas corpus* and freedom of the press, and promoted cattle breeding. In Vázquez Rial's *Historia del Triste* we come across the following dialogue concerning this true radical:

> they caught the train from the Once station: they walked towards the ticket office on calle Mitre, when Chaves pointed out the bulk of Rivadavia's mausoleum, across the plaza: 'Know who's buried there, Triste?': 'No, didn't know anybody was buried here in this plaza'; 'That's where Rivadavia is': 'He was a president, no?': 'Something like that, what one could do a hundred years ago; he was a mulatto... a black, with frizzy hair, go between for the English, so they say.'

Argentine sculptor Rogelio Yrurtia built the unfitting monument in 1932 in huge granite blocks on the backs of crouching figures, with two large bronze statues, one of Moses looking south, symbolizing pensiveness, the other a muscular young man of action, holding his stomach in a yoga position.

The vagabond, socialist poet Raúl González Tuñón was born on calle Saavedra 614 in the Once in 1905, mythologizing this *barrio* and tango writers in a poem: "I was born in the Once barrio, in the south part. / Nearby Julio de Caro was born / and de la Púa wrote his memorable lyrics.

/ At that time the moon still reached the patios. / And the tango and poetry were born in my barrio." Another great *porteño* poet from the Once was the tango lyricist Enrique Santos Discépolo (1901-1951), whose acerbic tangos *Que vachaché*, *Yira-yira*, *Cambalache* etc. are the most moving and urban of all tangos written. He was born on calle Paso 113.

The Argentine Nobel Prize-winning scientist Bernardo A. Houssay's house, where he lived from 1925 to 1970, is a museum, on Viamonte 2790, with a library and archives that you can visit. There is also a Cinema Museum, the Museo Municipal de Cine Pablo Ducrós Hicken on Sarmiento 2573; Ducrós Hicken was a collector of cinema artifacts and a painter.

Avenida Boedo

In the 1920s and 1930s this street and *barrio*, named after a man from the Congress of Tucumán, came to be associated with proletarian and socialist writers. Martínez Estrada compared Boedo with Florida to decide that "Boedo is more Buenos Aires than Florida," for this wide noisy street is easily understood and is typical of many similar avenues in the city. Baldomero Fernández Moreno wrote of this avenue in a poem as "a pandemonium of lorries and cars," with bizarre buses like "exhausted suitcases"; there were old houses, new cement ones, and a cafe where "I could hear all the languages of the world spoken." He ends: "An infinity of people strolled the streets / along packed shops and florescent stalls./ I captured Boedo full of movement." The group of writers associated with this street met in bars like La Perla (in the Once), in the studio of the painter José Arato (on Inclán and Boedo), at the printing press of Manuel Rañó, in the *boliche* of Francisco Munner's bookshop, or in the offices of the Editorial Claridad. They saw themselves as reflecting petit-bourgeois and proletariat life, as summarized in Leonitas Barletta's novel *Los pobres* [The poor] and Roberto Mariani's *Cuentos de la oficina* [Office stories, 1925]. Mariani, born in 1893, was buried in the Chacarita in 1946 and Borges attended his funeral—so much for the division between Boedo and Florida. In Mariani's stories all the characters work in a department store like Gath y Chaves on Florida and Cangallo, and in the story "Uno" losing a job through ill-health means falling below the poverty line and rotting in hospitals such as the Rawson in Constitución or the Ramos Mejía in the Once. The crucial word that links all Boedo writers' worries was *conventillo*, the slum peculiar to Buenos Aires, where the poor lived in overcrowded promiscuity and disease: Alvaro Yunque's poem "Conventillo" has leprous walls and the threat of tuberculosis; its door is a "foul mouth." *Porteños*, he complains, are seemingly indifferent to this urban squalor. One area, Puente Alsina, praised elsewhere by Raul González Tuñón, is defined by knife fights and tangos, bordered by the Arroyo Maldonado and divided by the Riachuelo, "nourishing police reports / a barrio famous for its knife fighters." Dante Linyera (a pseudonym meaning "tramp") wrote his tango "The Florida of the Suburbs" eulogizing Boedo as a "picturesque barrio and playing grounds of poets, / where the lads are the best, / and pick up the lovely young ladies / ... / Boedo, Boedo / everybody's street."

Flores

San José de Flores, a well-defined *barrio*, began life as a separate village, with its plaza, *almacén* [street-corner shop] and church, which Roberto Arlt called the "prettiest of the city." Flores is named after Juan Diego Flores, a landowner, and San José, to whom was dedicated a simple mud-brick chapel dating from 1806. This chapel was followed by a second church opened in 1831 complete with a clock donated by the tyrant Rosas. The actual large domed church—the *Basílica*—was begun in 1879 and finished in 1883. Germinal Nogués remarked that "Flores today does not have enough green spaces to honor its name" [flowers]. Because it was slightly higher and hence cooler than Buenos Aires, Flores became fashionable and people of means would summer there. One typical house from before 1857 is the Casa Marcó del Pont on calle Artigas 206, now a National Historical Monument and being converted into a cultural complex. A similar, but now demolished, villa was the Palacio Basualdo, with a hexagonal tower that was a landmark from afar. It was captured in Baldomero Fernández Moreno's words: "In the distance the tower of the Basualdo palace. / The tower of the Basualdo. / And tomorrow, emptiness."

Before urban spread engulfed it, Flores was joined to the city by the road that Rosas built in honor of General Quiroga (whose barbarous customs ignited the exiled Sarmiento to pen his polemic against Rosas, *Civilización o barbarie: la vida de Juan Facundo Quiroga* (1845). It was built on top of the old colonial *camino real* (today Avenida Rivadavia) which linked Buenos Aires with Lima. In 1857 the railway joined Flores to Buenos Aires, and people started living there, and commuting. Now, alas, the once grand railway station is falling apart. By 1900, Avenida Rivadavia reached Flores and it became a middle-class *barrio*. In 1922 the *barrio norte* rebel poet Oliverio Girondo mocked the girls who lived in Flores, who walk about arm in arm, "and if anybody stares at them in the eye, they squeeze their legs, scared that their sex might drop on to the pavement." With their overdressed mothers, they stroll the plaza in the afternoon letting men "ejaculate" words in to their ears. Girondo could have been mocking Luis Cané's poem "Slightly Vulgar Elegy to the Novias [fiancées] of the Barrio of Flores" which opens: "He who has worn out his heart / in false loves / should seek a novia in Flores / and it'll be his salvation." The poem ends "He does not seek / girls from Belgrano, / who teach the piano / or dress-making." Baldomero Fernández Moreno wrote a book with the place name as its title, *San José de Flores* (1934), a collection of down-to-earth poems about Flores, where he lived from 1938 to his death in 1950 in a Mansarded French château-style house in a car-free backwater on calle Francisco Bilbao 2384.

Roberto Arlt (1900-1942) was born in Flores of a German father and an Italian mother and later lived there in 1926 on calle Yerbal 2000. He left home at sixteen, educated himself, married early at twenty, and survived as a journalist, principally on *El Mundo*, and was for a while the *estanciero* writer Ricardo Güiraldes' private secretary. His writing exposes all the dreams and nightmares of the petit-bourgeois Man of Corrientes and Esmeralda (after Scalabrini Ortiz) of the 1920s and 1930s, who, like Arlt, wanted to be "rotten rich." From his self-imposed exile in Paris, the experimental writer Julio Cortázar chose Flores as most typically *porteño* for his character Oliveira's return home in disgrace after being booted out of France. The second half of his novel *Hopscotch* finds his protagonists living opposite each other on calle Cachimayo in a Flores *barrio* of low houses, once—famously—communicating between their flats across a plank.

Floresta

Another *barrio* with literary echoes in its name is Floresta, clustered around the Plaza Vélez Sarsfield, named after the man who drew up the *Código civil* and translated Virgil's *Aeneid*. It was where the railway ended in 1857. On the plaza is a neo-Gothic church dating from 1896. Baldomero Fernández Moreno lived there in 1905: "It was a true little village where everybody knew everybody: streets without paving stones; wire fences covered in ivy and honeysuckle... little woods of casuarina trees, of eucalyptuses." As a boy he wandered around the abandoned Vélez Sarsfield *quinta*, "a huge house with wooden balconies."

Caballito

The Caballito *barrio*, at the end of the Avenida Rivadavia, developed around another railway station on the western line going out from the Once station. Today it is centred around the Plaza Primera Junta, with the Mercado de Flores [Flower Market] and the Parque Rivadavia's huge second-hand book fair on Sundays. The novelist Juan José Saer claimed that Caballito began as a zone of co-operativists, socialists and utopians and that calle Pedro Goyena, with its enormous acacias, is one of the "of most beautiful in Buenos Aires."

Avenida del Trabajo

This long avenue that leads out to Ezeiza airport became the theme of Baldomero Fernández Moreno's poem of the same name written in 1942. The avenue is so long that "Chacabuco park / is a little leaf by its side." It points out to the empty *pampas* that surround the city of Buenos Aires, leading from skyscrapers and traffic congestion into the emptiness: "You begin in the city, / and dissolve in the country," wrote the poet. This avenue has been recently renamed Avenida Evita Perón.

Santos Lugares

On the railway out from Palermo you reach Santos Lugares, where the pregnant heroine Camila O'Gorman was shot on Rosas' orders, when the place was little more than a garrison. Argentina's intellectual conscience, novelist and essayist Ernesto Sabato, though born in Rojas (Buenos Aires province) in 1911, has lived most of his life in a large house in suburban

Santos Lugares. Sabato is the analyst of Buenos Aires' seamier side, the recorder of cloacal notes from the underground. The characters in his three novels (*El túnel, Sobre héroes y tumbas* and *Abaddón el exterminador*) roam the named, urban streets; the casual encounter or coincidence feature strongly; special sites are associated with love affairs and crimes, like Barracas, Belgrano's Rotonda, Parque Lezama, Plaza San Martín, as well as cafés and bars. Sabato chronicles the city, with cameos about anarchists and boutique owners, and old, perverted families like the Olmos in *Sobre héroes y tumbas*. It is the street and café life that stands out, as well as a deep concern for making sense of what he calls "Babylonia." Sabato is a patriotic writer, with his finger on the pulse of the national psyche, engaged psychologically and historically, writing in rambling sentences in infrequent novels compiled over long years. He plans to leave his house as a museum.

Hurlingham

Further down the tracks from Santos Lugares lies Hurlingham. The large Anglo-Argentine community in Argentina, many with dual nationality and historically linked to the railways, introduced boarding schools, football, polo and rugby. Professional Argentine polo players are sought around the world, and the Pumas national rugby team competes in rugby world cups. The area around Hurlingham railway station has so-called English-style or railway chalets and a club founded around 1888 which echoes the riverside Hurlingham Club in West London. In the following scene in Isobel Strachey's novel *A Summer in Buenos Aires* (1947), the English nanny flees from marriage to her stiff English boss with her Latin lover in a train out to his *estancia*:

> *"Look," he said, taking her arm, "we have passed Hurlingham and the polo ground. You have never seen it, have you?"*
> *"I went there once with Colonel Hamilton and the children," she replied. "We watched the polo while he played golf."*
>
> *There had been a lot of English people sitting in front of the club-house in deck-chairs, wearing striped blazers and calling loud and cheerful greetings to each other with an air of the close intimacy of a family party and a jolly almost aggressive appreciation of leisure spent in green and spacious surroundings.*

Golf at the Hurlingham Club (Dirección Nacional de Turismo)

In 1907 W. H. Koebel found that this club "stands as a monument to the sporting enterprise of the British in Argentina… it is difficult to conceive a more business-like fashion than that in which its numerous acres are laid out." He enumerated a racecourse, a cricket pitch and pavilion, polo grounds and a club house, concluding "the place is a paradise of sport." In 1932 Philip Guedalla portrayed Hurlingham as:

> something wholly British. Seventeen miles out of Buenos Aires a charming suburb clusters round an admirable club. It has its games, its dances, and its life; and its contacts with Buenos Aires are almost confined to the successful effort of its male population to catch the morning train to town or lunch on Saturdays at Harrods… one begins to wonder whether the prim British instinct of keeping oneself to oneself dictated this retreat.

When the Prince of Wales visited Buenos Aires in 1925 one of his days was timetabled in a local newspaper as: "10 A.M. St Andrew's College. 11 A.M British Hospital. 12:30 Lunch with the British Chamber of Commerce. 2:30 Polo at Hurlingham Club." In 1929 the British Ambassador is reported (by John King) to have said that "Argentina must be regarded as an essential part of the British Empire," just when British influence was on the wane.

Banfield

Another English-sounding *barrio*, Banfield, reached by train from Constitución station, is associated with Julio Cortázar, who was born in Brussels in 1914, moved back to Argentina aged four, but never lost his French "r." He was brought up in an English railway-house (sloping roof, black and white timbered gables, red bricks) on leafy, cobbled Rodríguez Peña, 585. Banfield is often cited in his great "childhood" short stories like "End of the Game," where adolescent sisters play the part of statues for passing train passengers on the British-built and owned railways in a rite of passage. All that is left of the once-handsome English station is a fine, rusty footbridge. There was plaque at Cortázar's Banfield school (Number 10) on Talcahuano 278 (but when we went it had been unscrewed).

Adrogué

Adrogué entered literature through Jorge Luis Borges' eerie parable "Death and the Compass," set where Borges and his family summered in a hotel (now demolished) with a turret like Triste-Le-Roy's in the story, with strong-smelling eucalyptus trees in the park, and fountains. Borges told Victoria Ocampo in 1967 about his Adrogué: "When I think of Adrogué, I do not think of the actual Adrogué dilapidated by progress, by telephones and motorbikes, but of that tranquil, lost labyrinth of quintas, plazas, and streets that met and diverged, with iron railings." Just the scent of eucalyptus, anywhere in the world, threw him back to that place. Estela Canto's personal memoir of her times with Borges evoked Adrogué's Hotel Las Delicias, where the Borges family spent summer because they could not afford the grander Mar del Plata hotels: "In the forties Las Delicias was a rundown building, with a nostalgic charm, and the unexpected elegance of the new poor. Palm trees and ferns in flower boxes had vanished, but the great windows with red, blue and yellow glass rhombi fascinated Borges. In "Death and the Compass" he described these rhombi, giving them a magical meaning." The most desolate vision of this place comes from Borges' poem titled "Adrogué," published in 1969, in which Borges intensely recreates this place where he was happy. Amidst its dust and jasmines and eucalyptus trees with their "medicinal smell," he remembers every detail from "mica paving stones" to a "lion's head" and the red and green colored glass. But the past is a "closed circle," inaccessible to Borges who is made of "time, blood and death's agony."

Adrogué was founded by Esteban Adrogué in 1874 as a place safe from the yellow fever epidemics. No longer fashionable, the *barrio* still retains some wealthy villas.

Villa Devoto and its Prison

The middle-class neighborhood of Villa Devoto is named after Antonio Devoto who copied the church in Superga, Italy, which now stands on Lincoln 3701. The church was finished in 1920, with expensive marble fittings, including a relief in marble of Leonardo's *Last Supper* and statues of the two dead donors. The Devotos built a 200-roomed palace in 1891, designed by Juan Buschiazzo, abounding in Carrara marble, but it was demolished in 1942 when no inheritors claimed it.

To end this guided tour of literary landmarks with one of the two prisons in Buenos Aires (the other is Caseros) is to end with both a place and a metaphor. First the metaphor: any critic remains trapped in his perceptual prison, since the city changes under his nose and other corners of this regenerating textual city will emerge in books unread or forgotten by me. So the routines and verbal tracks left by different writers will change future readings of the city. An anthology could be made about the actual prisons of the city, from the first Cabildo to the larger block on Las Heras, now demolished, to the Villa Devoto prison. This jail hit the news once when I was in Buenos Aires because the recently-elected President Dr. Cámpora opened its doors, and out came all the writers imprisoned for belonging to urban guerrilla groups. One of them was "Paco" Urondo (1930-1975) later killed in a shoot-out with the police. This, of course, was before the foul days when the military could not be bothered to imprison and simply made people "disappear."

The prison, then, like the lunatic asylum, is the subconscious of a city where the violent and scary are locked away, where the obscene happens. The anti-Peronist student Pablo Alcobendas is tortured and dumped in Villa Devoto prison in Beatriz Guido's novel *El incendio y las vísperas*: "Protected by the night, they brought them down to an inner patio. In a freight lift, they pushed them out in different floors. A voice ordered him: 'The judge doesn't want any more problems with students; let them have fun in the fifth.' Pablo overheard, semi-conscious. Then he realized he was in Devoto. He was welcomed with a high-pitched uproar of laughter, castrated, strident vocal chords."

The essayist who has clarified the social chaos of Buenos Aires more than most quoted in my guide, Juan José Sebreli, also spent time in Devoto prison:

> When we new ones arrived there were four of us, we were separated from the rest and held in a provisional cell until they found room for us on the fourth floor: a wide cement and iron warehouse with a double line of beds very similar to a hospital or barracks. Only the pitiless electric lights that were never turned off and the guard who walked up and down the high platform opposite the iron-grilled door with a machine-gun reminded us that we were in prison.

Ironically, as Germinal Nougués observed, to "live in Devoto" is a euphemism for being in prison. If living in a big city like Buenos Aires can seem like a prison, one sure way to escape is through reading.

Further Reading

I have listed background sources only. Creative writers are cited in the text.

Aguinis, Marcos, *Un país de novela. Viaje hacia la mentalidad de los argentinos.* Planeta: Buenos Aires, 1988.

Amorim, Enrique, *Buenos Aires y sus aspectos.* Editorial Galerna: Buenos Aires, 1967.

Arlt, Roberto, *Aguafuertes porteñas.* [1936] Editorial Losada: Buenos Aires 1976.

Arrieta, Rafael Alberto, *Centuria porteña.* Espasa-Calpe: Buenos Aires, 1944.

Barnstone, Willis, *With Borges on an Ordinary Evening in Buenos Aires: A Memoir.* University of Illinois Press: Urbana, 1993.

Bernhardson, Wayne, *Buenos Aires.* Lonely Planet Publications: Melbourne, 1996.

Bigongiari, Diego, *La guía Pirelli. Buenos Aires, sus alrededores y costas del Uruguay.* Editorial Sudamericana: Buenos Aires, 1993.

Bossio, Jorge, *Los cafés de Buenos Aires. Reportaje a la nostalgia.* Editorial Plus Ultra: Buenos Aires, 1995.

Burns, Jimmy, *Hand of God: The Life of Diego Maradona.* Bloomsbury: London, 1996.

Cánepa, Luis, *El Buenos Aires de antaño.* Talleres Gráficos Linari: Buenos Aires, 1936.

Canto, Estela, *Borges a contraluz.* Colección Austral: Madrid, 1989.

Carilla, Emilio, *Una etapa decisiva de Darío (Rubén Darío en la Argentina).* Gredos: Madrid, 1967.

Clemenceau, Georges, *South America Today.* Fisher Unwin: London, 1911.

Collier, Simon, *The Life, Music and Times of Carlos Gardel.* University of Pittsburgh Press: Pittsburgh, 1986.

Constenla, Julia (ed.), *Crónicas de Buenos Aires.* Editorial Jorge Alvarez: Buenos Aires, 1965.

D'Agostino, García de, Rebok, Asato, Lopez, *Imagen de Buenos Aires a través de los viajeros, 1870-1910.* Universidad de Buenos Aires: Buenos Aires, 1981.

Delibes, Miguel, *Por esos mundos. Sudamérica con escala en las Canarias.* Ediciones Destino: Barcelona, 1961.

Dieguez Videla, Albino, Orloff, Lucrecia & Wannier Mario, *La Recoleta. Una ciudad dentro de otra.* Libros de Hispanoamerica: Buenos Aires, 1983.

Durrell, Gerald, *The Drunken Forest.* Rupert Hart-Davis: London, 1956.

Escardó, Florencio, *Nueva geografía de Buenos Aires.* Editorial Américalee: Buenos Aires, 1971.

Fernández Moreno, César, *Argentina.* Ediciones Destino: Barcelona, 1972.

Floria, Carlos Alberto & César García Belsunce, *Historia de los argentinos.* 2 vols, Larousee: Buenos Aires, 1992.

France, Miranda, *Bad Times in Buenos Aires.* Weidenfeld & Nicolson: London, 1998.

Frank, Waldo, *South American Journey.* Gollancz: London, 1944.

Galeano, Eduardo, *Century of the Wind*. trans. Cedric Belfrage, Quartet Books: London, 1989.

Gálvez, Víctor, *Memorias de un viejo*. Jacobo Peuser: Buenos Aires, 1889.

Garasa, Delfin, *La otra Buenos Aires. Paseos literarios por barrios y calles de la ciudad*. Sudamericana-Planeta: Buenos Aires, 1987.

Giardinelli, Mempo, *El país de las maravilas. Los argentinos en el fin del milenio*. Planeta: Buenos Aires, 1998.

Gómez de la Serna, Ramón, *Explicación de Buenos Aires*. Ediciones de la Flor: Buenos Aires, 1975.

González Garaño, Alejo, *Iconografía argentina anterior a 1820, con una noticia de la vida y obra de E. E. Vidal*. Emecé Editores: BA, 1943.

Guedalla, Philip, *Argentine Tango*. Hodder and Stoughton: London, 1932.

Hirst, W. A., *Argentina*. T. Fisher Unwin: London, 1910.

Hutchinson, Thomas, *Buenos Ayres and Argentine Gleanings*. 1865.

Isherwood, Christopher, *The Condor and the Cows*. Methuen: London, 1949.

The Journal of Decorative and Propaganda Arts, 18, 1992, 'Argentine Theme Issue'.

Jurado, Alicia, *Descubrimiento del mundo*. Emecé: Buenos Aires, 1989.

— *El mundo de la palabra,* Emecé: Buenos Aires, 1990.

Kar-Wai, Wong, in Richard Williams 'King Kong', The *Guardian*, London, 10 April 1998.

Koebel, W. H., *Argentina Past and Present*. Adam and Charles Black: London, 1914.

— *Modern Argentina*. Francis Griffiths: London, 1907.

Korn, Francis, *Buenos Aires 1895, una ciudad moderna*, Editorial del Instituto Buenos Aires: Buenos Aires, 1981.

— *Buenos Aires: los huéspedes del 20*. Editorial Sudamericana: Buenos Aires, 1974.

Lanús, Archibaldo, *La causa argentina*. Emecé: Buenos Aires, 1988.

Leitner, Garry, *Argentina Travel Companion*. Mudgeeraba, Australia, 1990.

Lugones, Leopoldo, *La grande Argentina*. Babel: Buenos Aires, 1930.

McCann, William, *Two Thousand Miles' Ride through the Argentine Provinces*. [1853] AMS Press: New York, 1971.

Mansilla, Lucio, *Mis memorias*. 1904.

Marechal, Leopoldo, *Historia de la calle Corrientes*. [1937] Paidós: Buenos Aires, 1967.

Martínez Estrada, Ezequiel, *Radiografía de la pampa*. [1933] Losada: Buenos Aires, 1968.

— *La cabeza de Goliat*. [1943] Centro Editor de América Latina: Buenos Aires, 1968.

— *El hermano Quiroga y cartas de Horacio Quiroga a Martínez Estrada*. Arca: Montevideo, 1968.

— *Poesía*. Argos: Buenos Aires, 1947.

Matamoro, Blas, *La casa porteña*. Centro Editor: Buenos Aires, 1971.

Maurois, André, *My Latin American Diary*. The Falcon Press: London, 1953.

Mazzei, Angel, *La poesía de Buenos Aires*. Editorial Ciordia: Buenos Aires, 1962.

Moya, Jose, *Cousins and Strangers: Spanish Immigrants in Buenos Aires 1850-1930*. University of California Press: Los Angeles, 1998.

Mujica Lainez, Manuel, *Los porteños*. Ediciones Librería La Ciudad: Buenos Aires, 1980.

— *Letra e imagen de Buenos Aires*, with Aldo Sessa, Ediciones Librería La Ciudad: Buenos Aires, 1977.

Nogués, Germinal, *Buenos Aires, ciudad secreta*. Ruy Díaz-Sudamericana: Buenos Aires, 1996.

Ocampo, Victoria, *Autobiografía I*. Sur: Buenos Aires, 1979.

— *Diálogo con Borges*. Sur: Buenos Aires, 1969.

Palacio, Ernesto, *Historia de la Argentina, 1515-1983*. Abeledo-Perrot: Buenos Aires, 1986.

Prebisch, A., 'La ciudad en que vivimos', in *Buenos Aires 1936. Cuarto centenario de su fundación*. Edición de la Municipalidad de Buenos Aires, 1936.

Preston, Peter & Simpson-Housley, Paul (eds.), *Writing the City*. Routledge: London, 1955.

Rock, David, *Argentina 1516-1987*. I.B Tauris: London, 1987.

Ross, Stanley & Thomas McGann (eds.), *Buenos Aires: 400 Years*. University of Texas Press, Austin: 1982.

Rumbold, Sir Horace, *The Great Silver River: Notes of a Residence in Buenos Ayres in 1880 and 1881*. John Murray: London, 1887.

Saer, Juan José, *El río sin orillas*. Alianza Editorial: Madrid & Buenos Aires, 1991.

Salas, Alberto, *Relación parcial de Buenos Aires*. [1955] Sur: Buenos Aires, 1977.

Salas, Horacio, *El tango*. Planeta: Buenos Aires, 1995.

— *Memoria del tiempo*. Losada: Buenos Aires, 1966.

Scobie, James R., *Buenos Aires: Plaza to Suburb, 1870-1910*. Oxford University Press: New York, 1974.

Sebreli, Juan José, *Buenos Aires, vida cotidiana y alienación*. Editores Siglo Veinte: Buenos Aires, 1964.

Soriano, Osvaldo *Rebeldes, soñadores y fugitivos*. Editora 12: Buenos Aires, 1987.

Theroux, Paul, *The Old Patagonian Express: By Train Through the Americas*. Hamish Hamilton: London, 1979.

Vasconcelos, José, *La raza cósmica. Misión de la raza iberoamericana*. Espasa-Calpe: Mexico, 1966.

Vázquez, María Esther, *Victoria Ocampo*. Planeta: Buenos Aires, 1991.

Vázquez Rial, Horacio, *Buenos Aires*. Ediciones Destino: Barcelona, 1988.

— (ed.), *Buenos Aires 1880-1930. La capital de un imperio imaginario*. Alianza Editorial: Madrid, 1996.

Wheaton, Kathleen (ed.), *Buenos Aires*. Insight Guides: London, 1988.

Wilde, José Antonio, *Buenos Aires 70 años atrás*. 1879?

Index of Literary
& Historical Names

Index of Places